Kinship and Marriage in Medieval Hispanic Chivalric Romance

WESTFIELD PUBLICATIONS IN MEDIEVAL AND RENAISSANCE STUDIES

11

Kinship and Marriage in Medieval Hispanic Chivalric Romance

by

Michael Harney

**WESTFIELD PUBLICATIONS IN
MEDIEVAL AND RENAISSANCE STUDIES**

11

BREPOLS

British Library Cataloguing in Publication Data

Harney, Michael
    Kinship and marriage in medieval Hispanic chivalric
    romance. - (Westfield publications in medieval and
    Renaissance studies ; 11)
    1.Romances, Spanish - History and criticism 2.Kinship in
    literature 3.Marriage in literature
    I.Title II.Queen Mary and Westfield College
    860.9'3543

    ISBN 250350910X

© 2001, Brepols Publishers n.v., Turnhout, Belgium

D/2001/0095/31
ISBN: 2-503-50910-X

Printed in the E.U. on acid-free paper.

in memoriam

John K. Walsh

Contents

CHAPTER 1

Introduction

This book analyses social themes in four chivalric romances that were written, in their original form, during the century and a half before the unification of Spain under the Catholic Monarchs and their grandson, Carlos V. The political, administrative, economic, and social consolidation achieved under Carlos and his successors brings about the end of the Peninsular Middle Ages. If there is a date which marks this historic discontinuity, it is 1521, the year of the Battle of Villalar that saw the defeat of the *comunero* movement (Elliott 1963: 128–49).

Because the chivalric romances discussed here were composed before the existence of a unified Spanish nation-state, we might be tempted to say that this is why they show little awareness of nationalism. The protagonists of the romances are cosmopolitan, in that they travel far and wide and come to know many lands and peoples. But they show no sense of the cosmopolitan as a self-aware transcendence of the distinctive provincialism of modern state-stratified society. This indifference to nationalism, however, does not necessarily derive from the works' having been composed before the rise of the state. One observes, in the modern era, a similarly apolitical cosmopolitanism in many genres. For example, self-conscious nationalism is usually absent from the fantasy and adventure literature of our own century. The romances of Edgar Rice Burroughs and J. R. R. Tolkien, and the myriad novels, short stories, films, television series, comic books, and video games grouped under the heading of space opera — all these also tend toward a similar omission of the nation-state as a criterion of social cohesion.

The emergence of the chivalric romance and of its earlier affines does not take place in primitive, truly pre-national times; rather, the genre appears during a preliminary phase in the expansion of centralizing states in Europe. For instance, the two Castilian works addressed here, the *Libro del caballero Zifar* and *Amadís de Gaula*, are known to have existed, in some form, by the middle of the fourteenth century. Their appearance in literary history roughly coincides with such significant events as the official promulgation by Alfonso XI of the *Siete partidas* as the law of the land (1348). The initial reception of these two romances thus parallels two centuries and more of conflict between the forces of centralization and those of regional and clanic autonomy. It would therefore be difficult to contend that the romances' authors and audiences were ignorant of politics, in the way that tribal folk or illiterate peasants can be.

It would be more accurate to say that the apolitical posture of literary adventure and fantasy finds an audience in earlier stages of state formation, and continues to be popular with new readers in the age of the fully developed, centralized nation-state. Incorporating many elements from earlier genres, especially the French Arthurian prose romances of the thirteenth century (Williamson 1984: 29–69), the Spanish chivalric romances thus achieved maximum popularity precisely when the Spanish nation-state and its overseas empire came to prominence. The most popular work of the genre, *Amadís*, provided the prototype for the sixteenth-century romances which knew such extraordinary success (Whinnom 1980: 193; Sieber 204–09). *Amadís* and the sixteenth-century romances have continued, directly or indirectly, to influence the composition of works in thematically similar genres down to the present day (Harney 1993b: 202–10; 1994: 381–84).

The themes that dominate chivalric romance are analogous to those revealed by the romances of antiquity. The ancient romance arose in Hellenistic times, a period of emergent empires into which were subsumed many smaller, independent polities. The ancient romances, like their medieval analogues, show a preoccupation with the past, with a way of life lost, as Ben Edwin Perry phrases it, 'by a fatality'. Thus a focus on 'the private concerns of the individual man apart from society'; an inclination toward a 'spirit of wonder upon the endless varieties of nature and human experience'; a predilection for 'what is particular, personal, abnormal, strange, and sensational'; a preoccupation with 'the external novelties of a big, strange world full of accident and [...] purely personal hopes and concerns' (Perry 1967: 6–7). As a description of setting and thematic concentration, Perry's analysis of ancient romances could well be applied to the works discussed in this book.

The chivalric romance lives in the past, in that it affects to ignore political categories and political action. It sanctions partisan cooperation and confrontation, but conceives of collective action in exclusively personal terms. What is portrayed is a world of man-to-man honour, in which the spontaneous act of courage, generosity, or forbearance can convert an enemy into a friend. This is, to mention but one of a multitude of examples, the case of Amadís and the giant Balán. The latter explains to Agrajes, Quadragante, and others how he dreamed for years of avenging the death of his father Madanfabul at the hands of Amadís (in the guise of Beltenebros): 'como hijo de tan honrado padre y que tanto a la vengança desta muerte obligado era' (Place 1959–65: IV, 1313.113–16). It is the hero's courtly generosity, as well as his courage and battle prowess, that win the giant over: he has been vanquished, the giant declares, by the 'fortaleza' and 'cortesía' of one who 'lo vno y otro más complido que ninguno de los que biuen tiene'. Because of the formidable character of his erstwhile opponent, Balán explains, 'aquella grande y mortal enemistad [...] se tornó en mayor grandeza de amistad y verdadero amor' (IV, 1314.125–33). Thus is rancour transmuted to amity, vengeance to vassalage. It is the chivalric hero as these stories imagine him who can achieve such conversions.

Related to the apolitical sensibility expressed in the stories is their obsession with vows, pledges, boons, and other promissory formulae. These are factors suggestive of a primordial social reciprocity reflected in verbal exchange. Again, this does not indicate any genuine structural parallelism between primitive societies, the social world of later medieval Peninsular audiences, and the fictional domain of these chivalric adventure stories. Rather, the covenantal practices dramatized by the romances idealize the authors' notions of traditional social relationships.

The theme of boons and vows dates from earlier centuries of

European chivalric literature. Edwin Williamson has summarized the background of such promissory themes in Chrétien de Troyes in terms of a courtly chivalry whose 'principal instruments' are 'solemn pledges and the recourse to arms'. The chief function of these instruments is ethical: 'Vows and pledges commit a man to his word, fasten his will to a declared course of action, and allow no latitude for deception or changes of heart.' Failing such verbal guarantees, combat serves as a remedy by which 'truth can still be established' (Williamson 1984: 9).

In *Amadís de Gaula*, a typical episode shows a damsel who, having secured the pledge of an unconditional boon, leads Galaor, the hero's brother, to the knight who has stolen his horse and armour. Galaor dispatches the knight before she can reveal that the thief was her lover, and that the boon was to spare him. If Galaor does not grant another boon, she threatens: 'por todas partes serás de mí pregonado y abiltado' (I, 189.183–85).

Frequent pledges of mutual security exact forbearance from strangers, heralds, or foes. Thus, the protagonist of *El libro del caballero Zifar* demands of enemy messengers: 'Fazetnos omenaje que por vos nin por vuestro consejo non venga daño a la villa nin a ninguno de los que y son.' The knights in question, complying, impose a provision of their own: 'E vos seguradnos [...] que non resçibamos daño nin desonrra por esta entrada?' (Wagner 1929: 73).

A prioress in *Curial e Güelfa*, to cite a similar example, demands of a knight, who has been fighting the hero, a pre-emptive boon (i.e. one exacted before its nature is revealed to the guarantor): 'yous prech [...] que vos me vullats atorgar vna gracia.' The knight accedes, imposing — after she has revealed that the 'gracia' is peace between him and Curial — a condition of his own: 'ab condicio quem do la donzella per la qual hauem combatut' (Miquel i Planas 1932: 144)

The vow proper in the romances declares, as Williamson points out, a plan of action, a deed to be performed. The sacramental background to such a practice is evident in *Tirant lo blanc*, where the Hermit King (Guillem de Varoic) vows to avenge the treachery of a Moorish captain: 'Ara jo faç vot solemne [...] de jamés entrar dins casa coberta, si no és església per oir missa, fins a tant que jo haja llançat tota aquesta morisma fora de tot lo regne (Riquer 1969: 149).

The foregoing examples of promissory utterance reveal a verbal economy, an oral marketplace where reputation consists of positive or negative publicity circulating within an inquisitive milieu. The censure and praise of this watchful collectivity constitute behavioural controls. In other words, society in the chivalric romances is what modern social scientists call a shame culture. It has been argued that in such cultures it is not 'fear of active punishment by superiors which is implied in shame anxiety, but social expulsion, like ostracism' (Piers & Singer 1971: 29). The need to keep one's word, typifying a culture governed by the principle of shame, expresses the authors' desire to project the image of a world in which men feel honour-bound.

Developing his own model of compliance and avoidance, Julio Caro Baroja affirms that shame is the antonym of 'prestige', a concept expressed in medieval Spanish by the expression 'más valer'. The latter notion underlies a concept of honour 'which is not individual but collective'. The collectivity is, first, the lineage, of which every man considers himself a representative, and second, the community at large, which ascribes honour and shame through approval or disapproval of clans and their members. Honour and shame, viewed as a two-fold programme of reward and punishment, necessarily imply a proclivity for confrontation and vendetta. This elucidates the paradoxical linkage of rivalry and camaraderie in chivalric practice. Lineal solidarity disintegrates because clanic segments contest one another's standing and prestige, in fierce competition 'over the possession of honours and property'. From the shame system, in other words, emanates 'a fierce individualism' which eventually devastates the lineage system, and thus 'the basis of the morality founded upon that system' (Caro Baroja 1966: 89 & 92–93).

The contradictions provoked by shame explain, to a large degree, why assertions of old-fashioned, man-to-man honour proliferate in these texts. Composed in an age of nobles who viewed themselves as 'courtified warriors' the chivalric romances yearn for bygone days when knights had to answer only to other knights. Maurice Keen demonstrates that the 'nostalgia for a *temps perdu*', for a 'more ideal age of chivalry', particularly as expressed through a general emphasis on vows and promises, exercised a marked influence on the society of the later Middle Ages, 'prompting men to strive to maintain or to revivify past values' (Keen 1984: 216).

The definition of the terms 'knight' and 'knighthood' underwent constant amplification throughout the 'age of chivalry', defined by Keen as a period 'between the time when the triumph of the Norman horsemen at Hastings was recorded in the Bayeux tapestry and the triumph of artillery (1984: 1). However, chivalry may be generally defined, states Keen, 'as an ethos in which martial, aristocratic and Christian elements are fused together'. The resultant 'compound', he argues, is 'something new and whole in its own right'. Each of the constituent elements of knighthood, moreover, is itself complex. The apparently simple requisites of a horse and skill in horsemanship to use it imply 'a costly expertise which could be hard to acquire, for one not born to a good heritage'. Chivalry, then, is not only an ethos but 'a way of life in which we can discern three essential facets, the military, the noble, and the religious' (1984: 16–17).

In the twelfth and thirteenth centuries a type of literature emerged, primarily in France, that dealt with the adventures and lifestyle of knights. An earlier phase of this literature is conspicuously represented by Chrétien de Troyes, whose verse romances on Arthurian themes continued to inspire the creation of new works, at first in verse, then in prose. Toward the end of the thirteenth century, chivalric literature in the Peninsula begins with translations of French romances from the thirteenth-century Post-Vulgate cycle (Deyermond 1971: 156–57).

The dissemination of the chivalric romance as a historically important genre is furthered, during the fourteenth and fifteenth centuries, by the emergence of a greatly expanded vernacular reading public. The latter phenomenon, notes Jeremy Lawrance, implies a 'discovery of the self' and of a self-conscious appreciation of rhetoric and pensive style. These elements in turn were fostered by the convergent factors of expanding capitalistic economy, increasing literacy, growth in the number and size of personal libraries, and the emergence of a leisured elite for whom the intellectual life held a status-affirming appeal (1985: 79 & 87–90).

Juan Bautista Avalle-Arce points to *Amadís* and *Tirant* as representative of two distinct kinds of Peninsular chivalric fiction. The

Castilian book is 'repleto de encantadores buenos y malos y de gigantes malos y buenos'. The Catalan work, by contrast, is 'firmemente inscrita en la realidad diaria'. The two works thus represent 'dos planteamientos antagónicos' of the chivalric literary world (Avalle-Arce 1990: 15). The genre typified by *Amadís*, descending directly from the verse romances of Chrétien de Troyes, is characterized by marvellous elements: dragons, monsters, serpents, dwarves, giants, magical events and practices, 'exageradísma fuerza de los caballeros', exotic locales and long-ago and far-away settings (Riquer 1973: 278; cited by Avalle-Arce 1990: 17). The essentially realistic *Tirant*, summarizes Avalle-Arce, referring to Riquer's terminology (1969: 85), may thus be classed as a 'novela caballeresca' while the essentially fantastic *Amadís* is a 'libro de caballerías' (Avalle-Arce 1990: 18–19).

While it is true that *Tirant* and *Curial*, unlike *Zifar* and *Amadís*, do not contain exaggeratedly other-worldly or magical episodes, this difference between the two pairs of narratives does not imply so drastic a generic division as that proposed by Riquer. Each narrative, in fact, may be contrasted on several counts to its supposed generic counterpart.

The two Castilian texts, *Zifar* and *Amadís*, tell somewhat similar tales of the exploits, tribulations, and eventual triumph of hero-knights. Neither tale is set in Spain. These romances are about exotic locales: the 'India' of Zifar, the 'Gaul' and 'Great Britain' and 'Constantinople' of Amadís. Moreover, they are set in a fabulous past: the time of earliest Christianity in India (*Zifar*), the Gaul and Great Britain of a century after Christ (*Amadís*). Both works make extensive use of the interlace technique, alternating frequently among a number of separate subplots. The fourth book of *Zifar*, devoted to the adventures of the protagonist's younger son Roboán, resembles in general outlines the basic plot of *Amadís*. However, *Zifar* is extremely didactic and digressive, with a third book consisting of an intercalated set of *exempla* and tales, and a considerable number of tangential anecdotes and stories. *Amadís* is very long and episodic, yet, given the complexity of incident and the large number of characters, is remarkably coherent in its story line. *Zifar* has several miraculous interludes unlike anything in the more straightforwardly escapist *Amadís*; the latter work entertains its readers with scenes of magic and wizardry that are lacking in the former.

Curial e Güelfa (written between 1435 and 1462) and *Tirant lo blanc* (completed in its extant form in 1490), are both set in a more recent past than the remote eras that characterize the Castilian romances.[1] Neither of the Catalan romances engages in magic or witchcraft. Both portray an essentially realistic geography of Europe, North Africa, and the Near East. Yet they differ from each other as much as each differs from the two Castilian romances. *Tirant* seems strikingly novelistic in the detailed psychology of its characterizations and the realism of its dialogues; *Curial* alternates between mordantly lifelike scenes that seem to anticipate *Les Liaisons dangereuses*, incredible escapades reminiscent of Chrétien de Troyes, and allegorical, dreamlike episodes bearing a strong affinity to the *Roman de la Rose*.

All four works have in common what John Stevens has studied under the heading of the marvellous. Stevens defines this characteristic element in medieval romances as that which violates the principles of the everyday, the mundane, the customary. Consisting of things 'out of nature', or which 'do not obey the rules', the marvellous is 'a necessary concomitant of the hero's heroism, its necessary dramatic setting' (1973: 97). There are four aspects of the marvellous. Most closely approximating the realm of the normal is what Stevens calls the exotic. While not really magical or supernatural, that which is 'foreign, strange and remote' implies a natural order which is 'out of our reach, out of our experience' (99). Somewhat further from the commonplace is what he terms 'the purely *mysterious* — unmotivated, unexplained and inexplicable'. Examples of this include ships without helmsmen, talking animals, fabulous fountains, and so on (100–01). Still further from the mundane sphere is the *magical*, comprising 'the marvellous *controlled by man*'. Necromantic spells, rings, ointments, swords, invisibility cloaks — in short, the techniques, accoutrements and equipment of 'witches, wizards, warlocks' (101). Furthest from the ordinary is what he terms the *miraculous*. This is the marvellous '*controlled by God*'. It involves divine intervention in the 'natural

---

[1]   For the dates of composition of the two works, see, for *Curial*, Riquer 1964: 620–21, and, for *Tirant*, Riquer 1969: 83.

workings of the created world'. Stevens suggests that this factor is rare in the romances (101).

All four of the chivalric romances studied here, with their proliferation of place names and personages, their deliberate situation in the long-ago or the faraway, are characterized by the exotic as Stevens defines it. Even though the Catalan narratives avoid the extravagant fantasy of the Castilian works, they may therefore also be classed as marvellous narratives in the sense that Stevens regards as characteristic of medieval romance.

They are further characterized by the importance they attribute to knights and knighthood. This feature prompts the definition proposed by Daniel Eisenberg for the Spanish chivalric romance: 'a long prose narration which deals with the deeds of a "caballero aventurero o andante" — that is, a fictitious biography' (Eisenberg 1982: 7). Despite their many differences, all four works share a fascination with specific social themes that derive from the pseudo-biographical character of their narratives. Although punctuated by numerous detours and setbacks, the hero's many adventures and hardships, in each of these works, tend always toward the ultimate goals of marriage and foundation of a household and family. This heroic progress, however roundabout, involves the knight's habitual collaboration with his kinfolk, and recurrent confrontation with adversaries who rely on their own. It is this familial aspect of the chivalric romance — both as to the hero's objectives and the means employed to attain them — that leads us to the themes of kinship and marriage.

Before beginning the analysis of these themes as they are treated by the four romances to be discussed, the criteria for selecting the type and number of texts for study must be explained.

A generic approach imposes the logic of taxonomy, which classifies according to both structural and genealogical criteria. Taxonomy constrains the observer to go beyond the impressionistic perception of superficial characteristics. The literary critic feels compelled, at the same time, to focus on the singular text — the aesthetic must be a realm of the particular. As Claude Lévi-Strauss has pointed out, the observer loses in information what he gains in abstract comprehension, and vice versa. What the minute analysis of the singular phenomenon lacks in theoretical power, it offsets in its plenitude of details, its consideration — as Lévi-Strauss puts it

— of 'individuals in their particularity'.

This tug-of-war between ontogeny and phylogeny is nowhere more excruciating, for a literary critic, than when analysis has to do with texts that seem defined as a group by their shared characteristics, yet differ enough among themselves to defy uncomplicated categorization. A literary genre is a discernibly separate population of texts to the degree that its constituent texts adhere to rules of genre membership. When several works of one genre are compared, however, the more strictly they observe generic rules, the more repetitive and superfluous the extensive citations that make for accurate criticism. At the same time, the more atypical a given work — the more it deviates from the array of characteristics that delimit the genre — the more attention must be paid to justifying its inclusion in the genre.

The dilemma can be alleviated somewhat if we invoke elementary set theory. Cantor's well known definition of a set — the grouping of certain objects of perception or thought into a single whole — reminds us that taxonomic categorization is a kind of set theory. The arbitrary abstraction of set-fabrication does not detract from the cognitive authenticity of the sets so devised. An author who composes a text in accordance with the canons of a genre adds a member to the set of texts that make up that genre. The reader who selects a number of texts on the basis of features common to all likewise employs set theory, as does the critic or literary historian who classes texts by genre or shared theme, whether or not these analytic divisions coincide with those discerned by earlier authors and readers.

When the reader or critic classes a text as a member of a genre, he declares that text t is an element of genre G: $t \_ G$. When one refers to the entire genre, having established the criteria of generic membership, one states that the genre G consists of the texts t_1, t_2, t_3, t_4..., i.e. $G = \{t_1, t_2, t_3, t_4...\}$. The rules of set membership having been established, we can discuss the manner in which any number of member elements satisfy the requirements for inclusion in the set. The rules of set membership in the taxonomy of literary history are often deduced from observation. One notes the presence of analogous features in different texts; the list of shared features constitutes the rules for inclusion in the set. The literary historian who speaks of 'bourgeois novels', 'peasant ballads', or 'romances written for the nobility' thus engages, by virtue of this minimal enumeration of common denominators among texts, in a kind of set theory.

Brian Stock does essentially the same thing when he speaks of the manner in which literacy affects social organization. People's 'conceptualization' of the relations of 'the family, the group, or the wider community' influences thought patterns in ways that 'feed back into the network of real interdependencies'. The organization of such interdependencies around a text or set of texts, used to 'structure the internal behaviour of the group's members and to provide solidarity against the outside world' yields what Stock calls 'textual communities' (Stock 1983: 88–90). Although Stock applies his concept to heretical or reformist religious sects, his model of the textual community may be usefully applied to generic feedback between authors and audiences in the broader context of classes and societies. Stock refers to textual communities as groups defined by their adherence to the rule, the philosophy, propounded by a text. The elements of his model may be transposed, so that one may also consider groups of texts as defined by groups of readers. Instead of textual communities, we have communal texts.

Aesthetic genres belong to the set of sets which are not single-tons: i.e. sets with only one member. In fact, four as the number of texts covered here was chosen somewhat arbitrarily, as being greater than two or three, and less than five or six. The study confines itself to only four members of a set that I define as *late-medieval Hispanic chivalric romances*. I select four texts from this set, and not, say, five or six, chiefly because of the pragmatic factor of the length of the works in question. Texts in this genre tend toward prolixity. By reason of the ontogenic/phylogenic dilemma mentioned earlier, it is difficult to write a short study that does justice to such long works. *Amadís* in the edition by Place contains more than 1300 pages of double-column text; the Riquer edition of *Tirant* exceeds 1200; the editions consulted of *Zifar* and *Curial* each contain around 500 densely printed pages. The inclusion of other works of similar dimensions, even if only in the form of cursory references to parallel passages, would have considerably augmented the size of this book.

I propose to study the first of two phases in the development of the genre. In this first phase, a group of long narratives emerges

from a larger population of texts, of variable length and provenance, whose preferential treatment of knightly themes makes them
part of chivalric literature. This stage begins sometime before the
middle decades of the fourteenth century. At that time there
appears a text which condemns false knights who 'no facen fuerza
de cosa del mundo, sino de parescer e semejar caballeros e no lo
son'. The same source informs us that such charlatans habitually
recount the 'maravillas de Amadís e de Tristán e del Caballero
Cifar'.[2]

This initial phase, demarcated by the appearance of the earliest
text of our group (*Zifar*, *c.* 1300 or a little later) and the publication
of the last (*Amadís*, printed 1508, but based on Montalvo's version
from the early 1490s), gives way to an imitative later phase in
which the paradigm of *Amadís* yields a harvest of best-sellers in the
early decades of the sixteenth century. This period also marked the
rise — in a development parallel to and synergetic with the reception of *libros de caballerías* — of printing and of the publishing
industry in Europe (Eisenberg 1982: 30–32).

Here we must address the problem of originality. It has been the
occasion of some controversy, for example, as to whether *Zifar* and
Amadís are, in their original form, translations from languages
other than Castilian. The former work presents a particular challenge, in that it claims 'Chaldean' origin, and incorporates many
anecdotes, tales, and passages of non-European origin. *Zifar*,
however, is probably an original work in the sense that it is a
combination of narrative elements that had never been combined
before. Into this narrative the author inserted numerous elements
borrowed from the storehouse of didactic and folkloric materials
available in the Middle Ages, many of which were of Eastern

---

[2]   García de Castrogeriz 1947: III, 361. The quotation was first unearthed by
Raymond Foulché-Delbosc (1906: 815). An exhaustive and up-to-date listing of
references to versions of *Amadís* or to the hero himself is provided by Riquer
(1987: 8–25), followed by an illuminating discussion of the allusions to *Amadís* in
various works (26–35). A note on the edition of *Zifar*: Wagner's system of
brackets and subbrackets is complex and renders the text both difficult to read and
tedious to transcribe and typeset. Suffice it to say that there is scarcely a line of
text that does not reveal his complex intervention and interpretation. I have
therefore not typed in every instance of a bracket. The reader interested in appraising his editorial decisions is urged to consult his edition. See my review-article on
editions of *Zifar* (Harney 1989–90: 570–83).

provenance (Wagner 1903: 5–23; Bohigas Balaguer 1949: 531–39). It is the anthropological profile of the work, more than a comparison of sources, which provides conclusive evidence as to the culture in which the *Zifar* we know was conceived and composed. A work's depiction of kinship relations, marriage customs, notions of inheritance and succession, reveals its author's unconscious assumptions concerning these phenomena and practices, elementary and self-evident issues in any society (Harney 1989–90: 585–99; see Walker 1974: 27–50 & 52–69).

The controversy as to the two Castilian works' original language of composition, although somewhat less urgent than it once seemed, may cause lingering doubts in the mind of the reader who seeks reassurance as to the linguistic authenticity of texts chosen for their reflection of social themes. The issue is not relevant to a study such as the present one. In this book, I study the romances regardless of any prior controversy as to their original form, taking my cue from the canonical status of such works as the thirteenth-century *Libro de Alexandre* and *Libro de Apolonio*. These works, although adaptations of texts in other languages, are nonetheless properly considered Spanish masterpieces. Literary reception is a function of cultural reception, which in turn is largely determined by receptor tendencies in the receiver-community. Only things assimilable are assimilated.[3]

Literary reception is therefore tantamount to literary creation, particularly in the pre-nationalist, pre-copyright Middle Ages. Eisenberg and others, then, are perhaps ill-advised to dismiss some chivalric narratives because, though of demonstrably wide Peninsular readership, they are not indigenous. 'Only those romances of chivalry written in Spanish can be called, or should be treated together with, Spanish romances of chivalry.' We can, he asserts, 'take a great step forward in clarifying the subject matter if we

---

[3] I borrow the concept of cultural receptors from the anthropologist Julian H. Steward, whose ideas on cultural ecology have elicited controversial responses from his fellow ethnographers, and from sociologists and historians as well. A defence or even an explication of his position is impossible in the context of this study, which employs the idea of the receptor only for its heuristic value in the study of literary reception, the necessary corollary to generic diffusion (see Steward 1955: 30–39).

exclude works that are translations into Spanish from other languages'.[4]

Spanish versions of the Arthurian romance *Tristan*, although known to be favoured by fourteenth-century Peninsular audiences, do not present the complete chivalric profile as I shall outline it presently. The *Tristán* story will be consulted only in so far as it reveals the thematic configurations defining our main group of texts, dedicated more straightforwardly to knight-errantry and its implications in the life of the characters. *Palmerín de Olivia* and its continuation, *Palmerín de Inglaterra*, while historically important chivalric romances, are explicable in their correspondence to the chivalric profile in that they are obvious imitations of *Amadís* (Thomas 1920: 85–91). The same things may be said — as to century of composition and imitative nature — of such Portuguese romances as *Clarimundo*, and of the large number of chivalric romances in Castilian surveyed by Eisenberg in his study of this genre in its sixteenth-century heyday.[5]

Another kind of linguistic problem arises when we consider just how to interpret textual evidence. There are, argues Georges Duby, two discursive styles whose social usage must be evaluated by the historian: that of laws, charters, and all other documents 'designed to establish certain rights' and that of narrators. The former, necessarily more precise because preoccupied with the need 'to indicate with precision the quality of specific persons or groups before the law, in order to define exactly their position with regard to authority, notably judicial authority', presents 'the most stylized representation imaginable of social relations'. Singularly intractable to innovation, it makes room for new terminology — 'transposing that by which the perception of new social relations has already been translated in less rigid idioms' — only under duress and after long resistance. It is an inherently conservative language, always slow in its recognition of novelty; when an innovative term does creep into the repertoire, it is destined to be preserved

---

[4]   Eisenberg 1982: 4. While I disagree with Eisenberg on his dismissal of works because they are translations, his collection of articles and essays is an indispensable source of insight and information on the genre.

[5]   Eisenberg provides a very thorough survey of scholarship on the chivalric romances, of the late-medieval background and earlier versions before their sixteenth-century popularity, and of the sixteenth-century genre (1982: 9–54).

indefinitely; the 'official' language is, therefore, 'encumbered with relics'. Narrative language, by contrast, always shows a chronological gap between itself and the official dialect. A quite different style of 'situating people among the social categories' it is notably more fluctuant, more 'indecisive'. It is governed not by the desire to define persons and groups precisely with regard to legal authority, but rather by the need to please an audience. Even as the writer strives to meet the demands of rhetoric and metrics, he shows himself, by his desire to please, more ready to 'translate that which is said in the spoken language'. Thus, the social vocabulary of such narratives as chronicles conveys a 'less fragmentary image of society' (Duby 1976b: 40).

While accepting Duby's basic division, I suggest that legal documents are just as often meant to please an audience, and are never devoid of the nuance, the covert intention, of ideology. Moreover, legal texts of the Middle Ages not infrequently resort to the narrative mode, while texts classed as chronicles and romances can also be obsessed with the concise definition of relationships between persons and groups. The contrast between documentary and narrative evidence — the basis for the standard distinction between literary and historical texts — was never more blurred than in the case of narratives which, like these romances, purport to be biographical chronicles. Their stance requires us to read them as history, as sociology, as anthropology, as political science, written from within — an ethnography, as it were, conceived and composed by the informants. For, as we shall see repeatedly, these stories theorise about the social world. Our attitude toward these texts must therefore be one of studied ambivalence, of deliberately simultaneous reading strategies.

Law, which we will frequently have occasion to cite as it bears on our texts, is a theory of desiderate behaviour. A society which, by various statistical measures, shows a majority adherence to a law code, is deemed 'law-abiding'. When we have the impression that this is the case, we look to legal codes as verifiers of 'realism' or 'unrealism' in comparing them to literary texts that portray relevant behaviours. All texts, however, are equal before the law of textual analysis, which is that all texts are fictive until proven realistic, in the sense of reflecting social practice.

A text can be viewed as the dramatization of social relationships.

At the same time, one must bear in mind documentary evidence concerning past audience reception of specific textual embodiments of these social issues. To say that a text is a social dramatization, moreover, is not to deny its other functions, which may be aesthetic, social, political, etc.

It is the intention of the present study to define a set of texts classed as chivalric romances with respect both to their 'documentary' function (not in the sense of a realistic correspondence to any historical reality, but rather in that of their intention to substantiate a certain social perspective), and to their relationship to the social order as they perceive it. The task is facilitated by the fact that anthropologists are accomplished textual critics. Contemporary anthropology and sociology, we might even say, ponder the same issues as those dramatized and analysed in the romances. The hermeneutical insight that meaningful action is a kind of text has, tacitly at least, been a working axiom among many social scientists for decades. One notes, in regard to this hermeneutical tendency, a move away from earlier schools or tendencies (British structural-functionalism, American cultural or evolutionist anthropology, symbolic anthropology, cultural ecology, structuralism, structural Marxism, political economy). Sherry Ortner, for example, summarizes the characteristic tenets of several schools of thought in the area of social hermeneutics as an introduction to her account of current anthropological trends. These centre on 'a bundle of interrelated items', including 'practice, praxis, action, interaction, activity, experience, performance'. A secondary 'bundle of terms' focuses on 'the doer of all that doing'. The elements of this second list include 'agent, actor, person, self, individual, subject' (Ortner 1984: 144).

A social interpretation of these or any other medieval Peninsular texts is rendered somewhat difficult by the relative lack of scholarship on historical kinship in the Iberian Peninsula. An extensive bibliographic survey of world historical kinship studies (Soliday & Hareven 1980) reveals, in confirmation of this gap, only sixteen items among Peninsular studies under the heading of 'Medieval and Islamic Periods' and only seventeen for the same region's 'Early Modern' period. By contrast Great Britain and Ireland show 105 items for 'Ancient and Medieval' periods, 254 for early modern. France, under corresponding rubrics, shows 145 and 328.[6]

A more recent review of work on Peninsular family history points to significant progress. Historical studies of Peninsular kinship and family structure have tended to focus on dowry and marriage, household formation and postmarital residence, and inheritance. Sources consulted have included family chronicles, genealogies, 'census-like documents', church records, and so on. Medieval records tend, they observe, to be 'occasional and of variable quality and utility'. This is especially true, with a number of exceptions, for medieval Peninsular subjects (Kertzer & Brettell 1987: 89). William A. Douglass also describes significant recent breakthroughs in Iberian family history. He stresses the increasing precision of our knowledge of regional patterns of domestic economy, household organization, and kinship structure. Particular attention has been devoted to configurations preferred by certain regions, such as the Northern Iberian 'multiple-family households' or practices of partible inheritance and neolocal residence (i.e. the foundation of 'nuclear family households') preferred by central and southern Peninsular communities. The very success of such region-specific investigations points out the 'general lack of a pan-Iberian [...] perspective'. The regional bias also fosters a tendency to ignore 'transnational commonalities' (i.e. those of regions straddling the Spanish-Portuguese and Spanish-French frontiers). Douglass demonstrates, moreover, a neglect — 'in both the anthropological and juristic traditions' — of the urban in favour of the rural. The historical perspective of Iberian kinship and family history studies tends to be shallow, with very little research on medieval themes (Douglass 1988: 2–3 & 7 n. 1).

Applying the anthropological and sociological terminologies just cited, we can define several common social themes that define our four texts as a set. Marriage and its multiple functions in the lives of individuals and families preoccupy the heroes, their friends, and

---

[6]   They list items 2674–2704 for General Hispanic topics; 2705–20 for Medieval and Islamic Period; 2721–37 for Early Modern. Entries for Great Britain and Ireland include items 514–618 (Ancient and Medieval) and 619–872 (Early Modern); for France, 1249–1393 (Ancient and Medieval) and 1394–1721 (Early Modern); for Central Europe, including Germany, 1984–2028 (Ancient and Medieval) and 2029–2102 (Early Modern).

their enemies. Equally important in these narratives are the closely related issues of sexuality, family structure, genealogy, property, sibling rivalry, and bastardy. The common ethnographic themes that justify our inclusion of these texts in a single set are thus the following: kinship, marriage, lineage, inheritance and succession, and the related issues of marital consent, dowry, and social status. The romances studied here, moreover, are obsessed with kinship categories within a narrow range. First cousins are especially important, as are uncles and aunts.

Although their stories are largely based on issues and conflicts deriving from kinship, the romances do not implement an abstract concept of blood kin — what modern social science would refer to as genetic relationships. These, it has been observed, 'are unknown to (i.e. not posited by) the vast majority of the world's peoples [... and thus] could not possibly serve [...] as criteria for the ordering of their social relations'. The obvious fact that genetics is a science unknown to the vast majority of human communities does not preclude the elaboration of many 'folk-cultural systems' for de-vising concepts of 'consanguinity' as principles of group identity and membership, and as criteria for the allocation of rights and the assignment of obligations (Scheffler 1974: 749). While rejecting the idea — espoused by A. R. Radcliffe-Brown and other social scientists — that the elemental unit of kinship is the 'biological family', Claude Lévi-Strauss contends that kinship derives its 'socio-cultural character' not from 'what it retains from nature, but, rather, the essential way in which it diverges from nature'. Thus, 'a kinship system does not consist in the objective ties of descent or consanguinity between individuals'; rather, 'it exists only in human consciousness' and is 'an arbitrary system of representations, not the spontaneous development of a real situation'. When we speak, therefore, of kinship in the realm of social relationships, as opposed to that of population biology, we refer to a collective representation of relationships amongst individuals and groups. This representa-tion, based on the metaphor of shared blood, is the chief criterion in many traditional societies for the determination of statuses and roles at both the individual and collective levels (Lévi-Strauss 1963: 50).

In observing real communities working at the business of creating and maintaining family relationships, one inevitably responds to a perception of common denominators among seemingly disparate groups. The teasing out of the likely purposes and unintended side-effects of one arrangement inevitably — allowing for circumspection in one's conjectures — suggests analogous explanations for other, comparable configurations. On the other hand, suggests Pierre Bourdieu, that is precisely why ethnography is particularly vulnerable to acceptance of kinship as a collective presentation of a cognitive system, as an 'official discourse' set forth as 'gospel truth'. Informants, perceiving themselves as spokesmen 'mandated to present the group's official account of itself'' tend to present a definition of their group that 'dominates or represses other definitions'.

Bourdieu argues that there is always a latent 'complicity' which binds the ethnographer to the official kinship ideology of his informants. Accordingly, the latter's system of 'filiation and alliance', whatever is said about it by its participants (or practitioners), must be analysed 'with respect to the various kinds of uses the agents may make of it'. Kinship terminology is not simply 'a closed, coherent system of purely logical relationships, defined once and for all by the implicit axiomatics of a cultural tradition'. The ethnographers who treat such terminology on its own terms will tend to unwittingly bracket the practical functions of the terms and the real working relationships they portray. Official kinship, in this sense, 'presupposes and consecrates neutralization of the practical functions of those terms and relationships'.

Logical relationships are to practical relationships, Bourdieu goes on to argue, as the geometrical space of a map is to real topography. Where a map is 'an imaginary representation of all theoretically possible roads and routes' the real lay of the land is a 'network of beaten tracks, of paths made ever more practicable by constant use'. The genealogical diagram of the anthropologist is, in the very extension and completeness of its representation of a multi-generational grid of kinship relationships, an ultimately reductionist depiction. It makes of these relationships mere 'theoretical objects' in that it conveys them to the onlooker as 'tota simul, as a totality present in simultaneity'. The genealogical fabrications that have so impressed generations of ethnographers, each with its 'convenient language of norms and obligations', are themselves, as folk-theoretical systems, collectively improvised and modified over time, the result of a historical communal collaboration (Bourdieu 1977: 36 & 37–38).

Expanding on Bourdieu, we may say that kinship systems, whether official or unofficial, are necessarily theories of kinship, both in regard to the history of genealogical relations within the group, and in regard to what kinship is, a system of social organization. In this sense we could speak of a kinship system as a kind of cognitive ethnocentricity. It is always a matter, to one degree or another, of defining one's group in contrast and in opposition to outsiders. But we must not confuse our analytical awareness of the origins of kinship systems in the past, and of their apparent continued orientation toward the past (i.e. with genealogy), with their real focus. Official kinship is a theory serving above all as a mechanism of social control. In this political sense, official kinship — defining 'official' in terms of enforcing a particular kinship system as the governing social strategy of the group — is abstract. Because it is a reassurance of group identity, and therefore of continuity, it is, more than an account of the group's past, or than a prescriptive, normative distribution of rights and privileges, a forecast — almost in the sense of a political candidate's assurances to his electorate — of how things will continue to turn out.

Practical kinship, by contrast, is not about forecasting, but rather about outcomes, in the sense both of an acceptance of social events as a pragmatic throw of dice, and of the inclination, wherever possible, to rig the game to yield a desired result. Official kinship is wish-fulfilment fantasy; practical kinship is role-playing. Official kinship provides the outlines of character traits and expectations for the roles which its terminology defines (e.g. father, son, brother, cousin, uncle, grandson); practical kinship is expedient improvisation within these guidelines.

How then may we define the official and practical kinship of literary texts like the chivalric romances? In the case of these specific texts, we begin by noting that these are stories about feuds between individuals and clans. On the surface the stories are fictionalized biographies of knights errant. On a deeper level they dramatize what is essentially a conflict of generations in which each party represents not a different ideology or way of life, but rather an opinion, passionately defended, about who controls marriage. The senior generation, invoking parental (i.e. patriarchal) authority, insists on arranging daughters' marriages in furtherance of clanic allegiances and alliances. The junior generation, that of the lovers, seeks to make its own marriage, to found its own independent household.

Taking the romances at their word as to the themes that matter most to them, I will seek to determine — while avoiding, it is hoped, any temptation to view the texts as a gospel-truth depiction of a real kinship — the degree and intensity of kinship ties as represented. This will involve more than ascertaining the outlines of terminology, the network of relationships. In addition to the representation of relationships, kinship in a second, wider sense refers to a predisposition to organize social existence with reference to such representational systems. It is a tendency to view social obligations as 'kin ordered'. It is the axiomatic structuring of the entire social universe along kin-oriented lines. Chivalric romances present a kin-ordered world in this sense. It is this aspect of their narrative which obliges us to compare their world with other worlds of fictive art and ethnographic fact. Because they are ethnography composed from the inside, we may correlate them with the ethnography of other eras and other peoples that are comparable to the world of the romances because of a shared concern for a similar repertoire of social issues and practices.

Thus, for example, a study of the relationships between ancient Roman fathers and daughters may provide insight into father-daughter conflicts in our romances. From another angle, consultation of studies on present-day communities provides a valuable aid to historical kinship studies, particularly in light of the relative scarcity of historical kinship studies for Europe in general and for the Peninsula in particular. Studies of recent or contemporary European or Peninsular communities and populations, argue Kertzer and Brettell, are required in order to interpret past social practices: 'Even the questions posed by those anthropologists who focus primarily on present-day community relations can provide a context within which to frame appropriate historical questions' (Kertzer & Brettell 1987: 95).

By pointing out such similarities between the medieval and other historical eras, I do not allege a necessary continuity between past and present contexts, nor any essential connection between widely

separated contemporary communities. Other investigators of analogous customs in independent contexts have addressed similar
problems. Writing on inheritance and dowry in classical Athens,
for example, Harry L. Levy mentions four processes by which
ancient forms may be parallelled in modern settings. Although he
refers to parallels within a single cultural tradition, that of Greece,
we may apply his comments to parallels that crop up in various
times throughout Europe, and perhaps even in widely separate
regions outside Europe. The first process is that of 'unbroken
tradition common to a larger cultural circle than that of the
Hellenes' such as that of the Mediterranean world. A second
process, that of 'unbroken Hellenic tradition, transmitted by word
of mouth or in writing', is the sentimental favourite of both Greeks
and 'philhellenes' (Levy 1963: 137).[7]

The third process involves a conscious recreation and
'reintroduction', as Levy puts it, of past tradition into the world of
modern times. This often involves reintroduction of earlier forms
of law; it accounts, in the medieval context, for the revival of
Roman law. The fourth process, he concludes, involves 'independent and unconscious re-invention under the influence of a similar
environmental or cultural framework or both'. All four processes,
Levy implies, are inextricably involved in most cases of cultural
parallelism; we may say the same concerning parallelisms cited
between ancient or modern social usage and the patterns noted in
the chivalric romances. We may take as a working assumption that
the fourth process is the most likely explanation for parallels in
social usage in widely separated historical contexts. The personages of the romances, therefore, do not merely obey laws or
maintain customs; they rather observe social practice in response to
a specific set of conditions (Levy 1963: 137–38).

The connection between depictions of society within a literary
work and the real-world society contemporary to the work's
composition is not always demonstrable. That is why anthropologi-

---

[7] An analogous comment may be made about any nationality's perception of
apparent continuities between populations of the remote past which occupied the
national territory, and the current occupants of that territory. This, to cite a
hispanist example, is essentially the view of Claudio Sánchez-Albornoz and his
school with regard to the formation of the Spanish national character and its
linguistic, aesthetic, and social manifestations.

cal studies may not be cited as if they were factual glosses, in the same way that historiographic studies are referred to by literary historians in order to explain things like political background or vestimentary details as described in a text.

When consulting social science as an aid to literary interpretation, I take my cue from such anthropologists as Meyer Fortes and Maurice Bloch. I treat the text as an ethnographic informant whose testimony is crucial but which must be nonetheless judiciously processed. Bloch has summarized Fortes's approach as a refusal 'to set aside in any way data from informants whether it be linguistic or otherwise'. If informants stress, say, the moral nature of kinship ties, 'then *this* is what we must understand'. We ignore the informant at our peril: 'A method which minimises [...] data by dismissing it as "dogma", as "unreal", or a theory like game theory which has no room for it or like the type of functionalism which assumes that form is a direct epiphenomenon of use, these methods or theories will mislead since they are not "struggling" with what is perceived' (Bloch 1973: 86).

The texts scrutinized in this book are defined by a chivalry whose earlier definitions do not disappear, but live on in coexistence with newer meanings. Some of these meanings can be directly observed in texts; some must be inferred. Knighthood, we shall see, becomes simultaneously an age-group definition, almost synonymous with adolescence, and a civil status, in the same sense as 'bachelor' and 'spinster'. Often associated with the tripartite social organization of estates theory, chivalry is also an implicit functionalist justification of elite privilege. The age group set apart as chivalric was a subgroup of a specific category of people, the nobility. Chivalry, in the romances or in history, thus partakes of the same disguised and presumably unconscious logic inherent in many functionalist, 'division-of-labour' accounts of society. In this sense it may be profitably compared with other functionalist ideologies, most notably the ideology of the Indian caste system. Such systems, as I have demonstrated in a previous study, are never really closed, but are instead characterized by mobility striving, status emulation, and social climbing usually disguised as recovery of a lost birthright (Harney 1989: 17–23).

Naturally, the present study is not intended to reduce the works analysed to the status of mere compendia of kinship practices, genealogical charters, or pseudo-biographies. Rather it is meant to facilitate understanding of that component of the narrative which centres on matters relating to kinship, marriage, and their links to the greater social order. The authors of the texts that we know often reworked earlier materials, presumably tailoring their product to fit the perceived preferences and tastes of a target audience. To cite the most prominent example of the adaptive tendency: Juan Bautista Avalle-Arce has argued that Montalvo's transformation of earlier, Arthurian versions of *Amadís* converts an earlier text — in which Amadís's love affair with Oriana culminated in his unintentional death at the hands of their son Esplandián, and in the subsequent suicide of the princess — into a scenario whose happy ending, marked by the hero's triumph and a multiple wedding (book IV, chap. 125) would be 'inconcebible' in an Arthurian romance. Here Avalle-Arce points out what is perhaps the most startling and paradoxical aspect of these chivalric texts: that they represent to a very considerable degree a feminist genre. Despite the obsessive representation of machista elements (sword fights, duels, wars, etc.), the chivalric romances clearly were aimed at an audience of both sexes, in which the female side was by no means the less important (Avalle-Arce 1985: 25–27).

The term 'romance', a label of bibliographic convenience, designates a population of texts defined by a number of shared features. The present book is an exposition of my response to these texts, of my understanding of these shared features. The actions and motives of the characters — their performance as social actors — is the shared theme that is chiefly addressed. Again, genre becomes rigidified to the degree that writers themselves become aware of generic categories and parameters, and consciously adhere to diagnostic patterns. This is the full-fledged generic identity achieved by such historically significant genres as the fairy tale, the fabliau, the epic, or — to mention significant twentieth-century popular forms — the mystery novel, the western, or the monster movie. The four major texts in this study differ among themselves because they were written before chivalric romances became a self-conscious genre in the sixteenth century. Their very success, especially in the case of *Amadís*, contributed to the congruity of later texts as a definable population. We may put this another way: that a genre exhibits readily discernible characteristics to the degree that it is epigonal, which is to say, an imitation of dominant models. It may be supposed, as well, that a genre falls into neglect to the degree that it becomes merely an imitative exercise. The emergence, success, and decadence of the chivalric genre over time are topics beyond the scope of this book, which concerns itself with texts conceived in the proto-generic stage.

Shared characteristics reveal, if not adherence to similar literary forms, response to similar social conditions. Social conditions include, as this study will repeatedly make clear, a climate of opinions about those conditions. This milieu — this ecology of readership — encompasses the varied response of individual authors, writing for a variety of audiences. The limited repertoire of social circumstances accounts for the coincidence of thematic considerations. What lies beyond these areas is that realm of aesthetic criticism which I hope to facilitate, by rendering the social setting of the works more intelligible.

CHAPTER 2

Lineage and Clan

Understanding kinship and marriage in the chivalric romances requires that we first define our terms. Anthropology offers no unitary definition of kinship, nor is there agreement among anthropologists that such a thing as kinship exists. Fred Eggan, outlining a general definition, notes that the term kinship logically comprises 'regulation of behavior and the formation of social groups'. The behaviour in question involves 'social recognition and cultural implementation of relationships derived from descent and marriage'. This system of recognition and implementation of relationships requires some kind of terminology and 'an associated set of behavioral patterns and attitudes which, together, make up a systematic whole'. Descent and consanguinity, marriage, and affinity (i.e. relationships established through marriage), are components of kinship as both a 'network of social relations' and a systematic terminology and behavioural code for organizing and using this network. The network, in both simple and complex societies, 'plays an important role in maintaining group cohesion and solidarity and in orienting the individual members to the social maze' (Eggan 1968: 390).

Kinship is, in a still larger sense, one aspect of the social praxis of a specific historical group. It is an array of behaviours, attitudes, and beliefs employed by a group with regard to its members and with regard to members' interaction with other groups. This array of possible or preferred behaviours and motives is not, however, an immutable inheritance transmitted from generation to generation. It is rather a repertoire of preferred responses. These are highly susceptible to alteration in response to any number of stimuli.

Thus, one may speak of Germanic kinship as something shared by a number of historical populations, and containing such elements as cognatic (bilateral) descent, partible inheritance, a tendency toward certain practices of fosterage and pseudo-kinship, and so on. These elements, however, are unevenly distributed among the peoples classed as Germanic, and, within any one people, show variable distribution over time.[1]

The Peninsular chivalric romances, like most narrative genres, express themes comprised within the ample framework suggested by Eggan. The romances, however, are more concerned than most with such issues. The motivation of their characters and the outlines of their plots are governed by an obsession with the regulation of behaviour and the formation of social groups in terms of descent and marriage. The stories are preoccupied with descent and consanguinity, marriage and affinity. Their emphasis on these topics contrasts them with other genres, in other times and places, which portray the social universe from less kin-oriented perspectives. This is not to say that the romances are not also interested in themes that characterize other genres: politics, social class, philosophy, warfare, and so on. They are, however, a kin-ordered genre in that the stimulus to action is, ultimately, to be found in the social realm delimited by lineage and matrimony.

Our elucidation of kinship and its functions within these narratives requires a further refinement of terms. The romances themselves classify the social world in ways analogous to those proposed by modern anthropologists. The authors of these works engaged in social-scientific speculation. They did so centuries before the emergence of the specialized academic categories which we now invoke to study the texts they wrote. R. Howard Bloch, in his account of a literary anthropology to be discerned in texts of the twelfth and thirteenth centuries, has expressed the corollary between medieval and modern ethnographies in terms of a threshold represented by 'the fundamental reorganization of the orders of knowledge and of discursive practice at the time of the Renaissance'. Before this discursive proliferation, 'poetry remains crucial to the anthropological endeavor'. Vernacular literature, he asserts, 'was the privileged locus for the articulation of a notion of the self

---

[1]   Friedrich 1966; Barlau 1976: 97–106; Murray 1983: 11–38.

as a distinct inner space with a law of its own'. This aspect of vernacular literature was in turn revealed through a 'constant ideological tension between collective (epic) and individual (courtly) forms' (Bloch 1983: 14 & 17).

The distinction suggested by Bloch — that between collective and individual forms — is admitted as well by modern anthropology with respect to the realm of kinship. We study this domain, according to this classification, in terms of structures which are ego-centred, and those which are group-oriented. The romances, in their own way, conceive of the social universe in the same terms, and dramatize the events of their story in terms of the tension between the two extremes.

The notion of kinship as a phenomenon in the real social world, susceptible to study and classification, has been called the invention of a single man, Lewis Henry Morgan. Thomas R. Trautmann observes that Morgan's isolation of kinship as the 'object of anthropological study' instituted a methodology of 'doing kinship'; this method is an 'artifact of the will'. It is to Morgan that we owe the most commonly accepted approach to doing kinship. 'The critical observation', states Fortes, 'is the one which established the standard form of presenting a kinship terminology with Ego at the center'. In propounding this system of determining kinship systems from the vantage point of 'a central point, or Ego, from whom outward is reckoned the degree of relationship of each kinsman, and to whom the relationship returns', Morgan allows us to show how a person's ancestors and descendants can be traced in 'the several collateral lines, males and females'.[2]

Morgan's method is borrowed directly, notes Trautmann, from William Blackstone's *Commentaries on the Laws of England*. Blackstone, in expounding the method of calculation of degrees of consanguinity according to both canon law and the Justinian systems, employs a Latin terminology, with the term *propositus* representing what Morgan and later anthropologists call *ego*, and terms like *filius, pater, nepos, avus*, out to such terms (of the ninth degree) as *tritavi proavus* and *trinepotis pronepos*. Morgan's system, observes Trautmann, thus reflects the influence of both 'canon law and Roman civil law' (54), since these were the primary

---

[2]   Trautmann 1987: 4; Fortes 1969: 22; Morgan 1871: 17–18.

sources for Blackstone's scheme.[3]

Neither Blackstone nor Morgan originated the concept of an ego-anchored family tree. In his explication of how the Church implemented a system designed to emphasize a genealogical system based on 'the unity of flesh (*unitas carnis*) established by marriage (or *copula*)', and therefore on 'the married couple and their children', Jack Goody points out that Isidore of Seville is, ultimately, the principal influence in the development of a kinship system based on 'the central notion of an *ipse*, that is, an *ego*' (Goody 1983: 142).[4] The *Siete partidas* of Alfonso X display a catalogue of kinship terms in the Isidorean style in the law concerning degrees of consanguinity. All the terms in this list are ego-defined (that is, expressed in terms of position above, below, or to the side of ego, in an imaginary tree):

> Cuenta et departe santa eglesia que son quatro grados en el parentesco, e muestra que se deben contar de esta manera: en la liña derecha que sube arriba son el primero grado padre et madre, en el segundo abuelo et abuela, en el tercero visabuelo et visabuela, en el quarto trasabuelo et trasabuela. E en la liña que decende derecha á yuso son en el primero grado fijo et fija, en el segundo nieto o nieta, en el tercero visnieto et visnieta, en el quarto trasvisnieto et trasvisnieta. Et en la liña de travieso son en el primero grado hermano e hermana, en el segundo fijos de hermano et de hermana, en el tercero nietos et nietas de hermano et de hermana, en el quarto visnietos et visnietas de hermano et de hermana. (IV.vi.4)[5]

The *Partidas* thus conform to Christian orthodoxy in their expression of the logic of consanguineal reckoning as a means of defining permissible marriages ('En los grados de las liñas que suben ó decenden derechamiente, nunca pueden casar quanto quier que sean alongados unos de otros'). This logic, as explained by such influential writers as Gratian and Peter Lombard, was adopted

---

[3] Blackstone's influence on Morgan is discussed by Trautmann 1987: 50–57. Trautmann (52) reproduces Blackstone's 'Table of Consanguinity' (1979: II, 203) in support of his analysis of Morgan's application of the model to Iroquois kinship.

[4] Isidore's ego-centred genealogical schema (Isidore of Seville 1911: IX.vi.29) is reproduced in Goody 1983: 143.

[5] On the advice of Professor Jerry R. Craddock, the edition of the *Partidas* consulted is Alfonso el Sabio 1861.

into Canon Law, in a form that has remained essentially the same down to the present day, by the Fourth Lateran Council in 1215 (Brundage 1987: 373 & 415–16).

Consanguinity in the ego-centred sense, as calculated in the *Partidas* and in Canon Law, corresponds to what has been called kinship proper. This concept may be opposed to that of descent. The distinction was first clearly articulated and analysed by Morgan, who expressed the contrast in terms of 'kindred and gens' (Fortes 1969: 38). Pursuing the distinction between kinship and descent, we note that the former is 'egocentric', in that it focuses, as Harold Scheffler demonstrates, on 'each person individually' and divides 'the totality of persons considered to be genealogically connected to him (his kindred) into a number of lesser categories — categories of kin'. Because rights and duties are allotted to these categories with respect to Ego — and vice versa — each person becomes 'the center or hub of a system of social relations'. Descent, by contrast, involves the attribution of genealogical connections within a group of persons 'recognized as descendants or as some specified type of descendant of a [...] selected individual'. The group thus defined may be 'deemed to constitute a distinct set'. Scheffler thus distinguishes between kinship systems — 'egocentric systems of social identities and statuses' — and descent systems — 'ancestor-oriented' systems based on genealogical relationships to a 'putative founder or apical ancestor'. Relations of kinship and of descent differ in that the former 'relate or oppose individuals to one another', while the latter 'relate or oppose sets of individuals to one another or to other sets of the same structural order' (Scheffler 1974: 756 & 760–61).

While kinship centres on an Ego (as in medieval charts of the consanguineal degrees), with each person the potential nucleus of a 'system of social relations', the principle of descent attributes genealogical affiliation to persons, thus dividing society into a few groups. Goody defines these unilineal descent groups, such as agnatic (i.e. patrilineal) clans or lineages: '[they are] large ramifying descent groups organized on a unilineal basis by means of recruitment through the father'. Such systems, however, are never 'entirely agnatic', since ties also exist with and through the other parent, ties that are often of political and social significance. On the other hand, rigorously observed rules of unilineal descent, as in the case of *agnation* (patrilineal descent), mean that group membership includes persons of the sex opposite to that of the founding, defining member (male in the case of patriliny, female in that of matriliny), but not their offspring. For example, a man's sister in a patrilineal system is his agnate, but her children are not his kin; they pertain to the patrilineage of her husband. One may further distinguish between patrilineal and *patrilateral* kin; the latter are simply all relatives on the father's side, of which true patrilineal kinsmen are a subset (Goody 1983: 16). Membership in the set of persons defined as descendants of the apical ancestor is, notes Scheffler, a 'status shared with or by others who are also descended from the putative founder of the unit in the same way as oneself'. The statuses deriving from such membership involve relations among 'co-members of the same unit', and between members of 'different descent-ordered units'. Descent and kinship can, of course be present in the same society, and can lead to conflicts of status and of obligation in the same person.[6]

Marc Bloch argued that 'vast *gentes* or clans, firmly defined and held together by a belief [...] in a common ancestry, were unknown to western Europe in the feudal period'. Where the Roman *gens* had persisted firmly over centuries due to the 'absolute primacy of descent in the male line', the feudal epoch knew no such durable genealogical entities. The ancient Germanic pattern was for each person to reckon his relatives on both the 'spear side' and the 'distaff side'. Bloch attributes this to the relative weakness of the 'agnatic principle', in the face of vestigial 'uterine filiation' (Bloch 1961: I, 137).[7] In assuming vestigial uterine affiliation, Bloch was subscribing to an earlier idea, once prevalent among anthropologists and historians: that of matriliny as the primordial condition. A more recent consensus among social historians is to view bilateral orientation not as a 'weakened agnatic principle' but as the dominant kinship pattern of early medieval Europe. From the end of the eleventh century this traditional cognatic system was challenged by the emergence of a unilineal descent system, that of the agnatic clan which 'does not so much replace, as is super-

---

[6] Scheffler 1974: 761; for further discussion of these concepts see also Scheffler 1966: 540–47 and 1970: 251–58.

[7] Bloch (I, n. 137) follows the older school of anthropological interpretation of literary, particularly epic, texts, citing Farnsworth 1913 and Bell 1922.

imposed upon, the earlier, cognatic *genus*' (Herlihy 1983: 124).[8] Georges Duby, documenting a movement away from the primordial bilateral, relatively un-genealogical structures among the aristocracy of Mâcon, observes that this society had become, by the eleventh century, 'a society composed of heirs'. The earliest documentary evidence profiling the aristocratic society of the Mâcon region in the mid-tenth century is already 'firmly established in its allodial possessions [...] We do not witness the birth of this aristocracy; it appears completely formed once the shadows of unrecorded history have dissipated' (Duby 1976b: 24–25; see also Leyser 1968).

David Herlihy argues that this nascent patrilineage, 'ancestor-focused, rather than ego-focused', must be considered a unilineal descent group since it traced descent to a common ancestor, and, 'like all ancestor-focused descent groups [...] [tended] to grow with each generation'. The emerging patrilineage of the twelfth and thirteenth centuries proclaimed 'solidarity with the past [...] through the adoption of an agnatic family name, a coat of arms, mottoes, and sometimes even a mythology'. Like agnatic lineages elsewhere, it tended to exclude daughters and their children from inheritance, and revealed solidarity among males claiming common descent from the same apical ancestor (Herlihy 1983: 124–25). Similarly, Jacques Heers advances the notion of an emerging pattern of agnatic clans. He documents the existence of the so-called suprafamily group consisting of 'associations of individuals who all bore the same name'. Such a group could consist of from several dozen to several hundred persons. His work, mainly covering the fourteenth and fifteenth centuries, reveals the presence of such suprafamily groups in Italy, the Spanish Levant, and the south of France (Heers 1977: 10–13).

Herlihy suggests that the agnatic lineage appeared as a result of the 'diminishing opportunities and resources available for the support of the elite households'. The political and economic stabilization of Europe, reducing 'the profits of pillage', left the landed patrimony as the principal economic resource. Thus arose such practices as primogeniture, designed to conserve the holding

---

[8] For a nuanced explication of the socio- and ethnohistorical background to the emergence of agnatic practices, see Meinhard 1975.

in the patrilineage. Concomitant to this practice were other tendencies. Elite families, reports Herlihy, 'forced their younger sons to
delay or eschew marriage, or they sent them forth to make their
fortunes'. Daughters, if they received anything, 'were given [only]
the dowries they needed for marriage'. Save for unusual circumstances, such as the death of all her brothers, a daughter's dowry
'represented the extent of her claims upon the family patrimony'
(Herlihy 1983: 124). Heers affirms that the earlier form known as
the *Sippe* — 'a rather vague and uncertain group of allies', with no
fixed domicile, without family names, and with baptismal names
taken from the maternal line and daughters sharing in inheritance
— gave way to the *Geschlecht*, 'a dynasty which brought together
all those men who claimed a common ancestor', and in which
'wealth and authority were handed down through the male'. This
group identified itself with a geographical locus from which it took
its name (Heers 1977: 19–20).

The concept of property management as the principal reason for
the emergence of the agnatic principle in European inheritance
systems corresponds to trends noted in the ethnographic literature.
Goody, for example, points to considerable evidence in support of
the theory of 'a positive association between the presence of
descent groups and the amount and type of property to be transmitted' (Goody 1968: 402). In regard to descent groups, Robin Fox
notes that a principle of descent, which 'signifies group membership of a special kind, handed down, like property and office, from
generation to generation', defines so-called 'corporate descent
groups' which use membership to control 'relationships between
owners and heirs, incumbents and successors'. Such groups emerge
'when there is some form of *group property or obligation*, like the
ownership in common of impartible land, or the duty to avenge a
death' (Fox 1967: 51–52; also Goody 1968: 401).

For R. Howard Bloch, the tension between the individual and the
self arises in a milieu in which kinship and genealogy are elements
in an aristocratic 'bio-politics'. In this context, agnation is the
official genealogical discourse of the nobility (in this Bloch relies
on the consensus represented by Duby, Herlihy, and others). 'The
kin group as a spatial extension', argues Bloch, 'was displaced
from within by the notion of the blood group as a diachronic
progression'. Nobility thus became a matter of lineage, with

'linearity [...] the defining principle of the noble house'. Noting the 'partial homonymy' of linearity and lineage, he points out the dissociation of nobility from 'function or benefice'. Nobility became defined — here he quotes Duby — by the ability 'to refer to a genealogy'.[9]

Property, both the geographical anchor point and the metonymic identifier of a lineage, traces, in Bloch's words, 'a particular course of descent' whose principal channel is primogenital inheritance. The patrilineal holding becomes literally *immeuble*, the indivisible, inalienable, inherited possession of ancestors (1983: 73–74). Thus, the 'transformation of provisional benefices into heritable fiefs' converts the kin group from a 'spatialized, horizontal' clan to the 'more vertically and temporally conceived lineage'. This represents an emerging awareness 'on the part of the aristocratic kin group of the necessity for biopolitical management of its resources, both human and material' (75). This emergence of the clan as an interest group whose leadership felt the need to manage its resources was furthered by the practice of heraldry — 'the rhetoric of aristocratic possession' (77) — and by the development of patronymics. These represent 'a passage from topology to genealogy [in which] the aristocratic *cognomen* came to constitute a central symbol of the unity of lineage' (79). Such semiotic practices illuminate genealogical narratives couched 'in terms of a heroic foundation in [the] mythic past [...] of the founding ancestor'. There thus arises, argues Bloch, a tendency to equate 'social status with antiquity' (80). Fanciful genealogy, involving the 'invention of ancestors', is thus yet another 'discursive strategy' aimed at the establishment of 'the most ancient ancestry possible and to create the most coherent continuity between this mythic beginning and the present' (81).

Bloch characterizes the parallel operations of etymological grammar and agnatic genealogy in terms of their shared obsession with origins, antiquity, and the transmission of clan identity as an inherent personal quality of each member. A common 'representational model' and a set of 'representational practices' come to be characterized by a 'temporal linearity' centred on a territorial locus, and by the 'metonymic relation of lineage to the symbols of

---

[9]   Bloch 1983: 69–70. Georges Duby (1973c: 283) states: 'être noble, c'est d'abord se réclamer d'ancêtres connus, c'est se référer à une généalogie'.

traditional power' (83). Consciousness of the lineage is experienced as 'a diachronic sequence of relations', while the noble kin group is perceived as 'a series of successions, a race of heirs with a common past' (84). Familial continuity is construed in reproductive terms: 'thus the son reproduces the father, accedes to the paternal name, title, heraldic sign, and land [... and] represents an essential link in a genealogical chain' (86).

Goody cautions against confusion in terminology. Historians, he observes, variously employ such terms as 'clan', 'lineage', 'descent group', 'agnation', and 'cognation'. 'Clan', for example, refers in strict anthropological terms to a 'non-overlapping descent group' (and is therefore, by definition, unilineal). The problem, affirms Goody (and in this he points out the same distinction made by Bertha Phillpotts several decades before him) is that the kinds of membership patterns displayed by the groups called 'clans' or 'lineages' in the historians' analyses do not appear to indicate unilineal descent groups. Some historians use the word to indicate 'a specific line of ascendants', as in the expression 'a man of noble lineage'. For others the term refers to 'an aristocratic "house" (*maison*) whose identity over time is assured by a landed estate, claims to office, titles or other relatively exclusive rights'. It is in this second sense that Duby employs the term, in his discussion of agnatic lineages, 'practising primogeniture', which emerged in the late eleventh century. These noble houses bore names 'handed down from generation to generation and from male to male, and [were] endowed with a sense of genealogy'.[10]

The lineage in such a context, to employ Goody's terminology, is 'a narrow agnatic line of filiation rather than a branching lineage (descent group) of the African or Chinese kind'. The shift to such a hereditary system is prompted, suggests Goody, by increasing political stabilization, which removed war and pillage as sources of income: 'the aristocratic patrimony had to be preserved not by force but by adopting a system of devolution based on primogeniture' (Goody 1983: 228–29). This tenurial practice, making impartible family property that had traditionally been shared out among heirs, was one of a number of factors, including the introduction of patronymic surnames, that influenced the clan

---

[10] Goody 1983: 222–28. He refers to Duby 1977b: 10.

formation described by Duby, Herlihy, Heers, and others.

In the chivalric romances, lineage means several things. It can signify 'descent group' in more or less the strict unilineal sense (for which 'lineage' from the Fr. *lignage*, has, in Anglophonic social-science usage, come to be a synonym). In *Tirant*, the King Arthur of the masque in chapter 193 declares that of the 'béns de natura' the foremost is 'gran llinatge' (636). By this, apparently, is meant 'excellent family' in the sense of 'socially prominent agnatic descent group'. Lineage can also refer to 'house', or even 'house-hold', as when Agrajes speaks to Oriana of the grief Amadís's death would cause not only Mabilia but 'todos los [...] de su linaje', so that 'su muerte fuera vengada o acompañada de otras muchas' (I, 209.339–46). We see this broader sense of the term lineage in the reference to Perión's perceptions of his lineage as consisting of 'Amadís, que era la lumbre de sus ojos, don Florestán y Agrajes, y otros muchos caualleros de su linaje' (IV, 1133.1062–65). Lineage in the chivalric romance can thus mean simply 'family', as when queen Brisena says to Amadís, who has just told her of his brother Galaor, and of his strange upbringing: 'estrañas dos marauillas son la criança vuestra y suya, y cómo pudo ser que a vuestro linaje conosciéssedes ni ellos a vos' (I, 153.108–16).

An additional sense of the term lineage is that of 'faction organized according to kinship ideology', or even as 'bilateral kindred', rather than as strict descent group. This meaning, corres-ponding to the factionalizing clans described by Heers, is how we should understand the term 'linaje' as it is used in such scenes as that in which the forces on both sides of the war between Lisuarte and Cildadán are catalogued. We find here a reference to the giants who are principal allies of Cildadán, 'que eran muy esquiua gente, y con ellos veynte caualleros de su linaje dellos' (II, 490.202–04). It is clear from the context that these giants cannot be blood kinsmen. We may say the same of Tirant's followers, whom he often refers to as members of his lineage. Addressing his loyal 'gent d'armes' on the occasion of their sailing back to Christendom from North Africa, Tirant praises his followers' courage and the honour they have brought to their lineages. Their 'il·lustre valer e llinatge' is heightened by their 'singulars experiències' (1028).

The chivalric romances reserve their most fervent expression of kin-mindedness for another locus of solidarity, namely the bilateral kindred outlined in general terms by Scheffler, and described in detail by Phillpotts (1913). However, we do find occasional expressions, despite this cognatic bias, and despite the variable meaning of the term lineage, of real agnatic solidarity. We know in *Tirant* that asking after other people's lineages is the norm, since the hero makes a point, in his account of participating in a tourney, of being distracted by the business at hand: 'la mia pensa estava més ocupada en les armes que no en demanar dels llinatges' (207). We see Tirant himself concerned with lineage. In response to the four mysterious knights who have challenged all comers, he obtains

> quatre escuts e féu-los pintar tots en aquella nit, cascun escut de sa color, e féu-hi pintar en l'u les armes de son pare, en lo segon féu pintar les armes de sa mare, en lo tercer escut féu pintar les armes de son avi, en lo quart féu pintar les armes de sa àvia. (247–48)

Later we are told that in his second joust against these adversaries, he wears his grandfather's coat of arms ('les armes de son avi'), while in the first he had worn those of his grandmother ('de l'àvia'). The narrator does not reveal the very telling detail of whether the grandparents fall on the maternal or paternal side. A more unequivocal expression of the solidarity of agnates in seen in *Amadís*, in the passages depicting Briolanja's misgivings about Trion, the cousin who tried to usurp her throne. He is, she points out to the knights of the Ínsula Firme who saved her, the son of her paternal uncle Abiseos, who killed her father 'a tan gran tuerto y trayción'. The seed of 'tal mal hombre deuría pereçer porque, sembrada por otras partes, no pudiesse nascer della semejantes trayciones'. On the other hand, the close kinship tie ('deudo'), the knowledge that sons are often 'muy diuersos de sus padres', and that Trion was very possibly the victim of 'algunos malos consejeros', makes her doubtful of how to deal with her cousin (IV, 1067.530–42). Later, Briolanja resolves her conflict by sparing Trion. The latter, recognizing the legitimacy of her claims, de-clares: 'no queda para mí reparo saluo conoçiendo ser vos la derecha heredera de aquel reyno que de nuestros abuelos quedó' (IV, 1068.616–20). The mercy she shows Trion, her 'mayor deudo [...] en este mundo' (1068.586–87) is, the narrator assures us, exemplary: thus should leaders of all lineages treat those 'de vna sangre, de vn avolorio' (1069.640–48). Showing a similarly strong sense of clanic allegiance, Tirant identifies himself as 'Tirant lo

Blanc, del llinatge de Bretanya, e d'aquella singular conquesta de Roca Salada, Capità major de l'Imperi grec' (840). In his last will and testament he emphasizes his lineal membership, declaring himself 'del llinatge de Roca Salada e de la Casa de Bretanya' (1148), and expressing his desire to be buried 'en Bretanya, en l'església de Nostra Senyora, on jaen tots los del meu parentat de Roca Salada' (1149).

Lineal membership obliges kinsmen to risk everything, and to respond with unanimous alacrity to threats to the group. This explains why Diafebus, the hero's cousin, reacts to the incompetence of the hero's nephew, Hipòlit, with near-homicidal intolerance. When the wounded Tirant leaves his sickbed to go into battle, Diafebus reprimands Hipòlit for allowing the injured man to stir: '¡E tu [...] qui est del nostre llinatge de la casa de Roca Salada e del parentat de Bretanya, deixar partir lo nostre mestre e senyor!' Only Christian law and public opinion, exclaims Diafebus, can prevent him from soiling his hands with a kinsman's blood: 'si no fos per temor de Déu e vergonya del món, ab aquesta espasa jo faria pijor de tu que no féu Caïm d'Abel' (721). No such scruples, however, can curb his wrath toward the doctor whom Tirant has bribed to co-operate. Enraged by 'lo gran atreviment que ha tengut aquest indiscret metge qui ha volgut posar en perill d'apagar la llum del llinatge de Roca Salada', Diafebus splits open the hapless physician's head with his sword (721–22).

The ideal of one blood, one lineage required, among other things, a principle of internal arbitration. Indeed, one of the invariable means of obtaining control of clans is to impose a principle of exterior arbitration. The concept of common blood, notes Heers, 'made the duty to keep the peace still more compelling'. The maintenance of internal peace was a function jealously guarded by the clan, which tended to 'decline any intervention from the state' (Heers 1977: 105 & 107). The medieval European pattern of internal clanic arbitration in turn reflects wider cross-cultural patterns observed in connection with feuds. Summarizing a very wide range of work on this subject, Leopold Pospisil suggests that feud necessarily involves 'prolonged, often intermittent violence' between 'intimately related' groups. Arbitration may be performed by 'a formally designated authority with jurisdiction over both feuding groups'. A far more frequent solution, however, is the intervention of 'informal arbiters or go-betweens' charged by custom with implementing the principle of 'internal self-redress' (Pospisil 1974: 2–9). The case of Briolanja's judgement of her rebellious cousin (*Amadís*, IV, 1067) typifies innumerable incidents in the romances. What we see in this episode is a principle of internal arbitration. There is no state to impose a legal decision on Briolanja, who makes up her own mind, with the counsel and help of kinsmen. We may note that repeatedly, throughout the romances, we see the same tendency toward arbitration and negotiation by members of the clan, without recourse to exterior agency.

A clear statement of agnatic integrity is presented by an impoverished young Jewish oil vender in *Tirant*. Abetted by King Escariano, a conniving Jewish merchant of Tlemcen seeks to find a husband for his daughter; his chosen candidate is the oil vender. The young man explains (870–71) that the proposed marriage is impossible. Jewry, he states, is divided into 'tres llinatges'. The first consists of those who contrived Christ's death ('d'aquells que tractaren la sua mort'); the second of those who actually carried out the torture and execution ('d'aquells qui executaren l'acte com l'assotaren e el clavaren e el lligaren e el coronaren d'espines, e [...] com l'hagueren alçat ab la creu li escopien en la cara'). The young man cannot marry the daughter of the merchant of Tlemcen, since the latter is of this infamous second lineage, while the young man is of the third lineage, that of David:

> E com jo sia d'aquest llinatge, no em par que jo dega contaminar ne mesclar la noble sang ab aquella de perpetual dolor, e lo llinatge de mos fillls fos menyscabat, que perdessen la successió de son dret llinatge [...] (871)

The official agnatic ideology which had become a European norm by the thirteenth century, and against which, to one degree or another, the protagonists of the romances set themselves, is represented in the Peninsular context by the *Partidas*, which enunciate the principle of primogeniture by declaring that the sons of kings should be taught 'como amen et teman á su padre, et á su madre, et á su hermano mayor, que son sus señores naturales por razon del linaje' (II.vii.9). This endorsement of the principle of primogeniture — a fundamental element in the biopolitics of agnation — is further explicated (II.xv.2) in terms of the 'mayoria en nascer primero' enjoyed by the eldest sons of kings as a 'muy grant

señal de amor que muestra Dios'. Younger brothers, in obedience
to this manifestation of divine favour, should therefore honour and
protect the heir 'como a padre et a señor'. The Old Testament is
cited by way of authority: 'segunt él dixo a Moysen en la vieja ley,
todo másculo que nasciese primeramente serie llamado cosa santa
de Dios'. The integrity of the lineage, moreover, demands the
devolution of inheritance upon the single person of the eldest son.
Ancient custom, allow the *Partidas*, admitted partition among
heirs: 'los padres comunalmente habiendo piedat de los otros fijos,
non quisieron que el mayor lo hobiese todo, mas que cada uno
dellos hobiese su parte'. Nonetheless, the 'pro comunal de todos'
requires a more exclusive testament: 'esta particion non se podrie
facer en los regnos que destroidos non fuesen, segunt nuestro señor
Jesu Cristo dixo, que todo regno partido astragado serie'. For this
reason, it was ordained by 'homes sabios et entendudos' that
sovereignty should be bestowed upon 'aquellos que veniesen por
liña derecha'.

The legal principles of the *Partidas* are the legal analogue of the
sentiments expressed in a scene from the *Primera crónica general*,
in which Fernando III lies on his deathbed:

> fizo açercar a si don Alfonso su fijo, et alço la mano contra el, et
> santiguolo et diol su bendiçion, et desi a todos los otros sus fijos. Et
> rogo a don Alfonso que llegase sus hermanos a sy, et los criase et
> los mantouiese bien, et los leuase adelante quanto podiese.
> (Menéndez Pidal 1955: 772)

Primogeniture functioned as the principal strategy of agnatic
heirship in the maintenance of patrimonial integrity. That this was
taken for granted in the chivalric culture of the early thirteenth
century is suggested by the life of Guillaume le Maréchal, a real-
life knight errant whose exploits and successful career influenced
both contemporaries and subsequent generations. The eldest of
Guillaume's five sons, also named Guillaume, assumes —
completely without discussion or explanation — the title and
property of his father after the latter's death (Meyer 1891–1901: ll.
14873–81). Primogeniture is equally prominent in the romances,
but its implementation occasions debate. In *Amadís*, for example,
Oriana's father Lisuarte is referred to as the typical property-less
younger son, a *cavallero andante* by force of circumstance. Owing
to the grace of God and the 'fallescimiento de su hermano el rey

Falangris', he is transformed from an 'infante deseredado' into the king of Great Britain (I, 250.3–7). Also in *Amadís*, Patín is regarded as the rightful successor of his older brother the Emperor Sidón (or Siudán) of Rome, who is old and without heirs; the Empress is not considered an eligible successor (II, 385.11–15). Succession is through the line of the eldest surviving male. Later we are reminded of Patín's situation: 'seyendo cauallero sin estado alguno, solamente esperando de lo hauer después de la muerte del Siudán su hermano que emperador era, por no tener fijo qu'el imperio heredasse' (III, 790.573–79).

In *Zifar*, it is Garfín, the elder son, who receives the lands and title of a defeated rebellious vassal (chap. 118). Roboán, the younger son, receives only those lands routinely granted to him as a worthy vassal of the king (chap. 96). It is assumed that Garfín will succeed to the throne on the death of Zifar, as we see in Zifar's counsel to the elder son: 'tu sabes que has a ser rey despues de mis dias, por que ha mester que a Roboan tu hermano quel fagas muy bena parte del regno, en manera que aya su parte de la onrra e de la merçed que Dios a nos fizo' (252). Aware that whether he receives anything at all after his father's death is entirely in the hands of his brother, Roboan declares to his father: 'bien fio por la merçed de Dios Nuestro Señor, que el que fizo [...] a uos rey e a el en pos vos, que non querra a mi desanparar nin oluidar; e non quiera Dios que por parte que el quiera dar a mi en el regno, yo mengue de la su onrra en ninguna cosa' (252).

Primogeniture as a source of familial and dynastic strife is a frequent issue in *Amadís*. Amadís attacks Abiseos the Usurper for his 'gran trayción' in killing Briolanja's father, who was Abiseos's 'hermano mayor y señor natural' (I, 338.589–92). The opening of the second book of *Amadís* recounts how a Greek king had two sons by his wife, a sister of the Emperor of Constantinople. The king, 'muy rico de dinero y pobre de la vida según su gran vejez', ordered that Apolidón, 'por ser el mayor, el reyno le quedasse'. The younger son is desperate because he is only bequeathed 'grandes thesoros y libros'. Apolidón, seeing the sadness and despair of father and younger brother, abdicates in favour of his brother, and takes the books and treasure (II, 355–56.9–51). Later, the Emperor of Greece dies 'sin heredero'. His subjects, knowing of Apolidón's virtues, and that he was 'de aquella sangre y linaje de los emperadores por parte de su madre', unanimously elect Apolidón emperor (II, 357.134–63).

The effective disinheritance of eldest sons awaiting succession to their fathers' title, a commonplace of the agnatic culture of the later Middle Ages, is also suggested in *Amadís*. We know, for example, that Amadís is such an effectively disinherited elder son waiting for the death of his father. The narrator describes how he rejects a generous invitation, from the Emperor of Constantinople, to be an imperial vassal. The Emperor observes: 'Le sería el mejor partido y más honrroso que durante la vida del rey Perión su padre le podría venir.' Amadís, the Emperor understands, must return to where 'la su muy amada señora Oriana era, assí que ruego ni consejo no le pudo atraer, ni retraer de aquel deseeo que tenía' (III, 816.614–24).

Another aspect of the patrimonial question is the disposition of female claims. Herlihy notes that the agnatic innovation of the twelfth and thirteenth centuries did not replace the older, cognatic system. Traditional bilateral concepts of kinship continued 'to require that some support be given to daughters and younger sons'. On the one hand, families sought 'to recruit rich, powerful, and supportive affines through opportune marriages'. On the other hand, the effort of favouring eldest sons while balancing the needs of younger siblings of both sexes was destined to promote conflict of interest: 'The welfare of the lineage was not always the welfare of the kindred' (Herlihy 1983: 124).

While not uncommon among medieval agnatic lineages, the exclusion of brotherless daughters from inheritance, in favour of collateral relatives, is specifically disallowed by the *Partidas*, which summarize the wisdom of ancient 'homes sabios et entendudos':

> et [...] establescieron que si fijo varon hi non hobiese, la fija mayor heredase el regno, et aun mandaron que si el fijo mayor moriese ante que heredase, si dexase fijo ó fija que hobiese de su muger legítima, que aquel ó aquella lo hobiese, et non otro ninguno; pero si todos estos fallesciesen, debe heredar el regno el mas propinco pariente que hi hobiere [...] (II.xv.2)

The *Partidas*, while favouring the male, do not disinherit the female. Thus we are told (VI.xv.7) that when heirs share equally in an estate, the custodian of pertinent documents should be 'aquel

[...] que fuere mas honrado et mas anciano et de mejor fama'. If, however, one of the heirs should be a woman, even if she is 'mas honrada ó de mas alto logar que los varones', one of the males should nonetheless be placed in charge of 'previllejos ó cartas'. Women, then, are accorded equal status as heirs, but are not granted equal participation in custodial or executive functions.

Daughters' rights are defended in the romances; indeed, the negation or defence of such rights is a principal motive for action. Thus, Lisuarte is clearly shown to be in the wrong as, swayed by the insinuations of the two *mezcladores* Gandandel and Brocadán, he declares impossible the concession of the Isle of Mongaça to the disinherited Madasima, since he has shortly before given the island to his wife, for their daughter Leonoreta, the younger sister of Oriana. We are told, however, that he says this 'más por escusarse que por ser assí verdad' (II, 713–20).

In *Tirant*, to take another example of patriarchal control, the princess Carmesina states (referring to the County of Sant Angel which had belonged to her but which her father the Emperor has given to Tirant) that the title in question was granted her by an aunt. However, she declares, 'les coses que són mies són de la majestat del senyor mon pare, qui ací és present, e de tots los meus béns e de la persona pot manar a tota sa voluntat com de filla obedient, e aquells pot donar e llançar així com a la majestat sua serà plasent' (553). This compendium of the kinds of rights controlled by the leader of a lineage shows, nonetheless, that the Princess's consent is a meaningful component in the system of patrimonial control: 'E jo ara de present conferme la donació per a vós e als vostres'. The distaff side, then, is not to be ignored. Princess Carmesina is clearly, as the hero expresses it, the 'heretera del Regne'. For this reason, her father the Emperor encourages her to attend meetings of his council: '[...] perquè sapiau la pràtica que en semblants afers és mester, com per dret e per discurs de natura sou més vividora que no jo, que aprés mort mia sapiau regir e governar vostra terra' (388). The Emperor's reason is based on 'dret' and 'discurs de natura'. Later, we see his perception of her and her importance to her line as he laments the imminent collapse of his empire:

¿Què val ésser senyor e senyorejar l'Imperi grec puix tinc a perdre'l? ¿Què em valen tants béns de fortuna com tinc, que

d'aquells haja ésser deposseït? ¿Què em val tenir filla honesta e
bona que no puga succeir en los meus béns, e per mos grans pecats
e culpes veure'ns catius en poder d'infels? (460)

That female inheritance is clearly an accepted usage in *Tirant* is
further verified in the scene in which, after the death of her father,
Princess Carmesina declares: 'Bé sabeu tots generalment com, per
mort de l'Emperador, pare meu, jo só succeïdora en l'Imperi grec'
(1165). The legitimacy of inheritance by the daughter is underscored with similar zeal in *Amadís*, where, indeed, a daughter's
inheritance rights supersede those of paternal uncles. The queen of
Ireland after the death of King Abies is thus the latter's daughter,
not the younger brother of Abies, don Quadragante. The narrator
clearly refers to Abies as the queen's father: 'su padre, el rey Abies
de Yrlanda, muerto por la mano de Amadís' (IV, 1054.11–13). The
narrative contrasts such cases with those typified by that of
Briolanja and her uncle, Abiseos the Usurper. Presumably a
younger brother, Abiseos has assassinated Briolanja's father and
usurped the throne of Sobradisa, disinheriting the *infanta*. Rescued
by an aged vassal of her father, Briolanja takes refuge with her
aunt. Thereafter they daily set forth with a retinue of eight knights.
The knight who can overcome these guardians will be recruited to
fight against Abiseos and his sons Darasión and Dramis (I, 196–
97). The filiacentric emphasis of this 'save-the-heiress' episode,
whose folkloric overtones are the same as those of the episodes of
Galapia and Mentón in which Zifar saves a besieged heiress (chaps
20–37 & 63–80), is reinforced by the episode in which Arcalaus
the Enchanter, the nemesis of the hero, tempts Barsinán of
Sansueña. The evil wizard explains that once Oriana's father
Lisuarte is eliminated, Barsinán may attain the throne of Great
Britain: 'que seyendo él muerto y la hija en vuestro poder, que es la
derecha heredera, no aurá persona que vos contrallar pueda' (I,
252.149–53). The assumption, we note, is that the elder daughter
rightfully inherits. Oriana, concerned about her father's possible
defeat in battle, later considers 'el gran daño que a ella venía
perdiéndose la tierra que suya auía de ser' (III, 720.319–20). This
danger is a primary consideration in Amadís's decision to support
her father Lisuarte in the forthcoming war between Great Britain
and the coalition of enemy kings. The hero reflects that, despite
their differences, he must intervene on the side of Oriana's father

because 'su gente era mucho menos que los contrarios', and 'porque seyendo vencido perdíase la tierra que de su señora Oriana auía de ser' (III, 722–23.481–85).

Disinheritance of the female often takes the form of seizure of an heiress's kingdom upon the death of her father. Thus Elisena appeals to her lover, King Perión, for assistance when her brother-in-law, King Languines of Scotland (whose ward the young Amadís has ironically become) seeks to take over Little Britain upon the death of Elisena's father, King Garínter. Her letter recounts how her father Garínter 'era muerto y ella estaua desanparada [...] que la reyna de Escocia, su hermana, y el rey, su marido, le querían tomar la tierra' (I, 35.127–32). When Perión arrives in her kingdom he hears news that 'Languines auía todo el señorío de la tierra, saluo aquellas villas que su padre a Elisena dexara' (I, 35.147–50). Subsequently, after Perión and Elisena have declared their intention to marry before all her 'amigos y parientes', Languines, presented with the fait accompli of his sister-in-law's impending marriage, withdraws from Little Britain after attending the wedding feast (I, 35.155–71).

King Lisuarte of Great Britain is clearly shown to be in the wrong as he dismisses Madasima after his conquest of her dead father's kingdom. Declaring that since her mother Gromadaça has died, leaving him in de facto control of the disrupted society of the Isle of Mongaça, he assures Madasima that he has no intention of relinquishing the new possession, which he intends for his younger daughter Leonoreta. Galvanes sin Tierra, now betrothed to Madasima, states: 'en aquel derecho que es de Madasima aquella tierra que fue de sus abuelos, en aquél so yo metido; y ruégoos que os membréys de algunos seruicios que os fize, y no me queráys deseredar, pues que yo quiero ser vuestro vasallo y en la vuestra merced, y seruiros con ella lo más lealmente y mejor que pudiere' (II, 578.764–73). The confrontation escalates, as Lisuarte refuses to grant Galvanes's request, prompting the other to declare that, since neither 'derecho ni mesura' avails him, he must seek to recover his beloved's inheritance by whatever means possible, including seeking the support of Amadís and his companions, and by so doing remove it from Lisuarte's sphere of influence (II, 578–79.774–95). The elder daughter's rights to inheritance are clearly enunciated by Count Argamonte, uncle of Lisuarte and the spokesman of the latter's nobles, who reminds his king of the implications of the imposed marriage of Oriana to the Roman prince, which would effectively disinherit her in favour of her younger sister. To do so places the kingdom 'en gran condición con Dios y con su justicia, y con el mundo en gran deslealtad y aleue'. Oriana, Argamonte insists, is the legitimate 'eredera destos reynos'. Her right to the succession is 'ahun más fuerte' than that of Lisuarte himself in succeeding to his brother Falangriz. Argamonte urges his nephew to put himself in his daughter's place: 'mirad, señor, que tanto sintiérades vos al tiempo que viestro hermano murió, que haziendo a vos estraño de lo que de razón quer deuíades, lo dieran a otro que le no pertenescía' (III, 872.391–405).

Oriana describes her plight to Florestán chiefly in terms of disinheritance by her father, speaking of herself as 'alguna desauenturada, que agora su mal atiende en ser desheredada y llegada fasta el punto de la muerte [...]'. (III, 859–60.261–64). Later, Amadís will cite custom and public opinion, and the age-old obligation of knights to defend 'dueñas y donzellas' from this very 'tuerto y agrauio' intended by Lisuarte: that is, the proposed disinheritance of a legitimate heiress. Oriana, Lisuarte's own daughter, is the 'legítima sucesora de sus reynos'. To deprive her of her inheritance violates both 'todo derecho' and 'la voluntad de todos sus naturales' (III, 908.1235–45). Lisuarte contemplates, in other words, that which all knights are sworn to prevent: the disinheritance of a young woman.

The rule of descent and succession depicted in *Amadís* may be understood in the light of a frequent pattern of dynastic descent groups, summarized by Scheffler: 'Where an office such as a kingship is a "corporation sole" [...] the rule of succession to it may also establish and define the boundaries of a class of "nobles" or persons of "royal ancestry," all members of which are entitled (though not equally eligible) to succeed to the office'.[11] *Amadís* presents this successoral profile. The king of Great Britain, Falangriz, dies without an heir. His brother Lisuarte — 'de gran bondad de armas y de mucha discreción', and recently married to Brisena, daughter of the king of Denmark — is elected to the

---

[11] Scheffler 1974: 763. For a discussion of the clanic corporation using, among others, the example of the British crown, see Fortes 1969: 281–84.

kingship by the grandees ('altos hombres') of the kingdom (I, 38.355–82) on the basis of his prowess as a knight ('las cosas que este Lisuarte en armas auía hecho') and according to principles reminiscent of the 'corporation sole' as outlined by Fortes. The pattern explicated by him, typified by the principles of succession of (Fortes's examples) Tswana chieftainship and the British monarchy, shows the eldest son as first in the order of succession, followed by male siblings in order of age, then female siblings by age, then 'siblings of the reigning monarch in sequence according to the same rule'. *Amadís*'s insistence on the rights of a surviving daughter as against the claims of paternal uncles shows close conformity to this pattern (Fortes 1969: 282).

Another example of corporate descent, also in *Amadís*, appears in the episode in which the conflict between Bohemia and Rome is resolved by Amadís's defeat of Garadán, the arrogant cousin and champion of the Emperor Patín. We read, after the Roman contingent's decision to withdraw from the field, of 'vn cauallero mancebo de alto linaje, Arquisil llamado, assí como aquel que venía de la sangre derecha de los emperadores'. So closely related to the imperial family is this young man that 'si el Patín muriesse sin fijo, éste heredaua todo el señorío' (III, 766.770–78). Amadís, speaking to Arquisil after the hero's reconciliation with Lisuarte and his Roman allies, declares: 'según la liña derecha de vuestra sangre, que muerto el emperador de Roma, como es, no queda en todo el imperio ningún derecho successor ni heredero sino vos; y también sé que de todos los del señorío soys muy amado [...] (IV, 1167.1065–71).

We must be careful to distinguish descent-group affiliation from status-group membership. The *Partidas*, for instance, seem at first glance to express a concept of patrilineal affiliation. In reality they express the logic of status by means of the vocabulary of descent, in their affirmation that 'la mayor parte de la fidalguia ganan los homes por la honra de los padres'. Although the woman be 'villana', if the father is 'fijodalgo, fijodalgo es el fijo que dellos nasciere et por fijodalgo se puede contar'. A child born 'de fijadalgo et de villano', on the other hand, is not considered hidalgo, 'porque siempre los homes el nombre del padre paran siempre adelante quando alguna cosa le quisieren decir' (II.xxi.3). When the *Partidas* seem to endorse patriliny over matriliny, they in fact correlate purity of blood with social status: 'el mayor denuesto que la cosa honrada puede haber es quando se mezcla tanto con la vil que pierde su nombre et gana el da la otra' (II.xxi.3). What is really emphasized here is not so much the pre-eminence of the male line over the female (although this factor is also important), but rather a disguised marriage rule, namely, that the daughter shall not 'marry down', in the sense of marrying someone of non-noble status. This factor is of great importance in the analysis of marriage patterns which are the subject of a later chapter.

A variation of this scheme for assigning offspring according to paternal or maternal line is encountered in *Tirant*. Although it is expressed in the form of a Muslim ambassador's proposal of a peace treaty based on intermarriage of two lineages, the patrilineal principle formulated recalls that of the Alfonsine code, in that it favours the male line (the fact that a Muslim utters this statement does not, of course, oblige us to regard it as an ethnographically correct depiction of contemporary Muslim practice). The treaty is presented, declares the ambassador,

> sots aquest pacte e condició: que si fill ix, haja a pendre la nostra secta de nostre sant Profeta Mafomet; e si ix filla, sia representada a la mare e vixca en llei crestiana. A aquell viurà en sa llei, e la Princesa en la sua. (599)

Official, 'genealogical', 'terminological' kinship is best conceived, according to Pierre Bourdieu, as a kind of accumulated capital of 'genealogical markers', of onomastic insignia that provide the members of a lineage with 'indices of genealogical position' enabling, perhaps most obviously, the attribution of titles in distribution of rights to the group patrimony (Bourdieu 1977: 36). An onomastic pattern of the type referred to is seen in the rise of naming practices associated with the European agnatic clans. 'Family groups', notes Duby, summarizing his own findings on the aristocratic lineages of the Mâcon region, 'were clearly set apart by a cognomen, a family name that brothers and cousins bore in common'. Some of these cognomina were 'nicknames that had become hereditary', while others were 'names associated with the land, that is, with the family's landed patrimony, its inheritance' (Duby 1976b: 18).

This vicinal naming practice, generalized through the Middle Ages among the European nobility, gave rise to the noble particle, as in French and Spanish 'de', German 'von', Dutch 'van'. Werner points out the need for caution, however, in interpreting such shared names as a sign of widespread clanic solidarity. There were, after all, poor members and poor branches of aristocratic lineages. Such naming practices should be understood, rather, less in terms of 'un dogme du groupe familial et de la parenté', than as a 'grammaire de relations de parenté' within the emerging class structure of the later Middle Ages.[12]

Marc Bloch asserts that even Romance-speaking regions show a prevalent use of bilateral naming patterns of Germanic type. A renowned example is that of Jeanne d'Arc, who told her judges that in her home country she was also called Jeanne Romée, for her mother, Isabel Romée. Bloch maintains that the decline of the ancient kindreds led indirectly to the growth of modern naming patterns. Early in the feudal age 'genealogies were too well known for anyone to feel the need of a verbal reminder'. After the twelfth century second names — nicknames or second Christian names — were added to the given name, to distinguish among the proliferating homonyms by means of 'distinctive labels'. The practice appeared first among the greater nobility, then spread among the urban bourgeoisie, then diffused throughout society (I, 138 & 140–41). Duby concurs, noting an apparent modification in kinship structures 'in the direction of a progressive narrowing of lineal solidarity', so that 'indications of filiation or of kinship were much more numerous in 1100 than in 1000' (Duby 1976b: 18).

Thomas Glick confirms the same naming practices in medieval Spain. He argues that the use of the *cognomen*, at first based on that of a distinguished forebear, then adapted to signify the geographical centre of the family estate (e.g. Lara, Haro, Castro), is demonstrated in the name of the historical Cid. The name Rodrigo Díaz de Vivar contains a patronymic (based on the proper name of Diego Laínez, the Cid's father), while 'de Vivar' indicates the 'geographical locus' of the Cid's lineage (Glick 1979: 143; citing Barbero & Vigil 1974: 186–87). Ángel de los Ríos y Ríos, in his study of Castilian surnames, observes that the 'apellido de señorío', what later historians would designate as the vicinal cognomen, first appears in the tenth century, alongside the use of patronymics in

---

[12] Werner 1977: 25–29 & 32; see also Schmid 1978.

the rigorous sense. Thus we find such names as 'Gundisalvo de Aza' and the characteristic, alternate-generation patronymics of such lineages as those of the counts of Saldana and Carrión.[13]

Almost completely lacking in the romances are the ordinary names based on the Castilian patronymic suffix in -ez or its variants (since the mid-thirteenth century a paternal family surname, and thus only the remnant of a genuinely patronymic system, in which the suffix literally means 'son of'). Thus, standard Castilian forms (e.g. Gómez, Martínez, Rodríguez) are absent in *Zifar* and *Amadís*. Lacking the special patronymic suffix, Catalan patronymics were marked either by the preposition *de* before the father's name (e.g. Bernat de Miró), or, frequently, the father's name after the son's without intervening preposition (e.g. Arnall Ramon, Bernard Guillem); such ordinary forms are likewise missing in *Tirant* and *Curial*.[14] The lack of ordinary surnames could be explained in romances by the authors' desire to enhance the exotic, escapist nature of their fictional world by avoidance of normal forms. This cannot be the whole story, however, since other historically frequent naming patterns are continually in evidence in these narratives.

Vicinal cognomina abound in the chivalric romance. Even fairy-tale names like 'Tristán de Leonís', 'Amadís de Gaula', 'Palmerín de Inglaterra', would appear to reflect the vicinal pattern. Leonís, Gaul, and England, the names of regions or countries rather than specific locales, nonetheless follow the vicinal naming pattern. The transformation of the more strictly vicinal cognomen to one in which an entire country is the familial locus is not without historical precedent (as in Philippe de Valois, Charles of Luxembourg). *Amadís* contains, in addition to the hero, and among very many others mentioned in innumerable passages throughout the book, a few personages bearing the vicinal cognomen: Angriote de Estravaus (I, 159–63, and passim), Brian de Monjaste (II, 556, 566, and passim), Bruneo de Bonamar (II, 365, 484, and passim), Ladaderín de Fajarde (II, 556 & 567). Other such names, again not

---

[13] Ríos y Ríos 1979: 43–44; see also genealogical chart, facing p. 51. He notes that at first the vicinal particle could indicate mere residential locus, rather than feudatory possession (57).

[14] Moll 1982: 28–30. He notes (30) that Catalan has no special suffix corresponding, as does the Castilian -ez or -z, to the Latin genitive.

the largest group, include Gavarte de Valtemeroso and the Duke of Bristoya. However, the great majority of personages in *Amadís* bear either single given names (Agrajes, Ardián, Basagante, Dragonís, Gandales, Gordán, Macandón, etc., as well as the great majority of female characters) or such descriptive names as Dardán el Soberuio (I, 108–11 & 116–23), Galuanes sin Tierra (I, 86, 143–151, and passim), Guilán el Cuydador (I, 291 and passim), Madanfabul de la Torre Bermeja (II, 440 & 490), Urganda la Desconocida (I, 28–32 and passim), and numerous others (e.g. Madancil de la Puente de Plata, Nicorán el de la Puente Medrosa, Cartada de la Montaña Defendida). Amadís himself is known as the Donzel del Mar before his identity is revealed. Persons of obviously noble lineage in *Amadís* who lack a vicinally-associated name are more often than not 'hijos naturales', as in the case of Norandel, King Lisuarte's illegitimate son by the infanta Celinda.[15]

Tirant shows, among many others, Diafebus de Muntalt (Tirant's cousin), the Duke of Macedonia (chaps 125, 129, etc.), and Kirieleison of Muntalbà (chaps 77–80) and his brother Thomas of Muntalbà (in 81). *Curial* abounds in names like Melchior de Pando, Ponç d'Orcau, and Roger d'Oluge. The catalogues of participants or onlookers in duels, tourneys, and warfare are particularly rich in these names, as one would expect (e.g. *Amadís*, chaps 58 & 63; *Tirant*, chaps 132 & 140; *Curial*, pp. 101–03). Of course, the names observed are typical European patterns. The point is that the books make constant and self-conscious reference to such names.

Other personages in the romances are named by the given name alone (e.g. Zifar, Curial), by the vicinal cognomen added to a given name, or by a descriptive or vocational sobriquet. Names in *Zifar*, like that of the protagonist, are generally of the simple kind: thus his sons Garfín and Roboán, the hero's companion Ribaldo (later the Caballero and Conde Amigo), the knight Garbel (385 & 507); Count Ruben (390–91). When there is a vicinal cognomen, it accompanies a title rather than a given name: thus, the Kings of Ester (117 & 157), Grimalet (390–93), and Safira (485); the Emperor of Trigridia (439 & 444). The absence of the noble particle in *Zifar* can perhaps be explained by that work's exotic setting: the 'India'

---

[15] See the index of proper names in Place 1959–69: IV, 1365–79, and Cacho Blecua 1987–88: II, 1769–1807.

of St Bartholomew (8 & 175–77), and other fabulous locales adja-
cent to it in the work's fanciful geography, preclude, we might
guess, the use of names and titles that might be perceived as anachronistic or inappropriate by the audience. The exotic setting, in
temporal terms, of *Amadís* (the story begins 'No muchos años
después de la passión de nuestro redemptor', I, 11) may also
account, assuming a similar desire for ethnic verisimilitude on the
author's part, for the relative scarcity of vicinal cognomina in that
work. While the setting of these two works may partly explain
naming patterns, we should not, however, assume that ethnographic
or historiographic plausibility are the chief goals of the authors.
What is more, most other aspects of the social world depicted —
titles, feudal relationships, weapons and warfare — were quite
familiar to the medieval audiences, even if, as Riquer has
demonstrated in the case of *Amadís*, much of the trappings and
weaponry of the chivalric world is old-fashioned from the viewpoint of fourteenth- and fifteenth-century audiences (59–164).
Contrary to *Zifar*'s claims of being a genuine translation, from the
'Chaldean', of the story of an Indian Christian knight, the work's
ethnographic profile and geographic sensibilities are — allowing
for an occasional insertion of authentic Arabic geographical material — thoroughly European.[16]

The Catalonian romances, by contrast, are set in recent time
from the viewpoint of contemporary audiences. The noble particle
is, not surprisingly, much in evidence. *Tirant*, while showing
numerous single given names (Melquisedec, Menador, Palomides,
Sinegerus), shows a larger number of names in the 'French style'
(e.g. Count of Albí, Diafebus de Muntalt, Viscount of Branches,
Clarós de Clarença, Kirieleison and Tomàs de Muntalbà, Robert de
Sicília, Guillem de Varoic). The occasional surname of other types
reflects profession (Joan Ferrer, i.e. 'John Smith', 1028) or trade,
as in the case of the merchant amusingly named Bartolomeo
Espicnardi ('Bartholomew Spikenard', i.e. 'the Spikenard Vender',
767). *Curial* likewise presents single names (Ansaldo, Ambrosio,
Tancredi, etc.) or, more frequently, the familiar vicinal cognomina:
Jacob de Cleves, Jaques de Agravila, Otho de Cribaut, Dalmau

---

[16] See Harney 1983: chap. 2; also Harney 1982–83, 1987–88, and 1989–90.

d'Oluge, Carles de Borbo, Beatriu de Foix, Galceran de Madiona, Carles de Monbrun, etc.

Ríos y Ríos discerns two patterns (101–08): what he calls the Castilian fashion, involving the combination of the noble patronymic with vicinal name (e.g. González de Lara, Ruiz de Guzmán), observed from the twelfth century on, and quickly disseminated through imitation of elite practices, and the French style, showing given name with vicinal cognomen only (e.g. Gastón de Bearno, Centulo de Bigorre). By the early twelfth century, a variety of naming patterns presented itself, including straightforward patronymics, 'apellidos de señorío', and surnames referring to 'naturaleza, oficio y cualidades notables ó apodos' (108). The seigniorial cognomen at first appears as 'una moda francesa', introduced through Aragon and Catalonia (112), and soon giving rise to the prevalent 'forma mixta' of patronymic + cognomen, including the occasional appearance of a country as the territorial locus, as in *Raimundus Galleciae* (113). The spread of such practices, argues Ríos y Ríos, can be chiefly attributed to the influence of status-conscious fashion: 'la imitación, ó llámese emulación de los principales, junto con la novedad, han sido y serán siempre causa impulsiva de las modas, no menos tiránicas en los apellidos que en todo lo demás' (102–03).[17]

From the thirteenth century on, he observes, the patronymic proper grows increasingly rare, 'siendo muy contadas las familias que lo hayan usado constantemente, ó sepan cuál deban usar'. While the patronymic proper was gradually abandoned (though persisting in some lineages), the vicinal cognomen alone became more frequent, passing from fathers to sons from the fifteenth century on (although it did not become a codified usage until the seventeenth century). That this naming practice was a self-evident requisite of noble family names is suggested by Juan Manuel's attitude toward surnames based on familial possession of an estate or country: 'Et estos nombres liévanlos de aquella tierra donde son sennores' (Juan Manuel 1974: chap. 89).

It was common in the fourteenth century, and not unusual until

---

[17] I make no claim to anything like a detailed knowledge of Peninsular onomastics or heraldic history. Ríos y Ríos's method is useful here because of his sociologically oriented approach to the status consciousness underlying naming practices.

well into the sixteenth, that two sons of the same father 'usaran diferentes apellidos'. Surnames could be the patronymics of 'cualquiera de sus abolengos, ó señoriales, de los pueblos que heredaban y entre sí partían' (Ríos y Ríos 1979: 102). Quintanilla Raso has documented the spread of what Ríos y Ríos calls the mixed regime in Córdoba of the fourteenth and fifteenth centuries, with a persistence, in noble circles, of the old pattern of alternate-generation patronymics (e.g. Nuño Fernández, Fernán Núnez). The use of the vicinal cognomen alone, a mark of higher nobility else-where, was affected by 'la aristocracia de rango medio' in Córdoba (Quintanilla Raso 1982: 335).

Helen Nader summarizes the breakdown of the mixed regime among the fourteenth-century nobility. The patronymic, whether in the strict or the clanic sense, tended to be dropped or neglected in everyday usage, while the territorial cognomen was retained, along with given names. This observance of the French usage, 'inflexible among aristocratic families', was accompanied by additional and chaotic naming practices within families. Women did not change names at marriage, nor add their husbands' names. Nader's catalogue of the names of the children of Íñigo López de Mendoza, Marquis of Santillana, and his wife, Catalina Suárez de Figueroa, reveals that seven carried the paternal family name, two the paternal grandmother's name (La Vega), one the mother's family name. In this as in other families, given names were sometimes shared by siblings. Such uncodified and inconsistent practices confused both contemporary scribes and later historians, with traditional names and combinations of names (e.g. Íñigo López, never, for example, Íñigo González), leading to hundreds of de-scendants with identical names (Nader 1979: xi–xii). Quintanilla Raso describes similarly variable patterns for the Cordoban nobility, where social standing, sex, and position in one's lineage determined 'el mayor or menor grado de rigidez en el uso del apellido'. The designated heir observed 'fidelidad absoluta' to the traditional family name, while younger siblings showed great diver-sity in choice of names, with females showing greater flexibility than males (Quintanilla Raso 1982: 335). It is significant, in light of these naming patterns, that Amadís, the heir to the throne of Gaul, bears a vicinal cognomen 'in the French manner', while his brothers Galaor and Florestán, implicitly excluded by the rule of primogeniture, have only their given names.

In *Tirant* the vicinal pattern yields an apparent example of the strict meaning of lineage as a genealogically determined group, defined with reference to an apical ancestor. We read of the hero's attendance at the Greek imperial court along with 'tots los de sa parentela, los quals eren trenta-cinc cavallers e gentilshòmens' (677). These kinsmen of Tirant's are known as 'ells de Roca Salada'. This, the narrator informs us, is because 'en aquell temps que conquistaren la petita Bretanya, eren dos germans, e l'u era capità e parent del rei d'Anglaterra, lo qual era nomenat Uterpandragó, qui fon pare del rei Artús'. This captain and his brother captured a castle built on 'una gran roca qui era tota de bona sal'. Because this was their first castle taken 'per força d'armes' and 'gran treball e perdiment de molta sang', they dropped 'lo nom propi d'ells' in favour of that of the newly conquered fortress (677). The elder brother took the title of Duke of Brittany. All those who accompanied Tirant to Greece, the narrator informs us, 'eren d'aquella pròpia línea, qui eren de llinatge molt antic, e hi avia haguts tostemps de molt virtuosos cavallers, e singulars dones de gran honestat' (677–78).

This would seem to indicate a notion of apical ancestry, thus of a more strictly delineated principle of descent (although we recall that Tirant's surname is taken from his mother's given name). *Zifar* seems to supply another example of apical ancestry, referring to the founder of the hero's line, the wicked King Tared. The hero's allusion to his descent from a 'linaje de reys' (33) suggests a vague 'genealogy' that mimics the false pedigrees of social reality, designed to justify claims not to membership in a specific lineage — this would be the descent orientation approximated by the passage from *Tirant* — but to assert the status of *hidalgo*. Similarly, Curial, the son of a 'gentil hom', 'senyor duna casa baxa' (4), presents, as it were, the minimal qualifications for nobility. Although poor, he is of 'good family'. Laquesis, Güelfa's rival for Curial's love, justifies infatuation with the young man (dismissed by her mother as not 'couinent') in these terms: 'Curial, cert es a tots [...] esser fill de gentil home e de gentil linage, e com vos e yo' (236). In *Zifar* and *Curial*, the emphasis on kinship affiliation as a sign of status-group membership is quite different from the membership criteria of the traditional descent group based on apical ancestry (which is more in evidence in *Tirant* and, to a lesser extent, in *Amadís*). We may conclude that where genealogy in the strict ethnographic sense is referred to in the other romances, it is thus usually shallow, barely comprising two ascending generations.

We may turn for further illumination of this problem to Edmund Leach, whose characterization of Kachin genealogies may be applied to genealogies in general. Such pedigrees, he argues, 'are maintained almost exclusively for structural reasons and have no value at all as evidence of historical fact'. In other words, genealogy, even when historically verified and useful, might as well be legendary from the viewpoint of any generation that invokes it for political, economic, or invidious purposes, since these rarely coincide with those of the historian, whose investigations are descriptive and theoretical (Leach 1965: 127).

Concerning the shallowness of the knight errant's pedigree (Tirant is the exception, a fact suggestive of the audience at which the work was aimed), we may also mention another point on which Leach provides additional insight. He notes that 'commoners are only interested in genealogy as a means of establishing correct relations with their immediate neighbors in the same community'. Such localized genealogies are 'consequently usually quite short, four or five remembered generations at the most'. Chiefs, by contrast, seek 'to establish their legitimacy' and to affirm their 'seniority relative to other chiefs over a wide area' (Leach 1965: 127).

Despite the tendency of anthropologists to assume that the issue of kinship as a 'necessary and sufficient condition of group unity' is resolved, we cannot, as Bourdieu notes, ignore the possibility that 'uses of kinship which may be called genealogical are reserved for official situations in which they serve the function of ordering the social world and of legitimating that order' (Bourdieu 1977: 34). The depiction of apical ancestry, one of the diagnostic traits of descent groups, is therefore by its very nature a mythogenetic enterprise. In the Peninsular context prominent examples of mythologizing genealogy are not lacking. Thus, the accounts of the semi-legendary founder of Pedro López de Ayala's line. Reputedly the bastard younger son of Sancho I of Aragon, this personage was said to have received a fief from Alfonso VI of Aragon for services rendered. Michel Garcia points out the salient traits of this heroic, idealized 'fundador mítico': that he came from a foreign land for mysterious reasons, but very possibly having to do with the malevolence and injustice of enemies; that his exile and separation from past relations and obligations 'crea las condiciones de un resurgimiento por iniciativa propia'; that his foundation of a new house and dynasty 'se deberá únicamente a sus virtudes'; that the patronage of Alfonso VI is earned 'por los méritos propios' of the impoverished founder. Garcia concludes: 'lo que las circunstancias le habían quitado en parte — el beneficio de su origen noble — sus cualidades se lo devuelven. Resulta ser doblemente un Infante: por nacimiento y por reconocimiento' (Garcia 1983: 12–13).

In verification of their genealogical sensibility, we may test the romances for their use of heraldic symbolism. Ríos y Ríos notes that 'armas de linaje' are unknown until the end of the twelfth century (82). In the early decades of the thirteenth century, heraldic devices remained little more than 'apellidos ó señoríos figurados' (165). Just as they conform, in general, to the French manner of noble naming patterns, so too do *Amadís*, *Curial*, and *Tirant* — in contrast to *Zifar* — reveal a greater concern for heraldry. There are, however, significant differences among the first three works. Of the three, *Tirant* presents the most standard view of heraldry, as the straightforward symbolic expression of lineal identity. Thus, in chap. 71b, Tirant, responding to the challenge of four knights to all comers, purchases four shields. On the first he orders painted 'les armes de son pare, en lo segon [...] les armes de sa mare, en lo tercer [...] les armes de son avi, en lo quart [...] les armes de sa àvia' (247–48). In chap. 80, Kirieleson of Muntalbà, seeing the shields of the knights vanquished by the hero, 'conegué prestament les armes de son seynor e del rei d'Apollònia e dels ducs' (269).[18]

Amadís presents a quite different heraldic profile, revealing, as Riquer notes, the influence of the 'heráldica novelesca' cultivated in French romances from the time of Chrétien. This Gallic influence also holds true for the parts of *Amadís* apparently

---

[18] Quintanilla Raso (1982: 337) summarizing the lineage-oriented approach to heraldry, reports, for the clans of the Córdoban region in the fourteenth and fifteenth centuries, the use of heraldic symbolism as 'otro de los elementos distintivos y factor de cohesión para los miembros de un linaje'. She lists various family symbols referring to 'un señorío, una hazaña, o un enlace afortunado'.

reworked by Montalvo (Riquer 1987: 58–59). The heraldic imagery analysed by Riquer is not lineal in orientation, but rather 'de tipo personal' (165). This too reflects heraldic usage in such thirteenth-century French romances as the *Roman de Tristan* in prose. Indeed, points out Riquer, we encounter in *Amadís* the typical French phenomenon of knights changing their personal coats of arms, so that they go unrecognized. Thus, the hero, disguised as Beltenebros, changes his arms from two azure lions rampant on field of or (I, 77.77–81 & 123.52–55) to 'canpo verde y leones de oro menudos quantos en él cupiessen' (II, 450.14–16); thus, 'vert strewn with lions or' (Riquer: 'campo de sinople sembrado de leoncillos de oro', 168). Riquer notes that the arms of some personages reveal a certain inconsistency, as in the case of the hero's half-brother Florestán (168–69). When the hero fights along-side Florestán and their father Perión, all three sport shields with argent serpents, suggestive of a heraldic device indicating shared lineage. Numerous inconsistencies and departures from historical heraldic practice (such as metal on metal) hint at 'un carácter más ornamental que rigorosamente heráldico' (170).

Curial departs from the strictly agnatic pattern of heraldry. More often than not, no connection is expressed between coats of arms and other heraldic devices and the lineage of the bearer. For instance, in the scene leading up to the judicial combat in which the hero defends the Duchess of Austria against an accusation of adultery (36), we read of the accusing knights' arms: 'vn estandart blau clar, tot sembrat de renarts burells' ('azure [...] strewn with grey foxes'). The standard of Jacob and Curial, presumably belonging to the former (who, the friend and primary defender of the defendant, has sought the hero's help), is 'burell e negre, mig partit, e vn leo rampant en mig' ('grey and black [...] [with] lion rampant'; 36–37). A herald's announcement of a forthcoming tournament requires grey and black for knights in love with widows, royal purple for those in love with married women, green and black for those enamoured of virgins, green and grey for those whose beloved is a nun (63). Later, Curial orders his surcoat embroidered with a falcon (66), while his friend, the Catalonian knight Dalmau d'Oluge, uses 'vn escut vert ab vna barra dor quil trauessaua' (84). The context suggests that Dalmau's arms are those of his lineage, while Curial's symbol is of the personalized, decorative type observed in *Amadís*.

Thus, *Tirant* shows a clear awareness of heraldry as an indicator and confirmation of lineage affiliation, while *Amadís* and *Curial* present, with rare exceptions, heraldic symbolism as a function of the idiosyncratic ornamental preferences of knights eager to proclaim their individuality. Whether through studied indifference or from outright resentment of linealist ideology, *Zifar*, by contrast, avoids all mention of heraldry. This cannot be viewed as an accidental omission, since the work is well aware of lineage (as we see from its insistence on the royal ancestry of Zifar), and of the relevance of genealogy to the personal status of its protagonists. The absence of heraldry from *Zifar* must be correlated with other features, such as naming patterns. In *Amadís*, *Tirant*, and *Curial*, as we have seen, the French style, with the vicinal cognomen added to a given name, is quite common (although, for reasons mentioned, more in the Catalonian romances than in *Amadís*).

By contrast, Zifar and his son Roboán, while often confronting or collaborating with personages named by vicinal cognomina (or by titles associated with places or countries), lack such names themselves. When to this non-cognominal, non-heraldic profile of *Zifar*'s main characters we add (as will be shown presently) the absence of kindred networks surrounding Zifar and his family (at the same time that their adversaries and allies often do show membership in such groups), we encounter possible evidence of an intended original audience quite different from that suggested by the onomastic and heraldic patterns in *Amadís* and *Tirant*. The heroes of these works are depicted as of clearly aristocratic origins: the former is the son of a king, the latter of a duke. Zifar, by contrast, is — notwithstanding a royal ancestor, the deposed king Tared (33) — an ordinary knight with little property and no apparent family connections. We might add that Curial, while confronted and associated, throughout the story, with noble characters sporting titles, vicinal cognomina, heraldic arms, or combinations thereof, is the son of an impoverished 'gentil hom [...] solament [...] senyor duna casa baxa' (4). Protagonists of humbler circumstances, such as Curial and Zifar, are thus portrayed as further removed from such patrilineal accoutrements as vicinal cognomina and heraldic imagery than their counterparts, the sons of royal or ducal families. Their exclusion from these agnatic perquisites, despite the different settings of the works, suggests that exoticism of setting was not the only reason that *Zifar* presents characters bearing only given names. Perhaps the setting itself was a function of the desire to express a thematic point, before an audience both noble and non-noble, concerning the irrelevance of titles to the accomplishment of honourable deeds. As I shall demonstrate in a later chapter, *Zifar* clearly speaks to the youthful audience typically inhabiting the households of great lords. The work's gnomic intentions, in so far as they aim at influencing the attitudes and behaviour of chivalric youth of all ages, are best served by an egalitarian approach that strips the fictional knight of ancestral trappings. The alien setting of the tale allows Zifar to be the perfect Christian knight, the 'Caballero de Dios', uncontaminated by the status symbolism of European Christendom.

Amadís and *Tirant* — particularly the latter — would seem, therefore, by their admission of aristocratic naming patterns, to be aimed at the higher aristocracy; *Zifar* and *Curial*, by contrast, would appeal, by virtue of their protagonists' simple names, unadorned by patronymic or vicinal labels, to a wider audience, perhaps including lesser knights and bourgeois aspirants to chivalric status. To postulate such a division in their original intended audience in no way limits the works' eventual consumption by any number of subsequent audiences, from various status groups. The glamour of chivalry — its 'archaic cachet', to borrow Alain Renoir's expression — has proven to be endlessly adaptable to the tastes of centuries of readers (Renoir 1986: 106). The enduring prestige of chivalric themes is confirmed, in the present century, by numerous plays, stage musicals, films, and television programmes devoted to the loves and adventures of medieval knights. The persistent appeal of such heroes as those in our romances is based, in large part, on their ability to prevail through individual worth and meritorious accomplishment — what the modern sociologist would call their achieved status. The protagonists of all four works, despite their differences of origin, are more or less at odds with the agnatic ideology which, as we have seen, had become the official norm of noble families of the period. This ideology, chiefly a method of controlling familial resources and of managing political alliance, is the system against which they must struggle to prove their worth.

CHAPTER 3

Kindred and Cousinship

The agnatic representational practices described in the previous chapter really existed. The lineage was conceived as a succession of heirs, while familial continuity was experienced in terms of both a patriarchal replication and a transmission of patronymic, titular, heraldic, and patrimonial assets. But agnatic representation as a practice could only portray the lineage as a diachronic projection from the viewpoint of such heirs. Most people, by reason of age, sex, or order of birth among siblings, were not heirs. Even those destined by primogeniture to achieve eventual inheritance were often temporarily excluded from the reproductive cycle defined by official agnatic ideology. Those so excluded lived not in the diachronic dimension of agnatic bio-politics but rather in the synchronic realm of cognatic alliance and its fictive analogues.

This is precisely the pattern observed in the romances of chivalry. The protagonists of the romances depend on unofficial kinship, which is to say, kinship practices disallowed, unrecognized, by the elder, controlling generation. Resisting the inroads, the oppression of this traditional official kinship, the youthful protagonists are counter-cultural. Their resistance to an official kinship epitomized by stern patriarchs in control of political and economic resources (including the marriages of daughters) does not, however, preclude the eventual or intended assimilation of the knight into the ranks of the very people he resists as a youth.

Official kinship, argues Bourdieu, aligns itself with the collective and public dimension, rather than the individual and the private. Official kinship is 'explicitly codified in a magical or quasi-juridical formalism', while practical kinship operates within 'an implicit, even hidden state'. Official kinship functions as 'collective ritual, subjectless practice'; it is therefore 'amenable to performance by agents interchangeable because collectively mandated'. What we could call private kinship functions, by contrast, as adjustable strategy rather than as fixed ritual. It is 'directed towards the satisfaction of the practical interests of an individual or group of individuals' (Bourdieu 1977: 35).

Official kinship is collectively enacted within a framework of 'abstract units produced by simple theoretical division', such as unilineal descent units or age groups, that are 'available for all functions' (i.e. for 'no single one in particular'). Such units have 'practical existence' only for the most official, most public, most collectively relevant occasions. In this sense, Bourdieu explains, official kinship represents the group's theory of its own identity. This sort of 'representational kinship' is, therefore, 'nothing other than the group's self-representation and the almost theatrical presentation it gives of itself when acting in accordance with that self-image'. Practical groups, on the other hand, cannot rely on any such 'officializing', 'group-representational', or 'self-imaging' ideology. Tinkered-together not to epitomize but to perform, they exist 'only through and for the particular functions in pursuance of which they have been *effectively mobilized*' (italics in original). Such groups persist only when they continue to be useful, and are 'kept in working order' only through their continued enactment and maintenance by an ongoing 'community of dispositions and interests' (35).

Kinship relationships, therefore, are (Bourdieu continues) 'practices which produce and reproduce'. They are things that people make and maintain, rather than 'objects and intuitions'. Viewing social relationships as if they really possessed the stability and coherence of, say, genealogical charts, can lead us to forget that such systems of relationships are 'the product of strategies (conscious or unconscious) oriented towards the satisfaction of material and symbolic interests and organized by reference to a determinate set of economic and social conditions' (35–36).

The interaction of public and private kinship as Bourdieu defines them may be observed in the 'agnatization' of noble lineages in the eleventh century. Duby remarks on the absence in earlier times of a 'conscience proprement généalogique'. There was, he elaborates, no 'mémoire cohérente des ancêtres'. An aristocrat in this earlier time conceived of his family as

> un groupement [...] horizontal, étalé dans le présent, sans limites précises ni fixes, constitué aussi bien de *propinquii* que de *consanguinei*, d'hommes et de femmes liés à lui assui bien par le sang que par le jeu des alliances matrimoniales. Ce qui comptait pour lui, pour son succès, pour sa fortune, c'était moins ses 'ancêtres' que ses 'proches', par lesquels il pouvait s'approcher des sources de la puissance. (Duby 1973c: 283)

The sources of power, access to which is facilitated by such horizontal groupings, are king and local magnate — 'en tout cas, l'homme capable de distribuer les charges, les "bienfaits", les honneurs'. Alliances therefore served to establish and strengthen the individual's relationship to political and economic patrons — to link him, in other words, with the house of a prince or duke. Thus, what mattered most to the individual were 'ses relations et non son ascendance'. One was, summarizes Duby, 'bénéficiaire' rather than 'héritier' (1973c: 283). In another study of the same historical trends, Duby points to the essential attribute of the aristocratic society: 'a close cousinship', he affirms, 'united the entire aristocratic society into a homogeneous block' (Duby 1976b: 21 & 25).

Bertha Phillpotts, in her study of kindreds and clans in early Germanic society, used the term *clan* to refer to 'large groups of kindred organized on an agnatic basis'. A true clan system in the ethnographic sense, she points out, is impossible in the bilateral context which typifies Germanic kinship since earliest times. Phillpotts uses the word *kindred* in the more specific sense of the 'fluctuating group' defined by the consanguineal relations of an individual. This sort of organization, she affirms, 'can have no name, no permanent organization, and no chief'. Because the kindred centres on an individual, it is not a corporation; it is 'not permanently organized, and each time that it organizes itself its centre, and therefore its circumference, varies'. Her account of the kindred corresponds to the ego-centred kinship groups defined by Scheffler.[1]

---

[1]   Phillpotts 1913: 2–3. Her study encompasses Scandinavia (chaps 1–4), North Germany and Holland (chap. 5), Belgium and Northern France (chap. 6), and England (chap. 8).

Herlihy invokes the same concepts. Because the kindred is 'ego-focused', he points out, its composition 'is redefined for each new generation'. Thus, it does not 'continuously accumulate members over time'. Because it is cognatic, i.e. bilateral, it 'assumes that women, as authentic kin, also enjoy rights of inheritance'. Moreover, he notes, in an aside that will take on meaning in the course of the present discussion, such a system 'does not impose patrilocal residence upon newlyweds, but allows them neolocal or even matrilocal residence' (Herlihy 1983: 123).

The patrilineal biopolitics of later medieval European society is not strictly unilineal in the ethnographic sense. María Concepción Quintanilla Raso analyzes, to cite a Peninsular example of patrilineal strategies, the systematic and widespread use of the *mayorazgo*, whereby a lineage was granted the privilege of establishing 'un orden de sustitución por vía de primogenitura'. This Castilian refinement on the customary practice of primogeniture established, by royal concession, the foundation of an inalienable estate, often including towns as well as lands, to be transmitted *mortis causa* from eldest son to eldest son (or, lacking a male heir, eldest daughter or nearest male relative). Such practices, while intended to fortify the solidarity of 'la familia amplia o parentela', took place within a context of segmenting lineages, as younger sons sought and often obtained, from various sources (including advantageous marriages), 'un patrimonio como para no tener que someterse al cobijo del "pariente mayor" del linaje'. The objective in each case was 'su establecimiento en otro lugar y por la fundación de su propio mayorazgo' (Quintanilla Raso 1982: 346–47).

Primogeniture, designed to reinforce agnatic advantage, paradoxically threatens the destruction of the patrilineage by intensifying the segmentary tendencies inherent in unilineal descent. The dispersal of lineage members — who marry into other lineages, enter the Church, or found their own independent households — effectively reduces lineage membership to the person of the designated heir, thus threatening the line with biological extinction. The reality of lineal extinctions has been amply demonstrated by Salvador de Moxó, who has documented what he calls 'la crisis biológica' of the Peninsular fourteenth century, during which the majority of the prominent medieval lineages— including those of

Hinojosa, Villamayor, Aguilar, Haro, Lara, and Castro — were absorbed by the marriage of a female heir into another family, or were merged with collateral branches (Moxó 1969: 196–97).

The fear of lineal extinction is expressed by the giantess Arcabona in the *Sergas de Esplandián*. Having seen her brother (whom we subsequently discover to be the wizard Arcalaus) and her younger son Furión slain by the Black Knight (Esplandián), she begs the latter for the life of her surviving and eldest son, Matroco:

> si tú anduviste en tal vientre, que te obligue á haber piedad de las viudas y de los vencidos, demándote por aquel Señor en quien tú crees, que hayas mancilla de mí, y dejándome este solo hijo, te contentes con los otros caballeros que de mi linaje hoy has muerto. (Gayangos 1857: 415)

Disinherited kinfolk, in the context of primogeniture and other agnatic practices, fell back on the natural fluidity of statuses in a social order which had been bilateral since time out of mind. The apparent move toward 'agnation', in other words, actually heightened the naturally dissociative tendencies of the bilateral system. Beneficiaries rather than heirs, the fictional knights of our romances are, just as the aristocrats of the so-called pre-agnatic phase described by Duby, enmeshed in a network of synchronic relationships upon which they depend to secure benefices dispensed by a royal or imperial patron. Patronage, to be sure, must be read between the lines: the knights' search for 'honra y prez' is portrayed in terms not of mere political or kin-based affiliations, but of meritorious performance. The benefices attained are not depicted as such, but are glamorized, folklorized, as good marriages and political offices earned by heroic valour. There would, however, be nothing to win without royal or imperial sponsorship of the tourneys and wars in which the knight competes to prove himself.

Kinship in the romances is thus synchronic, in the sense proposed by R. Howard Bloch as the antonym of the diachronic emphasis of official agnatic kinship. Although, as we have seen, lineage is present in its heraldic or cognominal guises, it functions chiefly as verifier of the hero's status before his beloved, his comrades, and his audience. Genealogy, as noted in the previous chapter, has many functions, and is not exclusively the instrument of agnatic ideology. In the practical dimension, genealogy (fake or genuine; the intention and result are the same) confirms who one's relations are. It serves to bolster kinship solidarity and to establish and maintain political and economic alliances. In the status dimension (which is of course practical in its own way), genealogy is used to legitimate one's position within a stratified system of invidious distinctions. These may or may not correlate with the gradations of political or economic hierarchies.

The romances are ego-centred, which is to say, they tend to emphasize the dynamics of the bilateral kindred. Kinship in the egocentric sense is both a principle of solidarity, and the framework of collaborative action-groups created according to that principle. Within the cohort of knights errant, kinship solidarities are cognatic — i.e. bilateral — because the youth culture is placed in a position in which class interest, in the Weberian sense of communalization and group solidarity, is provoked, to a degree, by social circumstances. These compel the chivalric cohort — divided into kin-based groups now confronting, now allied with one another — to behave in ways approximating the conflicts and solidarities of class-structured societies. The marginal hero therefore engages in collective action organized, more often than not, along the lines of kinship conceived in terms of bilateral kindreds. The cognatic networks of tradition, which never disappeared, are the most obvious elements in the repertoire of social strategies available to him. The collective actions instigated and led by him are often pursued in furtherance of love affairs and marriages experienced as methods of social advancement, of outdoing the previous generation, of competing with rival knights and with competing groups analogous to the hero's.

The term cognation requires further clarification. It may refer, as it did in Latin, to kin of Ego defined through all links on both the paternal or maternal sides (thus, *cognati* as opposed to strictly patrilineal *agnati*). In contemporary ethnographic usage, 'cognation' tends to be used as an effective synonym of 'bilateral kinship'. Much of what defines the open nature ascribed by Duby and others to pre-agnatic kinship practices derives from the bilateral character of European kin relations.[2]

The second sense of *cognati* is that of one's maternal kin.

---

[2] For the subtle differences between systems of bilateral kinship and those of double descent, whose elucidation of these nuances need not detain us here, see Goody 1961: 3–12; Forde 1968: 179–85; Fox 1967: 135–39.

'Kinsmen', asserts Karl Leyser, 'gathered round and sought to stand as near as possible to their most successful relatives [...] on whichever side, so that the centre of gravity and even the sense of identity of these large families could shift, sometimes within very few generations'. Thus, the standing of maternal relatives was often 'as high as or even higher than paternal kin, if they were thought to be nobler and had better things to offer' (Leyser 1970: 126; see also Leyser 1968). Leyser argues, in disagreement with D. A. Bullough, that *cognati* meant more than simply 'kin from both sides', its strict Latin meaning. For medieval writers it probably also signified matrilateral kin. In support of this assertion, he refers to Isidore's *Etymologiae* (IX.vi.1.2), which state that *cognati* are the relations arising through females: 'Qui inde post agnatos habentur, quia per feminini sexus personas veniunt, nec sunt agnati, sed alias naturali iure cognati.' Because of the importance of female ancestors, *cognatus* came frequently to denote 'maternal kinsmen'; *cognatio*, in short, 'was heavily weighed on the maternal side'.[3]

Matrilateral affiliation is frequently emphasized in the romances. Tirant provides a good example. As we have seen, he responds to a challenge issued by four knights by exhibiting four shields on which he displays 'les armes de son pare', 'les armes de sa mare', 'les armes de son avi', 'les armes de sa àvia' (247–48). Later we are told that in his second joust against these adversaries, he wears his grandfather's coat of arms ('les armes de son avi'), while in the first he had worn those of his grandmother ('de l'àvia'). The narrator does not reveal which side the grandparents fall on — maternal or paternal. The passage may be correlated, however, with other evidence in the text. Tirant's father is mentioned only as the lord of the Tiranian March, while his mother Blanca is described as the 'filla del duc de Bretanya' (170). The fact that Tirant takes his name from Blanca and that her father and his title are specifically mentioned suggests that this is a case of matrilateral preference. The importance of Tirant's relationship to his maternal grandfather is underscored by the welcome extended by the Duke of Brittany to Tirant and his companions upon their return from England (294). Still later, Tirant is among the ambassadors selected by his grandfather (who include an archbishop, a bishop, and a viscount) in his

---

[3] Leyser 1970: 131; he refers to Bullough 1969.

embassy sent to the King of France to assist that monarch's rescue of the Rhodian Christians (303).

Tirant thus takes his first name from his father's vicinal cognomen, and his second name from his mother's given name. Francesc Moll, in his compilation of lineage names, notes that, while the 'segon nom' was commonly taken from the father's given name, 'no manquen casos documentats de l'aplicació del nom de la mare' (Moll 1982: 29). Although taken from his mother's given name, Tirant's second name, we note, is more a descriptive nickname than a strict matronymic; in this he participates in the whimsical and idiosyncratic naming patterns described earlier. A more straightforward variation on the matrilateral naming pattern occurs in the *Gran conquista de Ultramar*, where we see a hint of the mother's father-sister's son relationship, a significant feature, as we will see presently, of European cognatic kinship. The Swan Knight, who always travels incognito, takes his baptismal name from his maternal grandfather: 'ovo otro nombre quando lo bautizaron, ca le mandara su madre poner Pompleo, ca ovo assí nombre su abuelo, padre de su madre' (Cooper 1979: I, 119).

Yet another sense of 'cognatic kin', finally, is that of an assemblage of bilateral kinfolk, centring on an individual ego. This, in other words, is kinship as opposed to descent, a distinction, already referred to, which defines groups in terms of common relatives rather than common ancestors, or, in Fox's analysis, in terms of 'the degree of relationship of [...] members to a common ego rather than to a common ancestor' (Fox 1967: 164). The term kindred has been applied to such groups. A kindred, explains Derek Freeman, 'consists of all the recognized stocks of a given individual, these stocks being linked, by marriages, in the generations between this individual and his truncal ancestors' (Freeman 1968: 255–56). In such bilateral groups, the range of relationships is determined by 'cousinship'. A kindred of first-cousin range is defined as 'two stocks linked by a marriage in the first ascending generation'. A second-cousin range of kindred comprises three ascending generations, and so on. George Murdock points out that because the kindred is always 'composed of persons related to a particular individual (or group of siblings) bilaterally', the members of a kindred, aside from 'the core individual and his siblings', are not necessarily related to one another. Because kindreds 'necessarily overlap one another endlessly', they cannot be regarded as groups with permanent or clearly defined membership. Thus, a society can never be divided into separate kindreds in the same way that it may be 'segmented into discrete families, lineages, clans, or communities' (Murdock 1968: 239).

Kinship relations organized around bilateral kindreds readily lend themselves, as Scheffler points out, to the improvisation of impermanent 'ad hoc "action groups"' (Scheffler 1974: 761). Freeman, referring to kindred systems in a range of bilateral societies, speaks of the kindred as presenting 'a wide range of optative relationships [...which] it is possible for [the individual] to accentuate as he pleases or as suits his special interests'. A frequently observed concomitant of bilateral kinship is thus 'the formation of temporary, kindred-based action groups'. Ranging from five or six to forty or fifty in the number of members, these impromptu groups engage in a variety of activities (foraging or trading expeditions, raiding parties, etc.) which may sometimes last several years. Although tending to disband after the collective task is accomplished, the group exhibits coherent organization while it exists. Travelling as a unit, its members interact intensively: it is, observes Freeman, 'an in-group with a marked collective sense of unity', while its members 'possess a common estate and common purpose'. Membership in such groups is voluntary, with participation determined by the 'interests and predilections of individuals' (Freeman 1968: 266 & 269).

Kinfolk categorized as reliable, potentially recruitable collaborators in such activities constitute what Adrian Mayer has called 'the kindred of cooperation'. Repeated recruitment of the same individuals can lead, he suggests, to the formation of what he calls quasi-groups. These he defines as continuing, loosely organized associations which may in time consolidate into more enduring, all-purpose organizations. In any case, when kinship provides the pool of candidates, 'the outward content of recruitment is always at least partly one of kinship and its entailed moral obligations, whatever other incentives there may be to support ego' (Mayer 1966: 117–18).

Kinship, as revealed in innumerable casual references, is the circumstantial idiom, the assumed framework, of everyday life in the chivalric romance. Indeed, the frequency with which kinship relations are mentioned in tangential or digressive moments is one of the most significant indicators of the romances' obsession. To take an example from hundreds: the narrator describes, in the opening chapter of *Amadís*, how king Garínter comes upon a single knight (king Perión) in combat with two other knights, described as Garínter's vassals and as 'muy soberuios y de malas maneras, y muy emparentados' (I, 12). To cite yet another instance: for no particular reason, the narrator of *Curial* sees fit to mention that a certain sea captain and merchant on whose ship Curial and his companions embark — therefore a personage we will glimpse only for the briefest moment — 'tenia vn parent mercader en Genoua, lo qual, no obstant fos de Barchinona, tenia empero casa en Genoua' (403).

Kindred solidarity is most often expressed, in the world of the knight errant, in terms of cousinship. This phenomenon is seen in the biography of Guillaume le Maréchal. As a youth, Guillaume is sent by his father to the household of William II of Tancarville, described by the poet as the

> Chamberlenc kui pas n'avile
> Son lingnage ne jor ne ore,
> Einz l'eime & essauce & enore;
> E il ert lor cosins germains. (Meyer 1891–1901: ll. 746–49)

Later, revealing the same emphasis on cousinship, the *Histoire* recounts how the Young King (Prince Henry, son of Henry II) is received with great honour and affection by the Count of Flanders: 'Ce fu bien dre[i]z qu'il s'entramérent / Quer cosin e boen ami érent' (ll. 2459–60).

Amadís is particularly dominated by a fixation on cousinship. As with kinship relations of all kinds, the importance of cousinship is revealed through a myriad of offhand allusions to secondary characters: messengers, squires, felon knights and other background personages whose family relationships have little or nothing to do with the plot. When Galaor, seeking hospitality and medical care, is beset by treacherous knights in the Castle of the Arnida Forest, killing several, the master of the castle demands: 'Uos soys el que ha muerto mis cormanos y la gente deste mi castillo?' (I, 138.436–38). When the Damsel of Denmark, Oriana's handmaiden, sets forth for Scotland (II, 403), sent by her mistress in hope of finding Amadís there, the narrator makes a point of telling us that she is accompanied by her brother Durín and Emil, a nephew of Amadís's foster father Gandales (thus a cousin of Gandalín). When Florestán and Quadragante send Elián el Loçano to Lisuarte, they send along 'otros dos caualleros con él que eran sus primos' (III, 706.100–01). Arrayed against Tafinor of Bohemia, the narrator informs us, are the forces of Patín the emperor of Rome, who seeks to make Bohemia a tribute kingdom. The leading warrior in these forces is 'Garadán [...] primo cormano del emperador Patín' (III, 759.257–58).

The prominence of cousinship as a principle of social cohesion and political organization is equally evident in *Tirant*. The narrative imagines the collective actions of the Saracens in conflict with Christians, for example, in terms of cousinship. The Emperor, describing the arrival of reinforcements in the Infidel camp, refers to the King of Jerusalem, 'qui és cosín germà del Gran Caramany' (723). On the Christian side of the conflict, cousinship is likewise of pervasive importance. Hearing that his 'cosín germà' Agramunt has been 'malament nafrat', Tirant arrives with reinforcements and redoubles the attack on the city of Montàgata whose inhabitants have reneged on their promise to surrender. When, after a prolonged assault, they ask for terms, the hero replies that 'per lo defalt que ells havien fet a son cosín germà, anassen a ell, e lo que ell faria hauria per fet' (952). Strategy, tactics, and diplomacy, in other words, are heavily influenced by the logic of cousinship.

Tirant's military aptitude is couched, to a degree, in terms of his ability to attract the collaboration of kinsmen in military enterprises. One such kinsman is the Viscount of Branches, 'cosín germà de Tirant'. The Viscount comes to Greece because 'son oncle, lo pare de Tirant, era desijós de veure son fill', and because he wishes to participate in the 'molt gran empresa de guerra molt justa contra infels' led by his cousins Tirant and Diafebus. Moved by the desire to practise arms in so great a cause, and 'per les grans pregàries de la mare de Tirant', he arrives 'en ajuda de son cosín germà ab cinc mília francs arquers' (629). Later, again in reference to the kindred solidarity commanded by Tirant, the narrator refers to the kinsmen accompanying him at the Greek imperial court as 'los de sa parentela, los quals eren trenta-cinc cavallers e gentils-hòmens' (677).

Cousinship is regarded in many societies with the same intensity as fraternity in the strict sense. Significantly, in Indo-European cultures it was the general pattern that 'cousins were considered as brothers' (Schusky 1972: 16–17). In this regard the terminology in *Amadís* and *Tirant* is suggestive. The common term for cousin in *Amadís*, for example, is *cormano*; in *Tirant* and *Curial*, it is *cosí germà*. The latter expression parallels English 'cousin german', both reflecting the French *cousin germain*. Both *hermano* and *germà* come from the Latin *germanus*, meaning 'true, genuine, authentic'. Corominas notes (under the entry for HERMANO) that the Castilian *cohermano* (*cormano* in Amadís) derives from *co(n)-germanus*, literally 'co-brother', as a synonym for *primo hermano*.

The effect of the terms *cohermano* and *cosí germà*, in any event, was to classify cousins as if they were brothers. This practice participates in a cross-cultural trend toward employing terminology which both reflects and encourages cousinship as a principle of kin-based cooperation. It is very possible that the narrators of *Amadís*, *Tirant*, and *Curial*, in their emphasis on the social importance of cousinship, reflect the real social practice of their time, a practice which might well have continued to be recognized as normal by the audiences of subsequent centuries. In the system of bilateral European kindreds, the prevalence and the ambiguity of the term cousin make it useful as a generic label for 'mobilizable kinsman' (Schusky 1972: 21–24).

The narrator of *Amadís* frequently portrays the close collaborations implied by traditional cousinship, as in the scene in which the two ladies who lead Amadís to Lisuarte's court are 'hermanas y primas cormanas' of the woman he defends against Dardán (I, 130.564–65). Amadís tells Mabilia, his cousin, that because of their family tie he is obliged to love and cherish her ('querer y amar'). She responds, with no less intensity, by assuring him that, as a matter of their common *deudo* (blood relationship), she has taken pity on him, and intends to put at his disposal her life and her good offices (I, 129.530–40). The emotional equivalence of fraternity and cousinship is expressed in *Tirant* by the intensity of the hero's relationship with his kinsmen. At times this intensity leads to a merging of terms, as when Tirant, as he demands news of his beloved Carmesina, addresses his cousin Diafebus as 'Lo meu bon germà' (379).

This is a world of face-to-face relationships, of passionate commitments and instinctive allegiances. In *Amadís*, for example, there is a scene in which Galaor and Norandel meet their nephew Esplandián for the first time. Although they do not yet know that he is Amadís's son, they feel a powerful, intuitive bond: 'lo tomaron, y abraçáuanlo muchas vezes, como que naturaleza que con él auían los atraya a ello' (III, 779.438–40). The instinctive attraction of kin for kin partakes, we may be tempted to say, of the mentality described by Claire Bell for the Germanic epic: 'So powerful was the tie of blood relationship felt to be', she notes, 'that it was supposed to assert itself inevitably even in those who were unaware of their common descent' (Bell 1922: 77).

Cousinship as an action-group of 'mobilizable kin' is portrayed in the impending confrontation between King Lisuarte and the self-exiled knights who have rallied around Amadís. The nucleus of the fighting force sent out to rescue Madasima and the twelve captive maidens, held hostage by Lisuarte, is an impromptu action-group composed of cousins, as we see in the following catalogue announced by the hero:

> Uos, señor don Galuanes, seréys el primero, pues que el negocio principalmente vuestro es, y Agrajes, vuestro sobrino, y mi hermano don Florestán, y mis cormanos Palomir y Dragonís, y don Brian de Monjaste, y Nicorán de la Torre Blanca, y Orlandín, hijo del conde de Vrlanda, y Gauarte de Valtemoroso, y Madancil de la Puente de la Plata, y Ladaderín de Fajarque; (II, 567.965–77)

Later in *Amadís*, the Roman Emperor Patín, newly ascended to the throne on the death of his childless brother, turns, in his selection of an emissary to head a diplomatic mission to renew his suit for Oriana's hand in marriage, to 'vn cormano suyo Salustanquidio llamado, príncipe de Calabria, cauallero famoso en armas' (III, 791.630–33). The importance of collaborative cousinship in the matter of the arranged marriage between Oriana and the Roman prince is repeatedly invoked, as in the elaborate description of Salustanquidio's entourage (III, 825.1260–63).

Cousins in *Amadís* are more often than not related to the hero. At the same time, cousinship is portrayed in *Amadís* as of the first range, that is, limited — in so far as the text mentions details of relationships — to the collaboration of first cousins. The world of the romances, moreover, does not appear to distinguish between so-called parallel and cross-cousins. Agrajes, the hero's most important cousin, is the son of the Lady of the Garland, Elisena's sister (thus mother's-sister's-son from the viewpoint of the hero, i.e. a parallel cousin). The brothers Dragonís and Palomir, staunch companions and battle comrades of the hero and his brothers are 'fijos de Grasugis, rey de la profunda Alemaña, que era casado con Saduua, hermana del rey Perión de Gaula' (III, 664.344–48). The sons of the hero's father's sister, they are thus his cross-cousins.

Sentiments of kindred solidarity are a standard element of social discourse throughout *Tirant*. The hero, leading the garrison at the fortress of Mount Tuber, awaits the arrival of forces summoned by the recently surrendered King Escariano of Ethiopia, knowing that those on the latter's side 'havien tramesos correus per tota la terra dels moros amprant a molts parents que el Rei tenia en la Barberia, que li vinguessen ajudar' (895). Tirant, seeking to forestall the assault on the castle, orders prisoners, including the captured King Escariano, placed 'en dret de la muralla'. The effect is immediate: 'E com los de fora veien lo Rei en tal so estar e los altres presoners, que hi tenien pare o fill o germans, no consentiren que les bombardes més tirassen' (896).

Modern warfare also features such scenes of hostages, and of refraining from hostile action by their kinsmen. What is significant is that this measure causes dissension among the ranks of the besiegers: 'E per açò havia entre ells de grans debats, e moltes morts que s'en seguien' (896). There is no humanitarian policy, no consistent method for dealing with this sort of crisis; those whose relatives are not placed on the wall are for continuing the bombardment; those with relatives in danger are willing to fight their comrades in order to bring about a cease-fire. Meanwhile, the ensuing truce is prompted, in part, by the Muslims' assumption of the imminent arrival of the King of Bougie, 'germà' of Escariano and 'cunyat' of the King of Tunis (896). In addition, many other kings arrive to join forces in the attempt to rescue Escariano: 'Tots aquests reis', the story tells us, 'los de més eren en deute de parentesc ab aquest rei Escariano' (897). It is yet another example of the solidarity of kinsmen mobilized by appeal to a system of reciprocal obligations.

Similarly, *Curial* also shows kinship as a function of war at what we would call the international level. The Sultan of the besieging Turks, at the end of the romance, ponders the significance of the death of the Turkish champion, the formidable knight Critxi: 'E volguera mes hauer perduts molts altres', we are told, 'que aquell tot sol, com fos parent molt propinque, gran capita, senyor de moltes gents [...] vnica e sola sperança dels Turchs' (425–26). In *Curial*, kindred solidarity is often expressed in terms of cooperation against the rest of the world. At the same time, such solidarity often employs the vocabulary of feudalism, itself — as we have seen — a system which, borrowing the logic of dyadic kinship relationships, served as an extension of kinship ideology into the political realm. When the Lord of Vergues meets the King of Aragon, recognizing him for a kinsman, he declares, kneeling before the monarch:

> Yo, senyor, son de vostre linage, e port vostres armes, e, per conseguent, vostre seruidor contra totes les persones del mon. E no era cosa en lo mon que yo tant desijas, com conexer mon senyor, lo qual sots vos. Perque us suplich [...] que daciauant maiats per seruidor, em vullats manar totes les coses que a vostre seruey sien e a mi sien possibles de fer [...] (207)

Vendetta in the romances is, predictably, a primary function of the solidarity of kinship obligations. In *Amadís*, Lisuarte is reminded by the twelve mysterious damsels who have come to care for Galaor and for Lisuarte's fallen enemy Cildadán (obliged to fight a war of revenge because of the death of his father-in-law, Abies), that the latter had been 'vn buen rey y que faziendo lo que obligado era, la fortuna le hauía traydo en tan gran tribulación que ouiesse dél piedad' (II, 495.614–18). In another instance, one among many in the same romance, Mataleza, the arrogant giantess who had provoked the battle between Bruneo and her brother Madamán the Envious, seeing the latter defeated and thrown from a cliff, takes her brother's sword and, invoking the name of her uncle, Ardán Canileo (slain in the previous chapter by Amadís), declares that there will her blood also remain; stabbing herself with a sword, she lets herself fall to be smashed to pieces on the rocks below (II, 539.146–55).

Vendetta is part of the casual apparatus of social description; it is taken for granted as a motive for warfare, as we see in the description of Tirant's participation in the war between the newly converted Ethiopian king Escariano and the latter's Muslim and pagan enemies, 'en especial lo rei d'Africa: per la mort de son germà usava envers los crestians de molt gran crueldat' (930). When this vengeful monarch confronts Tirant in battle, two kindreds meet. This is dramatized by the intervention of Tirant's cousin Lord Agramunt, who attacks the King of Africa: 'e feren tantes d'armes ab tanta malícia que es daven de mortals colps, la u per defendre a Tirant, e l'altre per voler-lo ofendre, e cascú estava mortalment nafrat' (931). Later the vendetta will be prolonged, as the King of Africa (938–39) demands that the King of Tunis heed him, 'com a persona qui ha perdut son germà en batalla'. Vowing to pursue 'infinidament venjança', the King declares his readiness: 'confiant en les mies pròpies mans d'atenyer aquella glòria que, los meus ulls havent vista d'aquell famós Capità, que matar-lo puga'. Moved by the 'dolor inestimable' caused by the death of his 'amat germà', he has no fear of death, 'car morint és reviure en gloriosa fama' (939).

Estefania, the Duchess of Macedonia and wife of Tirant's cousin Diafebus, invokes kindred loyalty and the law of the feud as she implores Tirant to come to her husband's aid: '¡Moga's, senyor, la vostra sang! Lo vostre cosín germà, catiu, presoner d'infels [...] a mi ha lleixat en mortal desolació e pressura'. His cousin's capture represents, she declares, a 'vergonyosa injúria' for Tirant. He must therefore respond by seeking revenge: 'Venjau, Tirant senyor, la vostra ofensa' (1098). Her appeal is entirely on the personal grounds of kindred solidarity; there is no question of reasons of state, of ideological crusade, of pragmatic recovery of the services of a valued collaborator.

Although references to cousinship are far less frequent in *Curial* than in either *Amadís* or *Tirant*, the importance of the relationship in the social universe of the work is revealed by occasional allusions to cousin-based solidarity, such as that involving the Earl of Salisbury, fervently motivated to participate in an important tourney, in order to succour or avenge his 'cosin germa', the Lord of Gloucester (213). Solidarity of the kindred in the context of vendetta is portrayed with some frequency in *Curial*, as we see in the episode concerning the brother and uncle of the arrogant Lord Monbru, recently and justifiably slain by the hero (Curial had rescued a damsel abducted by the felon knight). Carles de Monbrun, the brother, challenges the hero: 'Caualler, tu has mort mon germa malament' (156). Here, as in other instances, chivalric romance, while obsessed with kindred, presents a subtle subversion of primordial kinship principles, in the sense that justice prevails over kindred loyalty. When Curial defends himself against this charge by defeating both men, the uncle, wounded and limping, declares, after hearing Curial's explanation of his nephew's death: 'Amich, anats en nom de Deu: yous he per quiti [...] car vos hauets fet ço que bon caualler deu fer; e si als fet haguessets, haguerets fallit a caualleria' (157). In truly traditional kin-ordered societies, as we know, the principle of vendetta does not allow for justification of the adversary's actions on the grounds of legitimate self-defence.

Curial, while portraying kindred solidarities, clearly disapproves of the unconditional loyalties they engender. Chivalry, meanwhile, is shown to transcend kinship as a principle of social action. Tournaments and challenges are not merely aspects of a chivalric lifestyle; they are often the occasion of enmity between kindreds, as well as the means of enacting vendetta. In this sense, they are incorporated into the kindred system. Thus, in *Curial*, a herald explains to the hero the King of Aragon's attendance at the tourney in Melu:

> Ell es lo millor del mon, sens falla [...] e vol mal al Duch dAnjou e a tota la sua casa, segons he oyt, per ço com ha mort lo Rey Mamfre, son sogre; e be li plauria que lo Duch dAnjou caualcas com a caualler errant, e, per ventura, lo faria penedir de ço que ha fet .
> (171–72)

Earlier in *Curial*, in a similar circumstance, a knight challenges the character known as Boca de Far, with the significant formula: 'E yo donare a aqueix caualler altre caualler de mon linatge, de mon nom e de mes armes' (87). Late in the story, with the hero recently returned in triumph from captivity in North Africa, he is challenged to judicial combat by Guillalmes de Chastell, who seeks to avenge the death of his brother, Bertran del Chastell, 'lo qual hauia combatut Curial, en lo cami que, a forma de caualler errant, feu al torneig de Melu' (416–17).

In *Tirant*, the long account given by the knight Diafebus (Tirant's cousin) of the hero's exploits, during and after the great tourney in England, shows Tirant repeatedly challenging and being challenged by knights. Having defeated the four mysterious knights who had previously challenged all comers, among them the king of

Frisia (whom Tirant killed in honourable combat), the hero is accused of treason and challenged to a duel, first by Kirieleison of Muntalbà, the dead king's vassal (chaps 77–80), then, after Kirieleison's untimely death in an apoplectic fit, by the latter's brother Thomas (in 81). In yet another instance of kindred solidarity in the context of a tournament, we hear the knight Diafebus describe his attendance on Tirant (as the latter confronts the four mysterious knights) in terms of 'tres de nosaltres, parents de Tirant' (254).

When Tirant, recovering from his wounds and unable to speak for himself, is accused of treachery, he is defended at court by 'alguns parents' (260). Later, in the Greek kingdom, the nature of their relationship is confirmed, as Tirant addresses Diafebus as 'cosí meu' (375). Solidarity in real warfare is shown throughout *Tirant* by the collaboration of Diafebus, the hero's cousin (374, 494, & 721). Another collaborating kinsman is the hero's cousin, the Lord of Agramunt (895 & 951). In *Amadís*, kindred solidarity is seen in the unanimous acceptance of Amadís as the paramount knight of his line, as we note in the reaction of his brothers Galaor and Florestán, and his cousin Agrajes, to his triumph in the adventure of the Arch of Faithful Lovers: they react 'con gran plazer [...] porque en su linaje ouiese tal cauallero que passasse de bondad a todos los del mundo presentes y cient años a çaga' (II, 368.548–52). When Gandalín and Mabilia bemoan the disappearance of his master and her cousin, the squire cries: 'qué gran sinrazón ha hecho Oriana a vos y a vuestro linaje, que os quitó el mejor cauallero del mundo!' (II, 433.429–32).

In *Tirant* the allegiance of kinsmen to their leader is shown to be unbounded, as we see from Diafebus's reaction when he hears of the commotion in the palace caused by Tirant's nocturnal visit to Carmesina's bedroom: 'armà's prestament', we are told, 'que allí tenia les sues armes per ajudar a Tirant'. He is ready to risk all that he has gained (the title and property of a duke) in support of his cousin: 'Hui perdré tota ma senyoria, puix Tirant és en tal punt' (706). A little later, the wounded Tirant replies to Hipòlit's offer to bring help by declaring that only a kinsman may approach him in his vulnerable condition: 'Si és del linatge de Bretanya, fes-lo venir' (710). The fact that the narrator makes a point of the exemplary excellence of these knights shows that the depiction of kindreds does not merely reflect a prevalent state of affairs in contemporary society. The text exalts kindred solidarity as an ethical precept.

The romances, then, deliberately confirm (allowing for the rightness of one's cause) that the solidarity of cousinship transcends that of other bonds. Thus the attitude of Brian de Monjaste, Amadís's cousin (the son of Perión's sister and King Ladasán of Spain). Brian declares (II, 575.510–17), in explaining his position as one of Amadís's companions, that he cannot be said to have taken his leave as Lisuarte's vassal ('yo no os dexé porque nunca vuestro fue'), although he is of the king's linaje (i.e. as explained in a previous chapter, 'house:' 'ahunque soy de vuestro linaje'). He came to Lisuarte's house in order to be with Amadís ('vine a vuestra casa a buscar a mi cormano Amadís'), and now that the latter no longer belongs to Lisuarte's household, Brian does nothing wrong by accompanying his cousin ('no errando vn punto de lo que deuía'). Kindred solidarity is expressly defended by Brian, when he explains why he will fight alongside Amadís and the other knights of the Ínsula Firme against Lisuarte in the matter of the possession of the Isle of Mongaça: 'que él es mi cormano y tengo de seguir en todo su voluntad' (II, 579.824–25).

This solidarity of the kindred is seen on both sides. The web of active relationships established by it is interwoven with the network of vassalic and amical relationships, as we see in the following catalogue of the combatants on Lisuarte's side:

> y hizo el rey dellos tres hazes. La primera huuo don Galaor [...] y con él yua su compañero Norandel, y don Guilán el Cuidador y su cormano Ladasín, y Grimeo el Valiente, y Cendil de Ganota [...] Y la segunda haz dio al rey Cildadán [...] y yuan con él Ganides de Ganota, y Acedís el sobrino del rey [...] y en medio desta haz yua don Grumedán de Nuruega, y otros caualleros que yuan con el rey Arbán de Norgales. (III, 705–06.27–45)

The catalogue of the opposing side — that of the knights of the Ínsula Firme, who support Galvanes sin Tierra in his attempt to reclaim the inheritance of his beloved Madasima — is similarly composed of brothers, cousins, nephews, sons, brothers-in-law, friends, and vassals:

> En la primera yuan don Florestán y don Quadragante, y Angriote d'Estrauaus y su hermano Grouedán y su sobrino Sarquiles y su

cuñado Gasinán [...] En la otra haz yua don Galuanes, y con él los
dos buenos hermanos Palomir y Dragonís [...] (III, 706.72–87)

As we have seen, kindred solidarity does not preclude a conflict
of obligations with other foci of solidarity. Indeed, the romances'
ability to convey such conflicts is an important source of narrative
suspense. Thus, in Amadís, Count Argamón feels constrained on
the one hand by his loyalty to do the will of his lord King Lisuarte;
on the other, he must speak out against the injustice of his sovereign's action in marrying Oriana against her will to the Roman
emperor. 'como yo sea de vuestra sangre y vuestro vasallo', he
exclaims, 'no me contento ni satisfago con lo dicho [...]' (III,
896.375–77). Similarly, the hero's brother Galaor is the vassal of
Lisuarte, and must choose between serving his brother Amadís or
his lord; in either event he will violate honour. The author avoids
this thorny contradiction by having Galaor take sick at his father's
court in Gaul during the confrontation (IV, chap. 100). At the same
time, Norandel, Galaor's close friend and Lisuarte's illegitimate
son, is bound to help his father in the war with the Ínsula Firme,
although he is also a friend of Amadís and all his lineage; that is
why Perión, as he marshals his own forces to support his son
Amadís, sends Norandel away from his court: 'Esto fizo el rey
porque Norandel cumpliesse lo que a su padre obligado era, y
también porque no viesse que él mandaua adereçar su gente y
apercebir sus amigos' (IV, 1048–49.114–18).

    At the court of Lisuarte, the four heroes — Amadís, his brother
Galaor, their cousin Agrajes, and the latter's uncle Galvanes sin
Tierra — dine together, 'sin que otro cauallero alguno con ellos
estuuiesse'. Their solidarity, destined to be maintained through
'grandes peligros y afrentas en armas', is cemented by 'el gran
deudo y amor que se habían'. This collaboration reveals the
kindred's versatile criteria of recruitment. Galvanes, we are told, is
a member of the foursome 'ahunque . . . no touiese deudo sino con
sólo Agrajes' (I, 249.346–62). When Amadís goes to restore the
kingdom of Briolanja, whose throne has been usurped by her
treacherous uncle, he is accompanied by his brother and Agrajes (I,
313.45–85). Later, Florestán, the half-brother of Amadís and
Galaor, is added to this select fighting unit: 'éstos eran', declares
the narrator, 'siempre en vna compañía' (II, 485.788–90).

    In the battle between the forces of Lisuarte and Cildadán of

Ireland, Amadís, ever watchful over the kith and kin who are his companions in battle, comes to the rescue of his cousins Agrajes, Dragonís, and Palomir, saying to Agrajes, as he hands over the horse of a slain enemy: 'Cormano Agrajes, caualgad en esse cauallo' (II, 494.491–92). After the battle, with Cildadán and his forces routed, Amadís cries out to his comrades: '¡Ay, buenos cormanos! miedo he que hemos perdido a don Galaor!' (II, 494.550–52).

Kindred solidarity, in terms of gratitude and generosity, is consciously expressed in Amadís's speech of appreciation to his cousin Agrajes:

> mucho deuemos agradescer a Dios los que de vuestro linaje y sangre somos por auer echado entre nosotros cauallero que en las afruentas tal recaudo de su honrra pone, y en las cosas de consejo con tanta discreción la acrescienta. (IV, 1040.102–09)

Cousins do things together even without a specific purpose at hand. Thus, to take one from a myriad of such casual references, the two cousins Eliseo and Landín, the nephew of Quadragante, roam in search of adventure together, leading them to the predicament in which Grasandor finds them in book IV of *Amadís* (IV, 1277). Cousinship, then, is not merely for warfare or marriage negotiation. It is, as well, an available companionship for adventure, an instrument of diplomacy, a vector of hospitality, a means of charitable assistance. Amadís, newly arrived in Bohemia and just accepted into the service of that realm's King Tafinor, is lodged in the palace with, as company, the king's son Grasandor, and the king's cousin Galtines. This companionship, the narrator explains, is so that the hero may feel 'más acompañado y honrrado' (III, 759.240–44). In *Curial*, the Aragonese ambassador who rescues the hero and his companion from captivity in Tunisia, recognizing the companion as a kinsman, cries out: 'O, cosi meu! ¿e catiu erets vos, e yo ne vostre parents no ho sabiem?' (400). The narrator is at pains to remind us that 'daquell linatge de Madiona, son exits tots los de la casa de Pallars, e aquells eren cap e principi de tot lo linatge' (400–01).

One of the most important functions of the kindred was the internal mediation of quarrels, a procedure facilitated by appeal to group feeling. This aspect of cousinship is evident in the episode in which Tirant's cousin Agramunt, thinking that Plaerdemavida is a treacherous Saracen vixen, tries to behead her. The hero intervenes, badly cutting his hands on his enraged cousin's sword. Seeing that 'son cosín germà li havia guardada tan poca honor e reverència', Tirant is moved to 'grant ira', accusing his cousin of 'gran supèrbia e grossera presumpció' (974), and — a grave condemnation — of being a disgrace to his clan: 'tu est lo més trist de tot lo nostre llinatge' (975). While Escariano, as Tirant's 'germà d'armes', shows himself the peacemaker (975–76), Agramunt, in words expressive of the 'extrema amor' which he feels for the hero, humbly begs Tirant's pardon. 'Lo vincle de la sang', he declares, 'no es pot tornar aigua' (978).

Where, in the case of *Amadís* and *Tirant*, we may speak of both primary and secondary references to networks of cousins and nephews (i.e. to relatives of principal and secondary personages), in *Zifar* and *Curial*, references to cousins and other collaborating kinsmen all involve secondary personages. Zifar and Curial, more self-reliant than their counterparts in the other romances, operate without benefit of kinship networks. At the same time, although Zifar, his son Roboán, and Curial are not themselves shown to be members of an extensive kin structure, references to the networks of other characters, often the protagonists' opponents, suggest the importance of bilateral kindreds in the social background of author and audience. For example, in chapter 67 of *Zifar* the protagonist sallies forth from the city of Mentón, besieged by the King of Ester, to reply to a challenge issued by two knights of the surrounding army. The latter two are described as 'el fijo del rey de Ester, e el otro su sobrino: los mas poderosos caualleros que eran en la hueste'. Zifar has already replied, when told that he needs 'otro conpañon', that he has need of 'conpañon ninguno', save for God alone. The emphasis on self-reliance (while assuming that God is on one's side) is an explicit repudiation of reliance on kinfolk.

Curial presents similar contrasts between mutual aid among kin and the self-reliance of a lone hero. In the episode in which Curial intervenes, as a free-agent knight, to defend the Duchess of Austria, accused of adultery, the narrator mentions that the German Empress is the 'cosina germana' of the accused (36). In another episode in *Curial*, the King of Tunis, madly in love with Camar, the daughter of one of his vassals, must turn to various extended kinsmen of the girl, after her father has been executed through a misunderstanding. He calls upon Junes, 'germa de la mare de Camar', promising the man political reward ('tu regiras mon Regne'). The king then summons the brother of the executed man, begging the man's pardon for the hasty beheading. Audalla, the brother, points out that the proposed marriage 'a ell e a tot son linatge era molta honor' (374); the king promises this uncle 'estat' and 'honor' if he can find a way to win over the intended bride (375). Here, as elsewhere, we must assume that the description of Muslim (or other non-European) kinship practices is, most probably, a projection of European notions of kinship, rather than any attempt at ethnographic accuracy by the romance author; what the text says about 'Moorish' kinship reveals the author's notions of 'normal' kinship.

Glick discusses the contrast between Muslim Spain, with its patrilineal groups 'forming a segmentary social system', and Peninsular Christian society, in which we observe, he contends, a 'general drift' away from the bilateral structures of primitive Germanic society towards agnatic structures. Emphasizing that 'class differentiation of kinship relations [is] possibly the single point which most distinguishes Christian from Muslim kinship systems', he points to a general deterioration, in Christian territory, of the extended family (whether of cognatic or agnatic orientation) due to socio-economic conditions favouring the nuclear family (Glick 1979: 141). Pierre Guichard, who develops this contrastive model of medieval Peninsular Christian and Muslim social structures, argues that the segmentary, agnatic lineage was pervasive in all sectors of Islamic society in the Peninsula, while, in Christian society, the 'parentèle bilatérale' (bilateral kindred) was maintained 'dans l'aristocratie seulement' (Guichard 1977: 19; cited by Glick 1979: 141).

José Ángel García de Cortázar accounts for social transformations between 1050 and 1300 in terms of a tendency toward dissolution of the extended family, and its gradual replacement by 'simples asociaciones de intereses comunes pero voluntarios, a través de las cuales el individuo, y no la familia ni mucho menos el clan aparece como único sujeto de responsabilidades'. The extended family, traditionally supported by the 'explotación y disfrute común de un patrimonio inmobiliario', was eroded by various interacting demographic, economic, and political factors. These included frontier conditions provoking the dispersal of kin groups, fluctuating markets and an increasingly complex monetary system, the emergence of the state with its attendant bureaucratic and fiscal impositions, population growth, and the practice of dividing up once impartible family holdings into *rationes* shared out among heirs. The extended family splintered into 'unidades autónomas y más pequeñas', with many members migrating into newly reconquered territories, while the individual's increasing disengagement from extended kinship networks contributed to an emphasis on the nuclear family. These demographic tendencies, meanwhile, threatened or hastened the decline of the manorial economy. This latter development, in the Peninsula as elsewhere in Europe, prompted the trend, among land-owning families, toward the essentially defensive scheme of agnatization. This included, in addition to primogeniture and the *mayorazgo*, such practices as the adoption of vicinal cognomina and heraldic emblems (García de Cortázar 1976: 264).

In his suggestion that noble families, presumably through some sort of conservative ethic, collectively retained traditional bilateral and extended kinship, Glick assumes the existence of nobility as a social class. Jacques Heers, by contrast, cautions against 'presumptive attitudes' that assume the presence of social stratification and employ an anachronistic vocabulary of class struggle (Heers 1977: 2–5). Despite this emphasis on the pre-stratified nature of medieval society, Heers, similarly to Glick, assumes some kind of class stratification when he affirms that 'nobles rejected family obligations much later than did commoners' (31).

We can put it yet another way. Nobles were those whose observance of family solidarity provided a foundation for the political, economic, and honorific advantages that supported noble status. Assuming, then, with Glick, that extended kinship is the mark of superior social class, at least in an earlier phase of class structuration, we may hazard — while taking into account Heers's caveat concerning the essentially kin-ordered nature of medieval society — that the differing treatment of cousinship among the four core works of our study confirms the conclusion that *Amadís* and *Tirant* (both thoroughly kindred-oriented) would originally have appealed to audiences of higher social standing, while *Zifar* and *Curial* (less emphatic in their portrayal of cousinship) were aimed at a broader range of lesser nobles, or non-nobles, whose reliance on extended kinship was limited.

Additional evidence concerns an aspect of kindred relationships closely associated with cousinship, namely avuncular relations. Uncles and nephews are almost as common as cousins in the chivalric romance. This is to be expected, since the solidarity of cousinship implies an association of uncles and nephews, given that uncles (and aunts) are the defining linkages between cousins. The emotional camaraderie deriving from cousinship is shown, in *Amadís*, to be predicated on the bond formed through maternal uncles. The narrator, for instance, is at pains to identify Brian de Monjaste as a 'cauallero muy preciado, fijo del rey Ladasán de Spaña y de vna hermana del rey Perión de Gaula' (II, 556.116–19). The establishment of cousinship through the avuncular link yields a passionate devotion between the cousins. The love of Brián for Amadís comes not only from the 'gran deudo que con él tenía como ser fijos de dos hermanos, que la madre deste don Brian, muger del rey de España, era hermana del rey Perión', but also because Amadís 'era el cauallero del mundo que más amaua' (IV, 976.97–103). We may speak in such instances of kinsmen who experience their relationship as, indeed, a kind of 'co-brotherhood'.

As with cousinship, avuncular relations are mentioned innumerable times in passing, as an element taken for granted in the social environment of the stories. The very numerous casual references to the avuncular relationships of secondary personages are therefore as significant as the depiction of primary kin relations. *Amadís* is particularly abundant in such casual references. For instance, Arbán de Norgales, we learn, is the nephew of Queen Brisena (I, 295–96); he leads the resistance against the usurper Barsinán de Sansueña (I, chap. 37). In another example, an old man accosts wayfaring knights, exacting an oath to refrain from attacking his nephew, Abies of Ireland (I, chap. 5). Being old and infirm, he explains, he could not help physically, so thought to help his nephew 'con los caualleros andantes' (I, 52–53.265–69).

When Lisuarte returns to London after a rebellion which has been put down, he assigns a nephew, Dinadaus ('vno de los mejores caualleros del linaje del rey [...] assí de cortés como de buenas caual lerías y proezas') to set forth with a search party to bring back the city's dispersed inhabitants (I, 300.237–52). A dwarf, vassal of the Duke of Bristoya and accused by Agrajes and Galvanes of bearing false witness, calls on his nephew to defend his case in judicial combat with Agrajes (who, of course, defends his cousin Galaor's good name: I, 145). When Agrajes has defeated the dwarf's nephew, the latter, while admitting Galaor's innocence, cannot pronounce his uncle a traitor: 'no queráys que diga del enano, que es mi tio y me crió, que es falso' (I, 147.439–41). On the Duke of Bristoya's side, after a later encounter with Agrajes and Galvanes, also in judicial combat, a description of the disposition of the bodies of the duke and his battle comrades reveals the militant solidarity of uncles and nephews: 'al duque y sus sobrinos leuaron sus parientes a su tierra' (I, 310.458–60).

Another example is the case of Landín, the young knight who announces to Lisuarte and his court the challenge of the grand coalition of Famongomadán and his allies: 'he nombre Landín', he declares, 'y soy sobrino de don Cadragante, hijo de su hermana' (II, 442.93–95). Likewise a sister's son is Lindoraque, the nephew of Arcalaus, the son of the latter's sister by her husband the giant Cartada of the Forbidden Mountain (II, 481.499–513). The old knight Abradán, speaking to his nephews, asks them what they think of the people of Cildadán: 'Sobrinos, ¿Qué vos paresce dessa gente que Dios maldiga?' They reply respectfully, addressing him as 'buen tío' (II, 488.40). In the great battle between the forces of Lisuarte of Great Britain and Cildadán of Ireland, the latter's uncle, Sarmadán the Lion, is described as 'el más fuerte y valiente en armas que todos los del linaje del rey Cildadán' (II, 492.372–74). The King of Araby, leader of the coalition of the Seven Kings against Great Britain, is accompanied into battle by 'dos sobrinos, valientes caualleros' (III, 731.1135–36). In the midst of battle preparations against Lisuarte, he sends 'vn sobrino suyo que auía nombre Esclauor, hombre muy sabido de guerra' (IV, 1140.63–65). Then there is the aged squire, whose sixty-year search for the world's most love-faithful knight has brought him to Lisuarte's court. He turns out to be the nephew of that same Apolidón who founded the Ínsula Firme and its Arch of the Faithful Lovers (II, 470.337–48). Finally, to cite the last of very numerous examples casually presented by the narrator of *Amadís*: we are informed that the physician Elisabad, in his mission to the Greek empire, is accompanied by 'vn cuallero, su sobrino mancebo que Libeo se llamaua' (IV, 1042.23–25).

The bond between uncles and nieces is also occasionally portrayed. This is the case, in *Amadís*, of the wicked Dinarda, daughter of Ardán Canileo and niece of Arcalaus the Enchanter. She assists the latter in capturing the hero, his brother, and their father Perión, by pretending to be a mute damsel (III, 738–39). Later, Galaor and his half-brother Norandel, travelling with Dinarda, are tricked into coming to the castle of her uncle Anbades, who is also the cousin of Arcalaus the Enchanter, the mortal enemy of Amadís and all his lineage (III, 749.952–55).

Although less numerous than uncles, aunts also appear in the romances. Amadís, encountering a group of damsels who happen to be on their way to his destination, the Castle of Miraflores, is informed by them that they are headed to see 'vna [...] tía que es abadessa de vn monesterio, y por ver a Oriana, la fija del rey Lisuarte' (II, 459.657–59). In *Tirant* (414), the Lady Estefania, a confidant of Princess Carmesina, is a member of the imperial household described as 'una donzella qui servia a filla d'Emperador, e [...] donzella de gran estima, neboda de l'Emperador e filla del duc de Macedònia' (she is therefore, we note, also the cousin of Carmesina). The most prominent aunt in the chivalric romances is the sorceress Urganda la Desconocida, the fairy godmother (amounting, we may say, to a fictive aunt) of *Amadís*, and guardian of his clan. As she takes custody of Talanque and Maneli el Mesurado, Urganda thanks Galaor and Cildadán, fathers of the lads (with the sorceress's nieces):

> pues que en mi propia persona ninguna generación engendrarse puede, que fuesse yo causa que de las agenas tan hermosos donzeles nasciessen como aquí veys que tengo. (IV, 1236.162–66)

To interpret the frequent instances in which such relationships play a part in the chivalric narratives, we must further clarify our terminology. The vocabulary of the avuncular relationships evolved in relation to those of cousinship. 'Cousin' derives from Latin *consobrinus*, 'cousin on the mother's side', with variant forms of *cossofrenus, cosinus. Consobrinus* and its variants were frequent synonyms of *consangineus*. Hence, perhaps, the persistent frequency of the word's use to designate any collateral relative more distant than a sibling, as in its former English meaning of 'nephew, niece' (cf. Shakespeare, *Much Ado about Nothing*, I.ii.2: 'Now now brother, where is my cosen your son?').[4]

Robert Beekes notes for *consobrinus* the original meaning of Mother's-Sister's-Son, with the 'sobrini [... the] sons of consobrini'. The term *consobrinus*, argues Beekes, 'must have ousted *sobrinus*, so that *sobrinus* originally was MoSiSo and came to be used for the next generations only when consobrinus had come into being'. The etymology of *sobrinus*, he affirms, derives from the Indo-European *suesr-inos, 'he of the sister'. Thus *sobrinus* very probably had an original meaning of 'Sister's-Son'. *Nepos* for 'nephew', a later development in Latin, emerges around AD 200; its earlier meaning of 'grandson' is preserved in the Spanish *nieto*, Portuguese *neto*, with *sobrino/a* reserved (assuming a generalization from the sororilateral context) for 'sibling's son/daughter' (Beekes 1976: 48–52).

Relationships between uncles and nephews have been studied under the rubric of the so-called avunculate. Important in many societies, the avunculate has different functions according to the specific requirements and tendencies of the local kinship system. A. R. Radcliffe-Brown, in an influential article, demonstrated that in a patrilineal society a person's most important duties and rights centre on his relationship to paternal relatives. A member only of his patrilineage or clan, he is not considered a member of his mother's lineage. Discussing the relationship of mother's brother and sister's son in the context of 'joking relationships' in patrilineal societies, Radcliffe-Brown refers to the 'privileged disrespect [exhibited toward] the mother's brother'. In cultures that emphasize the patrilineal lineage and thus 'a marked distinction between relatives through the father and relatives through the mother', authority is generally invested in the father and his siblings. Nurturing and indulgent roles are assigned to the mother, her siblings, and her extended kin. Maternal uncles, in such circumstances, play the role of companion and 'friendly counsellor'. In some patrilineal societies the maternal uncle is even called 'a male mother' (Radcliffe-Brown 1965: 97–98).

Lévi-Strauss reviews Radcliffe-Brown's analysis of the avunculate in terms of 'systems of attitudes' which are 'inversely corre-

---

[4]   See OED, entry for COUSIN.

lated'. He argues that where familiarity characterizes the relationship between father and son, the relationship between maternal uncle and nephew tends to be one of respect. Conversely, where the father is acknowledged as 'the austere representative of family authority', the relationship between maternal uncle and nephew is one of familiarity (Lévi-Strauss 1963: 41).

The role of maternal uncle as friendly counsellor has been associated with the concept of primordial matriarchy. William O. Farnsworth, for instance, mentions as evidence of vestigial matriarchy the fact that one notes in the epics covered by his survey a 'tendency to minimize the intimacy between father and son, while exalting that between uncle and nephew'. The uncle-nephew relationship, he notes, reveals 'the closest solidarity'. The father, on the other hand, tends to show an attitude of 'severity and injustice' (Farnsworth 1913: 21).[5]

Farnsworth assumed the rule of 'mother's-right' as a primordial phase of social evolution. Goody demonstrates the weakness of this interpretation of the pattern of inheritance and succession from mother's-brother (or father) to sister's- (or daughter's) son. 'The part played by the maternal lineage (or maternal family, or maternal uncle)', he argues, does not constitute evidence of 'the weakness of agnatic relationships, much less of the earlier existence of matriliny'. The mother's brother and her patrilineage play 'an intrinsic role for members of a patrilineal descent group, a role that is in no way incompatible with the system itself' (Goody 1983: 226).

The authoritarian functions of the mother's brother in matrilineal societies can rival the 'severity and injustice' observed in the epic

---

[5] In this he is indebted to Johann Jakob Bachofen, the doyen of those nineteenth-century social thinkers who considered matriarchy a universal elementary stage of social evolution. For Bachofen's outline of his theory of what he called the 'Gynaikokratie', see his Introduction (1948: I, 14–64). Appraising Bachofen's contributions and the defects of his model, as set forth in *Das Mutterrecht*, Robert H. Lowie points out the ethnographic inadequacies of Bachofen's scheme: the notion of universal evolutionary stages was long ago exhaustively invalidated by reference to voluminous countervailing evidence; the idea of universal promiscuity as a phase underlying emergent matriarchy was similarly discredited; matriliny as implying 'the ascendancy of woman' was likewise extensively disproved. At the same time, notes Lowie, Bachofen's concept of the 'gynaikokratische Kultur' focused the attention of social science on diverse practices and institutions observed in real societies (Lowie 1949: 629).

father of medieval French epic. Among the Ashanti, for example, the (classificatory) oldest living mother's-brother had 'sole legal authority' over his sister's children, while a maternal uncle's 'area of control over sister's children was extensive' (including control of marriage). From this state of affairs arose a highly ambivalent 'asymmetrical' relationship, 'particularly', notes Harry Basehart, as regards inheritance and succession. The proverb he quotes is suggestive: 'Nephews are your enemy'.[6]

Goody points out that the avunculate should not be considered from the sole viewpoint of nephews and nieces. Matrilateral relationships, he argues, 'though from the junior partner's standpoint traced through the mother', are also a sororilateral relationship from the senior partner's perspective (i.e. they are 'traced through a sister'). The patterns of relationship may thus be described as 'uxorilateral' in a patrilineal context and virilateral in a matrilineal system (Goody 1969: 48–51).

Indo-European kinship tends to equate mother's brother with mother's father, as when Latin derives the word for 'uncle' from the diminutive form of the word for 'maternal grandfather': thus, *avunculus* from *avus* (Bremmer 1976: 72–73; Beekes 1976: 57–60). In addition, Indo-European examples of avuncular fosterage generally show the fostering household to be uxorilateral in the sense adduced by Goody: either that of the mother's brother or maternal grandfather.

Jan Bremmer, tracing Indo-European uncle-nephew relationships in connection with the custom of fosterage, presents numerous examples from folklore, literature, and history. In the *Iliad*, Apollo appears to Hector in the shape of his mother's brother (XVI.717–20), while Tlepolemos, having killed Heracles' maternal uncle, must flee the vengeance of Heracles' sons and grandsons (II.662–66). Among ancient Germans, Tacitus observed, a man cherished his sister's children as dearly as his own offspring. In the Celtic tradition there are the relationships of Arthur and Gawain, Conchobar and Cuchulain, and (a story element retained by Chrétien) the Grail King to Perceval (the case of Mark and Tristan, also based on Celtic materials, concerns, by contrast, the relation-

---

[6]   Basehart 1961: 291–92. See also, in the same collection, Aberle 169–70 and Gough 1961a: 348–51, 1961c: 427, and 1961f: 600.

ship between the hero and his father's brother). Evidence of the extreme importance of the relationship between the hero and his maternal uncle, in both the French and the Germanic traditions, can be seen in the poems devoted to Roland and Charlemagne, Guillaume and Vivien, Hildebrandt and Wolfhart, Hagen and Patafried.[7]

A well known example of Indo-European fosterage is that of Odysseus, raised in the household of his mother's father, Autolykos. Autolykos declares at the birth of his daughter's son that when the lad grows up 'and comes to the great house of his mother's line', he, Autolykos, will freely give of his possessions, 'to make him happy'. The *Odyssey* confirms that the maternal grandfather has the right to name the daughter's new-born male child, expects to play an important role in the lad's upbringing, and considers him a principal heir (Homer 1967: 4, 399–412).

This is the broad historical and folkloric background to the mother's brother/sister's son relationships which play a significant role in the romances, particularly in *Amadís*. They confirm both the strong uxorilateral influence explicated by Goody, and the importance of uncles as linkages in the formation of cousin networks. A sister's son groomed as her brother's heir is seen, for instance, in *Amadís*'s second book, which opens, as we have seen, with the account of how a Greek king had two sons by his wife, a sister of the Emperor of Constantinople. These nephews, Apolidón and his brother, are therefore sister's sons from the viewpoint of the Byzantine emperor. The relationship explains Apolidón's succession to the imperial throne (II, 355–56). In another case of political succession, this time from mother's father to daughter's son, we learn of the giant Balán's son by a daughter of the giant Gandalac, lord of the Rock of Galtares. Amadís's informant, the governor of the Isle of the Infante, tells the hero (IV, 1254–55.190–94) that Balán's son will be his maternal grandfather's heir ('si biue, será heredero deste señorío').

In another significant case in *Amadís*, we have the Greek emperor — a descendant of Apolidón — and his nephew Gastiles, the son of the emperor's sister, the duchess of Gajaste. Gastiles

---

[7] Bremmer 1976: 67–69. See, in addition to the exhaustive references in Bremmer, Bell 1922: 105–64.

receives the important assignment of leading the Greek contingent sent to assist the forces of Amadís (IV, 1045–46.253–73). Then there is Elián el Loçano, 'sobrino de don Quadragante, fijo de su hermana y del conde Liquedo, primo cormano del rey Perión de Gaula' (III, 706.110–13). A mother's brother/sister's son relationship is seen in the case of Gasquilán el Follón, who is the son of the giant Madarque of Ínsula Triste and a sister of King Lancino of Suesa. Upon the latter's death without an heir, 'todos los del reyno touieron por bien de lo tomar por su rey y señor' (III, 670.807–16; IV, 1095.13–18). The Emperor of Constantinople, in *Amadís*, is described as 'su sobrino, hijo de su hermana la duquesa de Gajaste, que era buen cauallero mancebo' (III, 809.78–80). In the combat between the Roman knights and those of Great Britain, the Roman side includes the brothers Gradamor and Lasanor, nephews of Brondajel de Roca, major-domo of the Roman palace. They are 'fijos de su hermana, que era braua y soberuia' (III, 887.479–83).

The avunculate expressed through fosterage of nephews or nieces by an uncle, is seen in *Amadís* in the hermit Andalod's custody and upbringing of 'dos moçuelos, sus sobrinos de aquel hombre bueno' (II, 414.128–30). Nasciano, the most important hermit in *Amadís*, and foster father of Esplandián, has as his assistant a nephew who is the son of the hermit's sister (III, 702.826–32 & 703.895–96).[8] Tirant's bequeathing of the bulk of his estate to his nephew Hipòlit expresses the importance of the avunculate and fosterage in this Catalonian romance. Hipòlit is described at first, in chapter 141, as the son of the Greek knight Malveí (455), but later, in chapter 234, as 'de França natural' (709), then, in chapter 238 as of the 'llinatge de la casa de Roca Salada e del parentat de Bretanya' (721). Lastly, after designating several minor beneficiaries, the hero concludes his testament by affirming the nature of his relationship to Hipòlit:

> E de tots los altres béns e drets meus, los quals mijançant lo divinal
> adjutori jo m'he sabuts guanyar [...] faç e instituesc hereu meu

---

[8]   The narrator seems undecided as to the relationship between the hermit and the father of Amadís's *hermano de leche*; at III, 703.895–96, the foster brother's parents are described (from the viewpoint of the hermit) as 'su hermana y su marido'. At III, 775.141–42, Nasciano refers to his nephew's father as 'vn su hermano que llamaron Sargil'. This might reflect either an inconsistency on the the narrator's part, or a somewhat unusual use of *hermano* as synonym of *cuñado*.

universal a mon criat e nebot Hipòlit de Roca Salada, que aquell en
lloc meu sia posat, e succeesca [...] (1149).

We are not told if Hipòlit, presumably in the guardianship of his
uncle, is the son of Tirant's sister or brother; given the importance
of the distaff side, already pointed out in connection with Tirant's
surname, we may, however, hazard that Hipòlit is his sister's son.
The ever-present uxorilateral option insures that fosterage can also
be of a niece by an aunt. Thus Urganda, the Athena to Amadís's
Odysseus, has as her prominent assistants the two nieces just
mentioned, Julianda and Solisa, 'muy hermosas donzellas, fijas del
rey Falangrís, hermano que fue del rey Lisuarte'. Falangríz, it
transpires, had had, when he was a *mancebo*, a love affair with
Urganda's sister Grimota. They are, then, daughters of Oriana's
uncle — in the terms of the story, her *cohermanas*. From the
'visitación' of Galaor and King Cildadán (the erstwhile opponent
of Lisuarte, also in semi-captivity on Urganda's island) with these
two nieces of the Enchantress will come two sons, Talanque by
Galaor, Maneli el Mesurado by Cildadán. These personages —
destined to play an important role in *Las sergas de Esplandián* —
are, therefore, either a nephew of Amadís (Talanque) or a second
cousin of Oriana (Maneli) (II, 503.322–27). The fellowship of
cousins formed by Esplandián, Maneli, and Talanque, augmented
by Prince Garinto of Dacia (*Esplandián*, 435) renews the pattern of
the wandering band of youthful knights — mostly cousins and
other kinsmen, with an admixture of comrades-in-arms — established in the generation of Amadís and his companions.

Also in *Amadís* we encounter Sardamira, Queen of Sardinia,
described as 'vna muger muy apuesta y fermosa donzella, que
seyendo sobrina de la emperatriz se auía criado en su casa' (II,
385.18–20). Yet another instance of a 'materteral' relationship
(from *matertera*, Lat., 'maternal aunt') occurs in the scene in which
Gandales informs Mabilia — handmaiden and confidante of the
princess Oriana — that she must come with him. 'Vuestro fecho',
he assures the reluctant young woman, who is devoted to the
princess 'está muy bien parado, que quando de aquí vais, seréys
lleuada a vuestra tía la reyna Elisena de Gaula [...] y folgaréys con
vuestra cormana Melicia, que os mucho dessea' (III, 667.610–17).
Elisena, we recall, is the sister of Mabilia's mother, the Dueña de la
Guirnalda.

The active solidarity of uncle and nephew is seen in the case of Agrajes and his uncle Galvanes sin Tierra, prominent characters throughout *Amadís*. In one scene, outnumbered by the duke of Bristoya and his men, they fight fearlessly shoulder to shoulder. The latter tells his nephew not to be dismayed be the uneven odds, to which Agrajes replies: 'Cierto, señor tío, seyendo yo con os, poco daría por cinco de la mesnada del duque' (I, 149.621–30). The fellowship of uncle and nephew, as exemplified by Agrajes and Galvanes, provides a powerful model in the formation of fictive kinship relationships. Amadís, his brother Galaor, their cousin Agrajes, and the latter's uncle Galvanes form an inseparable company. Galvanes is the paternal uncle of Agrajes, being the younger brother of the latter's father, King Languines. Although Galvanes, the narrator informs us, 'no touiese deudo sino con sólo Agrajes', Amadís and Galaor 'nunca lo llamauan sino tío, y él a ellos sobrinos' (I, 355–62). Similarly, King Cildadán considers Quadragante his uncle (although an affine, i.e. a relative by marriage only), as we see when he says to Amadís after the rescue of Lisuarte and his forces: '—Señor, tornadvos al rey, y yo quedaré con don Quadragante, mi tío' (IV, 1158.405–07).

Such relationships retain their importance throughout *Amadís* and into the fifth book, *Las sergas de Esplandián*. We have already seen how the widowed giantess Arcabona, in begging the hero to spare her eldest son Matroco, refers to the 'otros caballeros' of her 'linaje' whom Esplandián has already slain (415). Those slain include a guardian knight, Argante (409), her brother the wizard Arcalaus, who had been Amadís's long-time nemesis (410), and Aracabona's younger son Furión (411). In the bilateral logic of the Indo-European avunculate, Arcalaus and Furión are of her patri-lineage, a group whose continuity is endangered by the peril to which her surviving son is exposed. Arcalaus, Matroco's maternal uncle, clearly plays the important role characteristic of the mother's brother: he is in charge of the fortress in his nephew's absence. The emotional relationship between uncle and nephew is conspicuous. When Matroco, the surviving son and lord of the castle, comes upon the body of his uncle, the depth of feeling in his lament reveals the intensity of the relationship: ''¡Oh mi buen tío, qué dolor es á mí tu muerte, en cualquier parte que murieras, y mucho mayor en esta donde yo tengo el señorío!'' It is only natural, in light of kindred solidarity, that his first thought is to vengeance: "Pues, ¿qué haré? ¿En quién tomaré la venganza?'' (413).[9]

In chaps 13–15 of *Zifar*, to cite another example, the author emphasizes, during the siege of Galapia, the importance of the besieging count's nephew. The death of the latter at the hands of Zifar is regarded as a disaster by the count and his followers: 'començaron a fazer el mayor duelo que podría ser fecho por ningunt ome' (45). In chapters 104 and 105 the defeat and wounding of Count Nasón's nephew again points out the significance of the relationship of mother's brother to sister's son. The nephew of Count Nasón is described as 'vn sobrino del conde Nason, fijo de su hermana' (208). We see signs in chapters 102–07 that the nephew is a prominent and active member of his uncle's household. In charge of the defence forces (208–09), he is also in command of his uncle's domain in the latter's absence. At the beginning of chapter 107, when the count comes upon his nephew, blinded in the combat with Roboán, he cries: 'Ay mi sobrino! que meresçistes vos por este mal vos aueniese?' The nephew replies: 'Çertas [...] por los pecados del padre lazran los fijos, e asy fize yo por los pecados vuestros' (218).

The relationship between Count Nasón and his nephew is clearly not the nurturing, indulgent mother's brother/sister's son relationship often encountered in the strictly patrilineal context described by Radcliffe-Brown (and, to a lesser and nuanced extent, by Goody). In *Zifar*, the authority exercised by the uncle (208–10), the position of responsibility in which the nephew has been placed (208), the very serious recriminations exchanged between uncle and nephew (218-19), scarcely reflect the avuncular indulgence associated with strict patriliny. At the same time, there can be no question, despite avuncular discord apparently similar to that ascribed by Radcliffe-Brown to matrilineal kinship, of matriliny as the dominant system, in *Zifar* or in any of the other romances. A

---

[9] For treatments of the much-discussed issue of editorial intervention and authorial reworking in *Amadís*, see Lida de Malkiel 1952–53, and Cacho Blecua 1979: 366–406, 1986, and 1987: 57–81. In the introduction to his edition, Cacho Blecua (1987: 81 n. 30), considers that the discrepancies and parallelisms between the versions of *Amadís* and its supposed fifth book are essentially 'indemostrable'. For a countervailing optimism concerning the possibility of reconstructing such inter-textual relationships, see Avalle-Arce 1990, esp. chaps 2, 3, and 4.

daughter has rights, to be sure, but these — as has already been mentioned, and as I shall demonstrate in chapter 4, below — are with respect to her functions as a member of her patrilineage.

Cognatic systems, notes Fox, often have 'a patrilineal tinge', and a tendency toward 'masculine co-residence for purposes of defence and solidarity in work' (Fox 1967: 153). Indo-European fosterage, with its emphasis on the paternal lineage of the mother's-brother/ sister's son relationship, could thus be expected to exhibit, at least on occasion, an authoritarian formality, even considerable tension, in the relationship between the maternal uncle and nephew. Because the mother's brother or father represents the authority of the mother's patrilineage, a full-fledged joking relationship of the nurturing, indulgent kind is perhaps less likely to evolve between mother's brother and sister's son in a cognatic context than in a strictly patrilineal one.

Avuncular familiarity or authoritarianism is not, in any event, an unequivocal indicator of lineal orientation. Without denying the importance of Radcliffe-Brown's contribution, Lévi-Strauss cautions that the avunculate 'does not occur in all matrilineal or all patrilineal systems, and we find it present in some systems which are neither matrilineal nor patrilineal'. One finds, he contends, a variety of patterns that do not correlate as closely with unilineal configurations (patrilineal or matrilineal) as Radcliffe-Brown had maintained: 'Different forms of avunculate can coexist with the same type of descent, whether patrilineal or matrilineal'. Thus, we may find indulgent fathers and forbidding maternal uncles in patrilineal societies, easy-going maternal uncles and strict fathers in matrilineal societies (Lévi-Strauss 1963: 43–44).

The avunculate, then, is to be understood less as a manifestation of descent rules, and more in terms of its functions within the synchronic network of the kindred. The relationships that constitute this system include those of the nuclear family, as well as cousin-ship and the avunculate. As the expedient response to shifting social, political, and economic circumstances, practical cognatic relationships are bound to be influenced by the stresses and emotional oscillations of family life. Descent principles are only one component — one type of practice — in the aggregate toolkit of kinship, which includes both official and unofficial practices and motivations. There is, in other words, no manual of avuncular behaviour; the same uncle can be indulgent and authoritarian by turns, according to the conditions and situations that present themselves.

It is in light of these considerations that we may understand such frequent avuncular functions as that of regent to the sister's son or daughter in the latter's minority. In the great battle between Great Britain and the alliance of the Seven Kings headed by the King of Araby (in *Amadís*), we encounter 'vn tío deste Barsinán, hermano de su madre, que fue gouernador de la tierra después que su padre Barsinán fue muerto fasta que este su sobrino entró en edad de la saber regir' (IV, 1146.92–97). The tutelary function is likewise observed in chapters 34 and 35 of *Zifar*, where the chief negotiator for the lady of Galapia is described as 'un cavallero anciano, tio de la señora de la villa' (75). Similarly Count Rubén, in *Zifar*, assumes the role of matchmaker (chaps 180–82) in the case of Roboán's proposed marriage to the Princess Seringa of Pandulfa (411). Seringa's speech to her uncle, concerning measures for resisting the King of Grimalet's invasion of her lands, confirms the importance of avuncular relationships in the society of *Zifar*: 'Conde', dixo la infante, 'mandat lo vos fazer, ca vos sabedes que quando mi padre morio en vuestra encomienda me dexo, ca yo muger so, e non he de fazer en ello nada, nin de meter las manos en ello; e commo vos touierdes por bien de lo ordenar, asy tengo yo por bien que se faga' (391). We recall here the stipulations of the *Partidas* (II.xv.2) concerning the legitimacy of inheritance and succession for female heirs; the inheritance rights of an uncle, paternal or maternal, are secondary to those of an inheriting niece with respect to her parents' title or estate.

Seringa, in *Zifar*, is the heiress of a king. Her guardian and counsellor, Count Ruben, is described as the 'tio e vasallo de la ynfante' (411). The text does not tell us if he is her paternal or maternal uncle. If the former, he must be a younger sibling of her father (if he were the elder, he would have already occupied the throne). We should have to presume, in that case, a very strict observance of successoral logic, favouring an only daughter of the dead king over his younger male siblings. As is well known, this pattern was not always strictly observed in the Middle Ages, when paternal uncles often sought the throne of deceased elder brothers, regardless of the presence of heirs, male or female. Be he Seringa's maternal or paternal uncle, this fact remains: that a situation in which a princess rules as the successor of a deceased father, while remaining in the guardianship of an uncle, paternal or maternal, does not reflect matriliny.

In a strictly matrilineal situation, in which the lineages are also the primary political units, the society becomes 'little more than a federation of matrilineages/clans,' and the politically dominant males will be those of the ruling matrilineage (Fox 1967: 104). At the same time, membership in the matrilineage, transmitted through the mother, determines property- and office-holding. Matrilineal succession and inheritance are through a man's sisters' sons, or their terminological analogues, rather than through his own offspring (who are the heirs of his wife's brothers and other male kin), or his brothers' children (who belong to the lineages of sisters-in-law). As a means of securing political succession, primogeniture is far less effective in this context than in the patrilineal. The matrilineal analogue of patrilineal succession from father to son would be that of mother to designated daughter. This solution, however, does not apply, given that, as David M. Schneider notes, 'authority is vested in male-held statuses' (1961a: 26). Likewise inoperative in matrilineal practice is the theoretically feasible alternative of succession by eldest son of eldest sister, and so on. All things being equal, observes Schneider, lateral succession (elder brother to younger brother, etc.) is more likely, since 'precise pairing' of male and female members of a matrilineage is relatively more difficult than the equivalent procedure in the patrilineal context (1961a: 26).

Schneider's observation on the difficulty of matching males and females for purposes of regulating inheritance and succession is based on a complex explication of the preconditions and limitations of matriliny. One of these is that, while a patrilineage is readily founded by a single male who recruits a female, a matrilineage can only be founded by a woman and a sibling or other male kinsman; they must then recruit a male as the progenitor of new matrilineage members, while insuring that this husband's lineage has no claim on these offspring (1961a: 7–8 & 16–18). For this and other reasons, matrilineages 'depend for their continuity and operation on retaining control over both male and female members' (8). While the matrilineage's control over its members may be expressed in terms of an interdependence of brothers and sisters, this interdependence of male and female is more often than not meta-phorical, since frequently a brother or brothers may be lacking, or the ratio of brothers to sisters may be uneven (11). Consequently, the descent group 'is organized as if it were composed of siblings' (12).

Under such conditions, the maternal uncle of an orphaned niece who is also a princess (i.e. the female member of a ruling lineage) is more likely to be himself the ruler than merely his niece's guardian or regent (a paternal uncle, not being a member of her matrilineage, would be categorically excluded from office). A princess-heiress with an uncle as counsellor or regent therefore matches the familiar historical situation of occasional female succession within a patrilineal context. The succeeding female functions in such a context as a surrogate male where no suitable male heir is to be found.[10]

The circumstances of the Lady of Galapia (*Zifar*, chap. 34), who is a widow rather than an inheriting daughter, likewise reflect essentially patrilineal principals of succession and inheritance. The widowed queen, besieged by enemies who wish to force an unwanted marriage on her, offers her dead husband's armour to the hero. Zifar replies: 'non lo quiero donado mas prestado; ca heredamiento es de vuestro fijo, e porende vos non lo podedes dar a ninguno' (54). Later he will remind the queen: 'esta villa e los otros castiellos que fueron de vuestro marido, todos fincaran a vuestro fijo' (71). The *Partidas* forbid precisely the type of re-marriage suggested, namely that of a mother having custody of the deceased husband's children: 'la razon por que defendemos que non case demientre que los mozos toviere en guarda es esta: que podrie acaescer que por el grant amor que habrie a su marido que tomase de nuevo, non guardarie tan bien las personas nin los bienes de los mozos, ó farie alguna cosa que se tornarie en grant daño dellos' (VI.xvi.4). Should such remarriage take place, the children should be remanded to the custody of 'alguno de sus parientes de los mozos al mas cercano que tovieren que sea home bueno et sin

---

[10] For additional discussion of the very complex question of political authority and succession in matrilineal contexts, see Aberle 1961: 169–70; Schneider 1961b: 209–13; Fathauer 1961: 252–53; Basehart 1961: 291–92; and Gough 1961d: 490.

sospecha' (VI.xvi.5). *Zifar*'s account of the situation in Galapia suggests that the children of the deceased ruler and the widow herself are already under the guardianship of an honourable kinsman. In negotiations concerning a possible marriage between the Lady of Galapia and the son of her enemy, her uncle, referred to as 'vn cauallero anciano, tio de la señora de la villa', speaks in favour of the match. 'En vuestro poder so', declares the queen, 'Ordenad la mi fazienda commo mejor vierdes' (75).

As with cousinship, so also with the avunculate: the core texts of our study are divided into the relatively kin-ordered *Amadís* and *Tirant*, and the relatively individualist *Zifar* and *Curial*. It is not that kindred networks do not manifest themselves in the latter two works, but only that the protagonists do not depend on such networks for their success as knights or suitors. We suggested earlier that the contrast between the two types might be the result of different intended audiences. The supposition of Glick — that extended kinship correlates with superior social class, while reduction of kinship to the nuclear family typifies non-nobles — provides a possible explanation for the differences observed. We see again that *Amadís* and *Tirant* would thus have been aimed at nobles, while *Zifar* and *Curial* were created to please an audience of commoners.

There are, however, alternative explanations. One is that the romances were all conceived to reach the broadest possible audience. It would be difficult to prove that the depiction of noble life styles, including kinship practices, was exclusive to works aimed solely and verifiably at noble audiences. Indeed, the principle of status-emulation, so frequently observed in the consumption of all manner of aesthetic and vestimentary forms in the history of human cultures, suggests that non-noble audiences might well have been avid readers of stories packed with details concerning noble life-styles and family structures. On the other hand, the individualism of Zifar and Curial, which the authors pointedly contrast with the coalitionist deportment of their adversaries, might have expressed ethical themes reflective of an ecumenical didacticism. The broad spectrum of readers implied by the latter possibility might well have included — might have especially included — the nobility.

The question of multiplicity of potential audiences, implied by the kinship practices represented in the romances, may be further explored by turning to the dimension of marriage and marital alliance. As with kinship, it is a dimension which presents diachronic and synchronic aspects that correlate with motivation and behaviour in the social universe of the romances. Kindred and cousinship, the primary dimensions of kinship as conceived by these narratives, are integral components of the plot of the chivalric romances. The length of these narratives, one of their most obvious traits, has sustained one of the enduring clichés of hispanist literary criticism: the 'plotlessness' of this genre. Textual duration, episodic proliferation and narrative *entrelacement* — the recognized techniques of romance storytelling — do not, however, necessarily make for a lack of plot. As Peter Brooks suggests, the term 'plot' comprises, among its several meanings, the notion of 'the scheme or conspiracy'. In modern literature, he asserts, 'the organizing line of plot is more often than not some scheme or machination, a concerted plan for the accomplishment of some purpose which goes against the ostensible and dominant legalities of the fictional world, the realization of a blocked and resisted desire' (Brooks 1984: 12).

Viewed from this perspective, *Amadís* and *Tirant lo blanc* are no more plotless than, say, *Moby Dick* or *War and Peace*. Like these and other modern narratives, the chivalric romances are about thwarted desires. Their plot is the account of a resistance campaign devised to counteract a complexly interlocking array of obstructions placed in the way of fulfilling those desires by the 'ostensible and dominant legality' of the aristocratic patrilineage. Kindred and cousinship represent an ideology of collusion that informs and justifies the junior generation in its struggle against the agnatic authority invested in the senior generation. To understand the objective of the chivalric heroes' desires, and thus the nature of the impediments that they overcome, we must now examine the concepts of marriage and household as they are presented in the texts.

Marriage and Consent

E dmund Leach classes marriages into two groups. The first 'results from the whims of two persons acting as private individuals'. The second, by contrast, is 'a systematically organized affair which forms part of a series of contractual obligations between two social groups'. The nucleus of the groups linked by the second, systematic type of marriage, is 'composed of the adult *males* of a kin group all resident in one place' (italics in original). Women and 'remotely situated kinfolk' are not prohibited from participation in marriage arrangements, but co-resident males, usually representing three generations (i.e. grandfather, father, grandson) are the controlling voice in marriage arrangements. The membership of these superintendent groups is usually based on descent as well as residence (Leach 1961: 56).

The authors of the romances classify marriage into essentially the same two types as those proposed by Leach. The principal conflict in the narratives occurs between those who regard arrangement of marriage as a patriarchal entitlement, and those who — whether from ideological commitment or amorous expediency — glorify marriage as an emotional and sexual bond between two individuals. The stories of Amadís, Tirant, and Curial are thus concerned with the secret or delayed marriage of the knight to his beloved. Zifar manipulates the ideology of marital consent to secure the benefits of an advantageous second marriage. What complicates the premarital or marital relationships of all four characters is the need to elude the surveillance of their wives' kin, for whom marital consent represents a threat to familial authority and patrimonial integrity.

Bourdieu's concept of 'official' vs 'practical' kin helps sort out the complexities and nuances of kin-ordered behaviour with regard to marriage. He accounts for the conflict between lineal and individual imperatives as a function of official, masculine culture, vs unofficial, feminine culture. Men tend to be nominally in control of the political interests of the lineage. Women, in charge of the domestic domain, look to the furtherance of their own children's best interests. Marriage in such a context often represents the outcome of intra-familial negotiations, of compromise. At the same time, the individuals in a potential marriage, within their respective families, tend to make no secret of their own preferences. What defines traditional marriage is not the absence of individual preferences but rather the predominant role of family interests, focused through the will and influence of a patriarch or of clan elders.

Traditional marriage, affirms Bourdieu, is a card game whose 'outcome depends partly on the deal, the cards held (their value itself being defined by the rules of the game, characteristic of the social formation in question) and partly on the players' skill'. The cards in question represent 'material and symbolic capital', but a family's success at playing its cards depends less on their inherent face value, than on the 'competence which enables the strategists to make the best use of their capital'. Since the 'hands' of this game are a 'combination of the strategies of the interested parties', matrimonial negotiations are 'the business of the whole group, everyone playing his part at the appropriate moment'. As a preliminary gambit, women employ their 'unofficial and recoverable contacts' to sound out the other party, 'without the risk of a humiliating rebuff'. With the successful conclusion of such preliminary contacts, the 'most eminent men, those most representative of official kinship', carry out, as 'authorized spokesmen', the collectively formulated mandate of the kin group. The families contemplating matrimonial alliance with another family verify the details of the social and economic history of the other group, with special attention to 'the symbolic patrimony [consisting of their] capital of honour and men of honour [... and] the quality of the network of alliances on which they count, of the groups to which they are traditionally opposed'. Families concentrate on 'the maintenance and reproduction of the family, not the production of assets'. Honour, in such a context, is not merely the 'transfigured expression' of economic and political factors. Everything that encompasses 'the vulnerability of the group' must be safeguarded through 'punctilious, active vigilance' (Bourdieu 1977: 58–60).

In the domain of traditional lineage, marriage exists to form advantageous alliances with other kin groups, and as a vehicle of inheritance designed to perpetuate lineal control over property or political office. By contrast, the realm of individual marriage is that of amorous relationships determined by the preferences and pre-rogatives of the two partners. Whether for emotional satisfaction, sexual gratification, or spiritual fulfilment, marriage in this latter context is ego-centred. The Church, for reasons both too numerous and too obscure to discuss here, promulgated the second type as official Christian marriage. The individualism thus encouraged — whether as a matter of deliberate policy, as Goody contends, or as a tangential element in an ideological program with unintended social effects — worked over the centuries to undermine traditional kinship and the marital practices employed to perpetuate it. Incorporated with variations and modifications into secular law codes, this consensual model of marriage continued to subvert the influence of extended kinship in the age of the emerging states of modern Europe.

Duby's two-fold model of medieval European marriage is essentially based on the same dichotomy as that proposed in more general terms by Leach. What Duby calls the 'lay model' unites two individuals 'born of two different houses in order to found a new house of similar form — or rather, to ensure the survival of one of these houses'. Marriage of this sort was 'an ostensible, ceremonial act', 'an agreement, a treaty [...] concluded between two houses'. The pact so confirmed involved an exchange: a woman's 'anticipated motherhood' was transferred to the lineage of her husband. The marriage, being 'essential to the future of both houses', was held to be 'too important to be left to the individuals concerned' (Duby 1978: 4–5).

The second type of marriage, conforming to what Duby terms 'the ecclesiastical model', was developed, he contends, to satisfy 'two contradictory exigencies'. One was the reproductive function, the other 'the carnal impulses of human nature'. Mankind, the Church allowed, had to reproduce itself. At the same time, the faithful had to beware of the perils of hellfire. Thus, marriage was 'tolerated, but only as a remedy against carnal lust', while the physical act was 'strictly subordinated to the desire to procreate' (Duby 1978: 16–17). Marriage was therefore principally a matter of the individual, freely given consent of the persons concerned. All other parties, however important in the lives of the couple, were bystanders:

> The Church thus unintentionally tended to take a stand against the power of the heads of households in matters of marriage, against the lay conception of misalliance, and, indeed, against male supremacy, for it asserted the equality of the sexes in concluding the marriage pact and in the accomplishment of the duties thereby implied. (Duby 1978: 17)

The question to be asked with regard to secret marriage in the romances is: why must love and marriage be secret, if the parties' freely given consent makes the marriage? The answer is that the ecclesiastical model does not yet prevail; the spouses' families cannot yet be discounted. Marriage is therefore carried out according to an ephemeral working definition, a compromise incorporating imperatives from the old exclusively kin-ordered world and the new world of individual choice. When we regard the apparently dominant agnatic system in the background of our narratives as a game played from weakness and vulnerability, rather than from power and security, we begin to understand the violence which intrudes on the relationship between daughters and fathers, between fathers and would-be sons-in-law.

R. Howard Bloch has eloquently summarized the effect of the individualist trend. 'Seen in generational terms', he remarks, 'it bolstered the claims of children against parents [while bringing about] a catastrophic short-circuiting of the biopolitics of lineage'. The traditional collective arrangement of marriage — focused on 'military, social and economic considerations [such as] obligations to vengeance and to armed service, political alliance, [and] legal and financial responsibilities' — could no longer be achieved with unfettered regard for clanic advantage (Bloch 1983: 162).

On the one hand, we may speak, according to William J. Entwistle, of the 'ill-regulated' household portrayed for Tirant's father-in-law, the Byzantine Emperor. Not, Entwistle remarks, that the Byzantine imperial household was really like that, but perhaps

Martorell's household was a disordered one in which 'young men penetrated without difficulty and at any hour to the rooms of unmarried girls', with only the 'casual perambulations' of a bemused and somewhat ineffectual emperor to impede their assignations. The marriage customs in effect before the Council of Trent (1564), are also, he points out, observed in *Tirant*. Wedlock is established by 'an exchange of freely given vows between the spouses', while church ceremonies were 'of merely secondary interest'. The secretive conduct of heroines in *Tirant*, *Amadís*, and other romances, he explains, must be understood in light of the earlier preference for 'the secret promise and consummation' (Entwistle 1949–50: 152–53).

Concealment and stealth, Justina Ruiz de Conde reminds us, were integral elements of the etiquette of courtly love: 'los amores divulgados se perdían pronto'. Ruiz de Conde explains the acceptance of secrecy as a function not only of chivalric discretion, but, in the case of Amadís, of the hero's psychological modernity. He is, for her, the 'hombre interior', capable of private spirituality and emotional fulfilment: 'Sabía ya gozar de su alma e inventarse placeres espirituales.' He is, therefore a solitary personage ('es antisocial por excelencia'), capable of doing without 'ciertas instituciones sociales tan importantes como el matrimonio y la filiación'. It is in light of this alienation, she argues, that we must understand the secret marriage of Amadís and of his parents before him (Ruiz de Conde 1948: 201–03).

Antony van Beysterveldt, attempting to distinguish chivalric from courtly love, suggests, in a manner somewhat reminiscent of Ruiz de Conde, that secrecy in the context of the former stems from the very character and psychological profile of the knight, and therefore derives from 'la situación novelesca misma'. Moreover, Amadís and Tirant, who love the daughters of 'personas reales cuyos vasallos son', risk death by an offence which may be defined as, essentially, a kind of treason: 'la necesidad del secreto se relaciona [...] con la vigencia de un código de honor' (Van Beysterveldt 1981: 413–14). Taking a somewhat similar approach, James D. Fogelquist notes that lovers in chivalric romances live in fear not of jealous husbands but of jealous fathers.[1] Fogelquist's

---

[1] Fogelquist 1982: 103; cited by Sieber 1985: 206.

definition of the controlling third party, however, is perhaps too narrow. In our core texts, the adulterous triangle of the knight, his beloved, and her husband that typifies courtly love is replaced by the knight, his lady, and her principal male kin. These kinsmen in *Amadís* and *Tirant* are fathers; in *Curial*, an elder brother; in *Zifar*, both fathers (in the case of Zifar himself, books 1 and 2), and uncles (the case of Roboán, book 4).

Herbert Moller, writing on the 'social determinants' of the 'courtly love complex', tends to explain the well-known aspects of courtly love as a set of attitudes and behaviours which characterized the aristocratic life style. The ethos in question was a 'configuration of specific anxieties and wishful fantasies' which was 'coterminous with the social confines of the secular upper classes', and focused on 'an unapproachable and demanding lady'. This beloved was usually already married, usually of a higher station than the lover. Such poets as Chrétien and Wolfram von Eschenbach, according to Moller, tended to equalize sexual relationships, rejecting service to women for its own sake, while seeking to merge 'courtly and marital affections' through an emphasis on 'attitudes of mutuality of sentiment', instead of the earlier convention of unilateral servility shown by an unmarried knight toward an elusive married woman. The unilateral aspect of courtly love — men adoring aloof women — was at least partly a response to demography. The 'high sex ratio' of men to women, the numeric predominance of bachelor knights and other male dependants in noble households, implied a 'shortage of marriageable women [...] in the lower stratum of the upper class' (Moller 1958–59: 138, 143–45, & 154–55).

Entwistle, Ruiz de Conde, Moller, and Van Beysterveldt, although writing from very different points of view on the relationship between social factors and narrative themes in courtly and chivalric literature, emphasize perhaps a bit too much the status-affirmative nature of chivalric discretion. Although strictly social determinants are present, especially for Moller, the inertia of custom, aided by the stimulus of fashion consciousness, accounts, in the view of these critics, for various aspects of the knight's life, including the secrecy of his amours. The importance of status consciousness is, of course, not to be discounted, and undoubtedly played a role in the depiction of secretive behaviours. Audiences, we may suppose, were assumed to recognize the knight's motives. The notion that discretion and secrecy derive from a chivalric etiquette and style of life is, however, too simple an explanation, of itself, for the extraordinary importance of secrecy in the amorous relations of chivalric heroes. For one thing, what these critics perceive as the older and simpler style of secret promise and clandestine consummation was itself a subversive innovation with respect to traditional kinship practices that were themselves associated with high status. For another, the knight's beloved, in the chivalric romances, is not passive, aloof, or unattainable, but rather an active co-conspirator in subverting the family's control of marriage.

We begin to arrive at an answer when, to the agnatic imperatives outlined by Bourdieu and the social historians, and the ethical and behavioural motives suggested by Entwistle, Ruiz de Conde, and other critics, we add the character of the beloved and the function of the woman in the chivalric world. The knight, according to Maurice Keen, must be discreet in the pursuit of deeds that enhance his *bonne renommée*; 'he does not', Keen affirms, 'bray his conquests'. For him, the need for discretion stems, perhaps most significantly, from the active role of women in the chivalric culture. To betray their reputation is to undermine a fundamental source of spiritual power. The place of women in this system reveals a mentality which we might construe as revolutionary: women in the view of the truly chivalrous knight are not, points out Keen, mere spectators, but rather a vital catalyst to chivalric accomplishment. Love, moreover, is 'a human passion which, rightly regulated, sharpens and refines the honourable ambitions of martial men' (Keen 1984: 13–14).

Robert Hanning, somewhat along the same lines, argues that the romance is characterized by the tension between the protagonist's 'yearning to complete himself or herself through union with the beloved', and such external factors as 'conventions of modesty' and 'familial prohibitions' which prevent fulfilment of desires. Hence the intimacy of the romance world, which 'lacks any context larger than the lives of its protagonists'. The defining attribute of the genre is the plot, 'which organizes incidents ranging widely in time and space around the life of the hero without any larger controlling narrative context', thus, a plot which is 'episodic as well as biographical'. The plot of romance, closely tied to biography, therefore shows 'little linearity', and readily focuses on stories of adventures, shipwrecks, misunderstandings, separations and reunions, amnesia, exile, disguise, orphanhood and fosterage, etc., since these are the vicissitudes of real lives. The hero's goal is limited to the simple, believable objective of reconciliation with an 'earthly beloved'. The governing tension is described in terms of 'a private world of love and the public world of responsibilities'. Thus, the dilemma of the hero often consists of his beloved's involvement in a forced marriage, or his own commitment to 'a pseudo-love identity [...] in the form of a socially sanctioned and apparently desirable marriage' (Hanning 1972: 9, 10–11, 12, & 21).

Ruiz de Conde accurately characterizes *Tirant*'s emphasis on 'la voluntad', that of a tension maintained between the will of Carmesina ('de conservarse pura'), and that of Tirant ('de respetar los deseos de su amada'). It is above all the feminine will — 'ya de una manera mundana, como Placerdemivida o la emperatriz, ya con clara intención moral, como Carmesina' — which emerges as the dominant element in the social world of Tirant. The same may be said, to a certain extent, of the other romances as well. Ruiz de Conde makes the point that this emphasis on the female will is due to the impact of courtly love culture on the social world of Catalonia, and thus of *Tirant*. The findings of the present study confirm this impact, in the sense that courtly (or chivalric) love itself may have something to do with the marriage practices observed in the text. The court in question centres on the female will; as a social domain it is, as it were (borrowing a term from Goody which I shall analyse in greater detail in the next chapter) *filiacentric*. This does not contradict the perception of Ruiz de Conde, the author of the most thorough study to date of love and marriage in the Spanish chivalric romance: 'El amor cortés, sí, pero de tipo realista [...] con relación física entre los enamorados, con matrimonio para asegurarlo en la vida y en el futuro' (Ruiz de Conde 1948: 161).

The medieval standard for marriage rules, especially for consent as the determining factor, finds its origin in the Pauline epistles (I Corinthians 7; Ephesians 5. 21–33), which provide the earliest evidence of a normative regulation. This and other precedents, from scriptural, patristic, and canonical sources, were developed by such influential writers as Hugh of St Victor (d. 1141), who declares that 'Conjugii auctor Deus est' ('God is the author of matrimony'). Although woman is 'quodammodo inferior' to man (in that she derives from him), she was made to associate with her mate on a basis of equality ('ad aequalitatem societatis facta'). Hugh's enunciation of equality of the sexes is all the more consequential for its insistence on the contractual nature of matrimony ('quae foedere sponsionis mutuae consecratur') (Hugh of St Victor 1880: 482–85).

Although consent of itself was generally considered the determining factor in making a marriage, ambiguity arose concerning the difference between marriage effected by consent alone, and marriage confirmed, or made somehow more official, by subsequent sexual consummation. This was a theme of controversy throughout the twelfth century. The ambiguous distinction between *matrimonium initiatum* and *matrimonium ratum* gave rise to controversy concerning the difference between betrothal and marriage. One historian of marriage speaks of 'the old, convenient confusion' between betrothal and marriage, which was not resolved until the Council of Trent, and which served the aristocracy on innumerable occasions as a pretext for dissolution of unwanted marriage.[2]

Gratian, in his highly influential *Decretum* (completed *c.* 1140) allowed that marriage required the consent of the interested parties, but questioned the categories of *matrimonium initiatum* and *matrimonium perfectum* (in other texts *m. ratum*). John Alesandro contrasts Gratian's theory of consummation as the determining factor in marriage formation to the Parisian school's consensual theory of marriage. In presenting his view of the *matrimonium initiatum/matrimonium ratum* (or *m. perfectum*) distinction, he defines the *matrimonium perfectum* as 'the end result of [a] process', while the *matrimonium initiatum* is 'the preparatory process of marriage formation' (Alesandro 1971: 45). For Gratian, those exchanging future consent are betrothed persons (*sponsi*), rather than lawfully married *coniuges*. The precursory stage, or *desponsatio* is not the same as marriage, although many speak of it as such. No real *coniugium perfectum* exists until it is consum-

---

[2] Casey 1989: 94. See also Joyce 1948: 85–86.

mated by the first act of sexual intercourse (48; referring to Gratian C. 27, 2 *dictum post* c. 39). Gratian clearly distinguishes, therefore, between *desponsatio*, referred to by many as *coniugium initiatum*, and true marriage. For Gratian, betrothal is not, summarizes Alesandro, an 'embryonic marriage', with marriage after consummation another kind of marriage. Rather, there is only one kind of marriage for Gratian, namely, the *coniugium perfectum*. Although *desponsatio* constitutes the 'start of the process' that leads to real marriage, it can only be called matrimony 'by anticipation of what is to come' (Alesandro 1971: 53–54). As James Brundage affirms (1987: 236), Gratian made 'consummation the key to marriage formation'. A marriage initiated but not consummated 'lacked the binding power of consummated union'. The latter term was reserved by Gratian and his followers for the true and indissoluble marriage which symbolized the union between Christ and His Church.[3]

The consensus-copula debate of the twelfth century was resolved by Alexander III (1159–81), in a series of influential decisions that prepared the way for the Fourth Lateran Council of 1215, and, eventually, the commissioning of the *Liber extra* by Gregory IX (Brundage 1987: 325–27 & 331–46). The Church's concept of marriage and the role of consent in its establishment have remained essentially the same since the promulgation of the latter work in 1234. Consent by freely exchanging, baptised parties constitutes the sacramental, indissoluble bond of matrimony (Doyle 1985: 737).[4]

Charles Donahue, summarizing the marriage rules enunciated by

---

[3] Joyce 1948: 58–72 & 380–86; see also Brooke 1989: 126–41. The relevant section of Gratian's *Decretum* is Causa XXVII, Quaest. 2 (numerous clauses). The issue of consent vs consummation, in Gratian and elsewhere, has been studied by innumerable scholars; Brundage 1987: chap. 6, is a recent, complete survey. The other principal model of marital consent (emphasizing consent over consummation), is espoused by Peter Lombard, another influential voice (see Lombard 1981: Distinctio XXVI.i.6; Dist. XXVII.ii-v; Dist. XXVIII.i, iii, etc.). Brundage (236–37) contrasts in some detail the French and the Bolognese models of marriage formation.

[4] Joyce summarizes the impact of Alexander III's compromise in terms of a rejection of the Bolognese canonists' notion that until consummation the partners are not truly married, with consent only a formal commitment to enter the married state (Joyce 1948: 430).

Alexander III, remarks that their significance resides in the freedom of the partners to define marriage by their freely given consent. What is most notable about these rules, he affirms, is 'not what they require but what they do not require'. They do not require, among other things, the approval of parents or lords. They do not even require sexual consummation, in the case of present consent. A marriage established through vows of present consent remained valid and indissoluble. Unless the consent of other parties is expressly stipulated as a condition, the couple's mutual consent remained the sole prerequisite for matrimony. Moreover, continues Donahue, there was no requirement of 'solemnity or ceremony of any kind'. Even witnesses were unnecessary. Only if either party disavowed his or her pledge of consent would litigation ensue, with the consequent calling of witnesses and presentation of evidence (Donahue 1983: 145).

These marriage rules established a union by words spoken *de presentii* ('I take thee'). Matrimony also resulted if the couple exchanged vows of future consent ('I promise'), and subsequently engaged in sexual intercourse. The different ages of consent for men and women present a pattern significant for the interpretation of our literary texts. For marriages of future consent, the requisite minimum age was seven for both sexes. In the case of present consent, the more immediately binding of the two types of matrimonial vow, the ages were fourteen for the husband, twelve for the bride. In addition, conditions were specified. Marriage was established if neither party had been previously married to someone still living; if neither had taken a solemn vow of chastity; if the parties were not too closely related (Donahue 1983: 120).

The decretists of the twelfth and thirteenth centuries were the dominant influence in the establishment and imposition of the concept of consent which would become the Catholic norm. While emphasizing individual consent in its many aspects and implications, the decretists not infrequently condemned traditional marriage patterns, such as arranged marriage between cousins. The emphasis on the freely given promise of the partners thus inevitably undermined clanic prerogatives. The prohibition on close marriage, remarks Rudolf Weigand, 'verfolgt das ausdrückliche Ziel, damit zur weiteren Verbreitung der Liebe beizutragen'. Love, in other words, was extolled by the decretists as an expansion of that emotion from the realm of kinship into the broader realm of general social relationships. Marriage for them was therefore not so much the consequence of love as a strategy for extending the influence of love, 'unter Einbeziehung der gesamten neuen Verwandtschaft, als Ziel und Folge der Ehe' (Weigand 1981: 48–49).

The *Partidas* reflect a strong ecclesiastic influence, having assimilated the principal tenets of church views on marital consent and related issues (Gibert Sánchez 1947: 709–43). In regard to consent, the *Partidas* declare, for example, that 'maguer sean dichas las palabras segunt deuen para facer el casamiento, si la voluntad de aquellos que las dicen non consiente con las palabras, non vale el matrimonio quanto para seer verdadero' (IV.ii.5). The distinction between *matrimonium initiatum* and *matrimonium ratum* is also made in the *Partidas*:

> Diferencia nin departimiento ninguno non ha para seer el matrimonio valedero, entre aquel que se face por palabras de presente et el otro que es acabado ayuntándose carnalmiente el marido con la muger. Et esto es porque el consentimiento tan solamiente, que se face por palabras de presente, abonda para valer el casamiento: pero el un matrimonio es acabado de palabra et de fecho, et el otro de palabra tan solamiente. (IV.i.4)[5]

The *Partidas* state that although words spoken 'de presente' at betrothal may seem to be those of marriage, they represent something different. It is as if, the *Partidas* declare, the man said 'yo te rescibo por mi muger si ploguiere á mi padre', or the woman the equivalent. Thus, we have betrothal rather than 'desposajas' because when one person 'pone su casamiento en alvedrio de otro, non vale el pleyto que face, si el otro non lo otorga'. Consent is valid, meanwhile, whether the parties grant it 'manefiestamente o callando'. In fact, consent is tacitly understood from a number of conditions: 'que consienten quando morasen en uno, ó quando rescebiesen dones el uno del otro, ó se acostumbrasen de se veer el uno al otro en sus casas, ó si yoguiese con ella asi como varon con muger' (IV.i.3). These individualist criteria, accentuating the

---

[5] Esteban Martínez Marcos demonstrates the detailed reliance of the fourth *Partida*, that treating of marriage and family law, on book IV of the *Liber extra* (1966: 8–12 & 31–36). See also Gregory IX, section on 'De sponsalibus et matrimoniis', book IV, titles i–xix (including discussion of clandestine marriages under title iii).

actions and intentions of the two partners, are later reinforced by a specific rejection of familial intervention: 'los padres non pueden desposar sus fijas, non estando ellas delante et non lo otorgando' (IV.i.10).[6]

The medieval ecclesiastical concept of marital consent — a concept adopted, in its essentials, by the *Partidas* — defines marriage in the romances. In chapters 31–37 of *Zifar*, for example, the story deals with the decision of the queen of Galapia as to whether or not she will marry the son of the count who has besieged her city. Although she consults others, the decision is shown to be entirely her own. Another example of the importance of feminine choice in marriage is that of Seringa, the princess of Pandulfa. Count Ruben can only try to persuade her of the advantages of a marriage to Roboán; although he is her uncle and apparently the senior male of her lineage (he is 'tio e vassallo de la yfante'), Ruben cannot oblige her to do more than think about the matter. 'Non vos podria yo agora responder', she replies to his suggestion of a match with Roboán. To this her uncle responds by urging her: 'Pues pensad en ello [...] e despues yo recudire a vos' (*Zifar* 411).

Churchly intervention in marital matters, always implying a recognition of the priority of individual consent as a defining factor, is typified in *Amadís* by the actions of the saintly hermit Nasciano. Knowing from her confessions that Oriana is Amadís's secret love and that Esplandián is their child, the hermit recognizes the great danger that they run 'en hauerla de casar con otro' (IV, 1119.28–33). He resolves therefore to inform Lisuarte of the situation ('con su licencia de ella, que de otra guisa no podía ser'), thus facilitating 'paz y concordia' through the marriage of Amadís and Oriana (IV, 1119–20.40–45). Nasciano, whom we must take as the voice of the Church, sternly points out to Lisuarte the impossibility of marrying his daughter to the Roman emperor. Oriana, Nasciano asserts, is Lisuarte's 'legítima heredera y successora'. He reveals, in addition, that, 'según la ley diuina y humana', Oriana 'es junta al matrimonio con el marido que nuestro Señor Jesú Christo tuuo por bien, y es su seruicio que sea casada' (IV, 1124.341–59).

---

[6] See also Hugh of St Victor 487–88.

Consent is clearly stated in standard ecclesiastical terms in
Tirant, as we see in Plaerdemavida's appeal to the hero in chap.
357, in which she reminds him of his responsibilities toward
Carmesina and the Greek royal family: 'Car no ignores com los
turcs han subjugada tota la Grècia, que no els fall sinó la ciutat de
Contestinoble, e pendre l'Emperador e sa muller e la dolorosa
Princesa, muller tua, que has promesa ab paraules de present'
(967). Numerous scenes in *Tirant* reveal the importance assumed in
that work of the issue of female consent. Marriage is arranged, but
the bride, it is clear, must be consulted. There is, for example, an
element of coercion in the marriage to be arranged between
Carmesina and Tirant, but her consent is vital. In the betrothal
scene in chap. 452, her father, having pointed out the virtues and
accomplishments of Tirant, as well as the need to reward him with
a suitable prize, speaks to her in terms of both paternal authority
and fatherly persuasion: 'us prec e us man, ma cara filla', he says,
'que el vullau pendre per marit e senyor, e serà la cosa de què més
me poreu servir' (1118). The irony of the situation, deriving from
the reader's knowledge that Carmesina does not need to be
persuaded, does not negate the emphasis placed on consent.

In *Zifar* (chap. 77), the king of Mentón asks his daughter if the
newcomer deserves the prize destined for the saviour of the
kingdom, namely her hand in marriage: 'E creedes vos fija, que es
asy?' When she replies in the affirmative, the king asks: 'E plaze
vos [...] de casar con aquel cauallero de Dios?', to which she
responds 'Plazeme pues lo Dios tiene por bien' (159–160). The
Greek Emperor in *Tirant*, like the old king of Mentón in *Zifar*,
anxiously requests his daughter's opinion as to a suitable marriage
candidate: 'Tu volries al nostre Capità per marit?' (696). In
Amadís, Lisuarte, like his counterparts in *Zifar* and *Tirant*, feels a
similar constraint to seek his daughter's consent. He tells Patín of
Rome, who has proposed a match between himself and Princess
Oriana: 'yo y la reyna emos prometido a nuestra fija de la no casar
contra su voluntad, y conuerná que la fablemos ante de os
responder' (II, 387.130–34). We are told that Lisuarte says this
merely to temporize — that he has, in fact, no intention of giving
her in marriage to anyone 'que de aquella tierra donde él auía de
ser señor la sacasse' (II, 387.136–9).[7] He sends queen Sardamira,

---

[7]   The passage presents a slight difficulty of interpretation. Lisuarte is already the

sent by Patín along with an entourage of maids of honour to accompany Oriana in the voyage to Rome, to meet with his daughter in Miraflores:

> y le contasse las grandezas de Roma y la grande alteza en que sería con aquel casamiento, mandando tantos reyes y príncipes y otros mucos grandes señores. Esto fazía el rey Lisuarte porque de su fija conoscía tomar mucho contra su voluntad aquel casamiento, y porque esta reyna, que muy cuerda era, la atraxiesse a ello. (III, 843–44.31–41)

Carmesina, as her father solicits her approval, blushes and finds nothing to say: 'tornà roja e vergonyosa e no pogué res dir' (*Tirant* 696). Güelfa as well, although a widow and something of a woman of the world, reacts demurely as the moment of betrothal to her beloved finally arrives, after so many years of estrangement and vicissitude: 'Callaua la Guelfa, e de vergonya no sabia ne podia respondre' (455). *Zifar*'s Lady of Galapia, in the public discussion of the proposed marriage pact (concerning which, as we have seen, she has engaged in very pragmatic speculation), stands speechless: 'non dezia ninguna cosa e estaua commo vergoñosa e enbargada' (74). This aptitude of otherwise mature and purposeful women for blushing when asked for their consent seems a demure concession to patriarchal decorum.

The king of Sicily shows himself a good father in his answer to Tirant's advocacy of the match between the Infanta Ricomana and Prince Philip of France, the hero's friend:

> d'aquests afers jo no clouira res sens voluntat de ma filla, perquè a ella té de servir. E si ella és contenta, per ma part vos ofir lo matrimoni e dar-li he tot lo que li he oferta. Jo de bon grat ne

---

lord of 'aquella tierra'. Cacho Blecua reads: 'mas no tenía en coraçón de la dar a él ni a otro que de aquella tierra donde él avía de ser señor la sacasse' (I, 696). Cacho Blecua observes that 'Estas palabras se contradicen con los desarrollos narrativos posteriores' (I, 696n7). Cardona de Gibert and Rafel Fontanals (1969: 323) present the plausible but unexplained emendation: 'de la dar a él ni otro que de aquella tierra donde ella había de ser señora la sacase'. Place is silent on the apparent contradiction, never resolved within the text, between Lisuarte's reluctance here and his entire subsequent course of action, which sets in motion the principal conflict of *Amadís*, that between Lisuarte, who seeks to force Oriana to marry Patín, and Amadís and his men, who seek to rescue her from this match.

parlaré ab la Reina e ab ma filla e, sabuda llur intenció [...] lo
matrimoni se fermarà. (313–14)

The king's brother, the Duke of Messina, when questioned as to his
opinion of his niece's marriage to Philip, counsels the king with
regard to the issue of female consent and suitable marriage
partners: 'com a les donzelles los parlen algun matrimoni de què
elles se contenten, e tan prest no ve a conclusió segons l'apetit e
llur voluntat, resten molt agreujades' (319). His preoccupation
extends to the consent of the young man as well, but in, as it were,
the opposite sense: he is very concerned that the young man's
family approve of the match: 'aquest matrimoni se deuria fer ab
consentiment de son pare e de sa mare' (319). The Duke is
concerned that a compromise be effected. Both the family and the
prospective betrothed, it is clearly shown, have a legitimate say in
the arrangement of marriage. The narrator, however, makes it very
clear that the consent of the bride is essential for marriage to occur,
as we see from Ricomana's resolution to test her suitor: 'Si jo puc
trobar en Felip tal defalt que sia grosser o avar jamés serà mon
marit'. The same declaration sees her determined to further test the
prince: 'E d'ací avant en altra cosa no vull pensar sinó en saber-ne
la veritat' (342).

The world of *Tirant*, then, is not one in which daughters humbly
accept the husband imposed on them by the imperatives of familial
or political alliance. Shortly after her she enunciates her desire to
further test Philip, the Sicilian Princess Ricomana declares to
Tirant:

> Ans elegiria renunciar a la vida e als béns que pendre marit grosser,
> vil e avar [...] Si jo prenc aquest per marit e si no m'ix tal com jo
> volria, hauria ésser homeiera de la mia persona, que seria forçada
> de fer actes de gran desesperació, per què a mi és semblant que més
> val estar sola que ab mala companyia. (345)

Carmesina's declaration of love and of marital consent (chap.
271) kindles in Tirant a 'goig inefable', as he contemplates the
certainty that he is 'en camí per poder posseir la corona de l'Imperi
grec per mijà de les novelles esposalles'. The narrator emphasizes
Tirant's awareness of Carmesina's sincerity: the hero rejoices
'veent que l'excelsa senyora ab tanta lliberalitat e amicícia li havia
volguda mostrar la infinida amor que li portava, e ab verdadera fe e
sancer esperit l'havia tractat' (784). Obviously aware of the impli-

cations of sincerity in the giving of consent, Tirant nonetheless requires of Carmesina earnest intentions: 'per major seguretat sua pres un reliquiari que ab si portava en què havia del *Lignum crucis* [...] e féu-hi posar les mans a la Princesa, conjurant-la com ella ab pura fe e sancera intenció demanava lo matrimoni. E ella ab molta alegria féu lo jurament [...]' (784). Tirant also shows awareness of the need for sexual consummation as the absolute confirmation of marriage. It is more than sexual urgency that makes him say to the princess: 'ab aquella confiança que per tantes ofertes m'és estat afermat, e si les mies suplicacions troben en l'altesa vostra algun lloc, estimadament me façau gràcia e mercè que d'açò no se'n pare més, sinó que ab voluntat sancera donem prest compliment en nostre matrimoni' (793). A little later, he insists:

> Jo no vull vostra corona ni la senyoria d'aquella; dau-me tots mos drets a mi pertanyents segons mana la santa mare Església, dient semblants paraules: Si les donzelles ab treball són ajustades a matrimoni verdader, qui pot e no ho fa, peca mortalment si en lo matrimoni no s'hi segueix còpula. (795)

Tirant's prayer in the storm (chap. 297) reveals that the hero really considers Carmesina his wife. Addressing his absent beloved as 'excel·lentíssima Princesa e esposa mia' (838), he confirms the sincerity of his own intentions. Sexual consummation as a crucial component of marriage in *Tirant* is further revealed in Plaerdemavida's 'dream'. Actually an ironic summary of the events of a night during which Diafebus and Tirant visit their lovers, Estefania and Carmesina, her account relates what Estefania said after receiving her lover: that no one will ever again find her trustworthy, nor she will ever again be able to guard another damsel's honour having lost her own. However, Plaerdemavida continues, there are consolations:

> que no he res fet que perjudique la honor de mon marit, sinó que he complida sa voluntat a mal grat meu. En les mies bodes no hi són venguts los cortesans, ni cappelà no s'és vestit a dir la missa; no hi és venguda ma mare ni mes parentes; no han hagut treball de despullar-me les robes e vestir-me la camisa nupcial; no m'han pujada al llit per força, car jo m'hi só sabuda pujar; no han hagut treball los ministres de sonar ni de cantar, ni los cortesans cavallers de dansar, que bodes sordes són estades. Emperò tot lo que he fet resta en grat de mon marit. (564)

At the same time, we see a reflection of the equivocal perceptions of this factor. While it is clear that Tirant and Carmesina consider themselves married, both by virtue of their mutual consent freely exchanged and by the fact of their sexual relations, the Princess says to her father confessor, the pious Franciscan and 'gran doctor en la sacra teologia' (1161): 'he pecat greument, car consentí que Tirant, marit e espòs meu, prengué la despulla de la mia virginitat ans del temps permès per la santa mare Església' (1162).

Zifar's Queen of Galapia, we have seen, accepts a suitor who had been an enemy; all she required was that he ask her politely. By contrast, Madasima, in *Amadís*, wants nothing of any marriage to the boorish and arrogant Ardán Canileo, despite the latter's promise to avenge the death of her kinsmen. We see her resistance in her response to Ardán's plight during the judicial combat: 'de lo qual a ella no pesaua, ni ahunque Ardán Canileo la cabeça perdiesse, porque su pensamiento tan alto era que más quería perder toda su tierra que se ver junta al casamiento de tal hombre' (II, 533.980–85). However, Galvanes sin Tierra, her eventual suitor, does satisfy the criteria imposed by her 'pensamiento tan alto'. The crisis in the kingdom of Great Britain, confronting Amadís with his contingent against King Lisuarte and his allies, is eventually precipitated by Amadís's desire to facilitate this match: 'Siendo por Agrajes y don Galuanes y por mí', declares the hero, 'demandada en merced al rey a Madasima con su tierra para que con don Galuanes casada fuesse, quedando en su señorío y por su vassallo' (II, 551.1035–40).

In *Curial* we see indifference to the official advantages of a suitor, such as the prestige and personal attainments of a noble knight of the highest pedigree. Güelfa, in love with the hero 'sens tota mesura', shows herself aware of the charms of Boca de Far ('qui era molt bell e bon caualler, de molt gran linage e marauellosament heretat'), but remains nonetheless unmoved in her faithfulness to Curial (90). *Curial* clearly presents a scene, in another episode, in which the marital schemes of a family impinge upon the preferences of a potential bride. We read of the lady Laquesis, madly in love with Curial; she is, we are told,

> molt treballada per les instancies grans que sa mare, qui era molt tenguda a propri, per lo Rey, que donas sa filla per muller al Duch dOrleans, e a la mare plagues, la volia forçar ques fes aquell

matrimoni; enpero Laquesis, postposada tota pahor, li responia que
mort li podia donar, mas no marit. (224)

Another daughter who resists arranged marriage is the Moorish
girl Camar, in *Curial*. In love with the hero, a captive in her
father's household, she refuses to accept the marriage proposals of
the King of Tunis. Camar reacts to her mother's announcement of
this proposal (in which agnatic advantage is stressed above all else;
the girl, her mother rejoices, is about to become Queen) with total
dismay. Like Laquesis, she rejects the good match out of hand: 'la
mort me pot donar, may yo nulls temps en tal matrimoni
consentire' (269). The affinal advantages are pointed out by her
father: 'tu auras honor e molt de be, e nosaltres serem per tu
honrats e auançats molt', as are the attractions of a future royal
progeny: 'tos fills seran Reys'. Above all — here the lineage
orientation, in terms of the continuity of her own family, is
expressed most overtly — she is all they have: 'Tu sabs que yo no
he altre be sino tu' (370). Made hopeless by her father's impor-
tunate severity, she stabs herself with a knife, prompting her
mother — in a scene highly reminiscent of Bourdieu's contrast of
masculine official and feminine unofficial kinship — to execrate
Faraig, the father, calling him 'traydor' and 'alcauot' (372). Later,
the poor father having been executed due to the king's mistaken
assumption of paternal guilt in the matter of Camar's wound, the
girl's maternal and paternal uncles seek to intervene as match-
makers in the monarch's favour. Camar, ignoring the king's gifts,
assures her uncles that she will give herself a thousand more such
wounds rather than accede to their demands (378), prompting her
relatives to remonstrate:

> que lo Rey, volent e demanant la filla dun son vassall, per rich que
> fos, [no] deuia trobar repulsa [...] que poria esser que no serie a
> temps de penedir, e, per ventura, poria, aquesta sua follia, esser
> causa de la destruccio de tot son linage. (378)

The author puts into the mouth of this Moorish girl enamoured of a
Christian hero the essence of Christian doctrine on marriage: 'No
es matrimoni', she assures her mother, 'aquell ques fa per força;
car, entre persones liberes, se vol liberament contractar; e, com hi
esdeue força [...] pert lo nom e encara lo efecte de matrimoni'
(384).

A correlative of the concept of consent is that women can take the initiative in proposing marriage, as we see in the scene in which Briolanja, in love with Amadís, 'estuuo muchas vezes mouida de le requerir de casamiento' (I, 337.501–03). Later, when Briolanja has come to suspect that Amadís is secretly in love with Oriana, she explains to the latter why she has not made this hero 'tan bueno y de tan alto lugar', as Oriana puts it, lord of the kingdom which Amadís restored to her. Briolanja reveals her attempt at a marriage proposal: 'le cometí', she tells Oriana, 'con esto que agora dexistes y proué de lo hauer para mí en casamiento, de que siempre me ocurre vergüença quando a la memoria me torna' (II, 497.742–47).

Consent binds, as we have seen in Lady Estefania's letter of intent concerning her relationship with Diafebus. Referring to her free will ('llibertat de fer de mi lo que vull'), she proclaims:

> de grat e de certa ciència, no constreta ni forçada, tenint Déu davant los meus ulls e los sants Evangelis de les mies mans corporalment tocats, promet a vós, Diafebus de Muntalt, ab paraules de present prenc a vós per marit e senyor, e done-us mon cos lliberalment sens frau ni engan negú. (*Tirant* 494)

At the same time, the family and issues of lineage are not to be completely ignored. The romances' endorsement of consent is but one factor in a regime comprising both traditional and modernizing elements. A clear example of this blend of practices is shown in *Zifar*. Hearing the proposal of marriage from the young son of her enemy, the Lady of Galapia reflects on his attributes: 'el cauallero era mançebo e mucho apuesto e muy bien razonado e de muy grant lugar, e de mas que su padre non auia otro fijo sy non este' (71). The prospective groom is, therefore, an heir unencumbered with siblings whose pretensions on his own estate could be potentially hazardous to the lady's material interests. Not, we see, that traditional elements (e.g. social standing, the man's status as an only child) are not taken into account in arranging marriage: only that the woman's say matters most of all. The ecclesiastical model is influential, but not absolutely dominant. If it were, there would be far less concern to keep consensual amours a secret.

A hint of the complex perception of consent is obtained in that passage in which Tirant pleads with the Emperor to bless the union of the Emperor's niece Estefania and Tirant's cousin Diafebus. The Emperor is, as it were, given first choice in the sequence of persons who have a say. He yields his vote to his wife and daughter: 'tot mon lloc e poder jo done a ma filla, que ací present és, que ho faça ab consentiment de sa mare' (668). We see the importance of the Emperor's opinion by the reaction of the unhappy Estefania. Thinking that his naming of wife and daughter as proxies reveals his disapproval, she retires alone to a room to weep (668–69). All the young people present, including the hero and his beloved Carmesina, beseech the Empress to 'consentir en aquest matri-moni', to which she replies that she is indeed 'molt contenta' (669).

The author of *Tirant* reveals himself a theoretician of consent, as we see in the speech of the hero to the Queen of Tunis. He explains that words are 'senyals ab los quals nostre intencions se mostren, car en altra manera, elles, closes dins los corporals murs e segellades ab lo secret segell de nostra voluntat, sols a Déu són descobertes'. He shows that he considers his relationship with Carmesina a marriage because of the words he uttered to seal their union. At the same time, he shows, in making this offer of assis-tance, the typical desire to assume the matchmaker's role:

> si jo vixc, sereu senyora del regne vostre; e dar-vos he marit rei coronat, jove e virtuós, que de mi, com vos he dit ab tota veritat, no puc muller pendre, que ja en tinc; e si tal cas cometia, no seríeu dita muller, mas amiga, e la vostra excel·lència mereixedora és de major de mi. (902–03)

In the harangue delivered by the Viuda Reposada to her charge, Princess Carmesina, we see reference again to the importance of consent. The widow reminds the princess of her vow not to be 'sujeta a negun altre, rei o emperador, del món, e que si marit havíeu de pendre no seria sinó sol Tirant'. If, however, she intends some day to be Tirant's wife, if she does 'res, qui deshonest sia, ab ell', no sooner would she become his wife, than he would dismiss her as a 'mala dona' (687).

Secret marriage, without parental and familial consent, is permitted, but is a second-choice alternative. Much to be preferred are betrothal and marriage confirmed by familial approval and finalized in public celebration. Nonetheless, the sufficiency of consent is never forgotten. 'Qui promet en deute es met', chides Tirant. His beloved Carmesina retorts that the promise 'no es féu ab acte de notari', to which Plaerdemavida, who seeks to further Tirant's suit, counters that

promesa de compliment d'amor ni en exercir aquell no hi cal
testimonis ni menys acte de notari. ¡Ai tristes de nosaltres, si
cascuna vegada s'havia de fer ab escriptura! No hi bastaria tot lo
paper del món. (695)

Love is a function of consent, in that love exalts the importance
of the couple over all other considerations. The conflict between
the traditional and the modern is between the requirements of the
kin group and those of the individual. The texts themselves often
show their conscious awareness of this dilemma. Thus, Princess
Carmesina declares of Tirant that the 'extrema amor' which she
feels for him, above 'totes les persones del món', is so great that
she forgets 'a pare e a mare e [...] quasi a Déu' (738). Oriana tells
her confidante, Mabilia (Amadís's cousin), when Amadís arrives
for the first clandestine tryst, that the man at their window must be
Mabilia's 'cormano', to which the confidante replies: 'Mi cormano
es [...] mas vos auéys en él más parte que todo su linaje' (I,
127.407–11). Thus is expressed the supremacy of the affinal relationship over the consanguineal. We see the same clash of
priorities in Oriana's later exasperated remark to Mabilia, that
Amadís has no consideration for her: 'Siempre me acontece con
vuestro cormano, que mi catiuo coraçón nunca en ál piensa sino en
le complazer y seguir su voluntad, no guardando a Dios ni la yra de
mi padre [...]' (II, 505.462–67). Mabilia, upbraiding Oriana for her
unfounded jealousy, points out the nature of her cousin's love:
'aquella fuerte ventura suya, que tan vuestro sujeto y catiuo le fizo
que aborreçiendo y desechando a todo su linaje por os, señora,
seruir, teniéndolos por estraños [...]'. He has, in benefit of Oriana,
'fecho seruir a su linaje y sus hermanos', for the good of his
beloved. Mabilia declares that she has seen the very 'flower of her
lineage' die before her very eyes, all for the love of Oriana (II,
506.501–16). At issue is the tension provoked by the conflict of
obligations. Mabilia, a woman of Oriana's household mobilized, as
it were, to facilitate her mistress's love, cannot, in her anger, forget
the ancient imperative of kindred vendetta: 'Esta crueza que en
Amadís fazéys, Dios quiera que dél y su linaje vos sea demandada;
ahunque bien cierta soy que su pérdida, por grande que sea, no se
ygualará con la vuestra' (II, 506.525–30).

Oriana's dilemma is expressed in terms significant in the light of
the historical contradictions surrounding the concept of marital

consent and its impact on lineage. In terms reminiscent of Helen of Troy, she exclaims, at the sight of the battlefield where the two sides are deploying themselves:

> ¿Qué haré? que mi coraçón no puede sofrir en ninguna manera lo que veo [...] que de vn cabo está [...]la lumbre de mis ojos y el consuelo de mi triste coraçón, sin el cual sería impossible poder yo biuir; y del otro estar mi padre, que ahunque muy cruel le he hallado, no le puedo negar aquel verdadero amor que como hija le deuo [...] Que qualquiera déstos que se pierda, siempre seré la más triste y desauenturada, todos los días de mi vida, que nunca muger fue. (IV, 1063–64.262–78)

The consensual precepts of the Church, as dramatized and endorsed in the romances, stand in obvious opposition to the principles of marital alliance as practised in traditional societies. The life of Guillaume le Maréchal demonstrates the continued importance of traditional marriage arrangements in the chivalric society of around the turn of the thirteenth century. Guillaume, his biographer tells us, has five daughters. The poet is at great pains to recount the details of each marriage. They are advantageous matches, and in each case they are arranged; there is never any question of consent as an issue. The eldest, for example, is described as possessed of 'sens e largesse, / Bealté, franchice e gentillece'. Her father ('qui molt l'ama') gives her in marriage to Hugues Bigot ('Al mielz e al plus bel qu'il sout'), the future Count of Norfolk (Meyer 1891–1901: ll. 14919–28). All of her sisters but the youngest, the poet declares, likewise find noble husbands during the lifetime of their father, while the youngest is well married by her eldest brother (14929–56). The same is true of the marriage of the eldest son to the daughter of Baldwin, Count of Aumale. The latter's case matches that of several situations in the chivalric romances: 'N'out enfant fors la damisele' (14970). The two fathers confer ('Del marïage, ce me semble, / Parlérent entre eus deus asemble'), and the match is arranged ('Otrïé fu le marïage'), with Baldwin leaving all his lands to his daughter ('tote sa terre / E aliors par tot li donout'). No mention is made of any concessions made by Guillaume. The marriage contract is finalized by an appeal to the king to ratify its provisions, and to produce a written charter (14973–96). Despite the significance of consent in the texts, the romances frequently remind us that betrothal and marriage are an essential part of relationships between lineages. In *Amadís*, for example, the Emperor of Constantinople expresses a frank assumption as to the multifarious political utility of matchmaking as he expresses hopes that the woman Amadís loves resides within the confines of the Greek empire:

> que tanto auer y estado le daría yo que no ay rey ni príncipe que no ouiesse plazer de me dar su hija para él. Y esto faría yo muy de grado por le tener comigo por vasallo, que no le podría hazer tanto bien que él más no me siruiesse, según su gran valor. (III, 816.580–87)

Later, when the hermit Nasciano speaks to Amadís, he demands if the hero really wishes to restore 'paz y amor donde tanta rotura y desuentura está', and specifically makes a spiritual appeal: 'quise saber de os [...] si ternéys conoçimiento más a Aquel que os crió que a la vanagloria deste mundo' (IV, 1130–31.853–62). The hermit tells Amadís the message conveyed to the king, Oriana's father: 'le dixo que Oriana era casada con él, y que el donzel Esplandián era su nieto'. Furthermore, the hermit concludes, he must extract a promise from the hero: 'que él diesse orden cómo, quedando casado con aquella princesa, se concertasse la paz entre ellos ambos'. The emphasis, in other words, is on lineage and alliance, although couched in spiritual terms, and duly emphasizing consent. This constitutes a compromise. The church invokes consent as justification for the marriage of Oriana and Amadís, but the political function of marriage is allowed to persist, as it were, on sufferance.

Amadís is perhaps chiefly about the conflict between lineage and individual for the right to determine marriage; neither side in the controversy enjoys an unequivocal advantage. The work is obsessively conscious of the contradictions and dangers inherent in the notion of free will. In chapter 1 of *Amadís*, Elisena is described as Perión's 'amada' and his 'señora'. While they make love for the first time, Elisena's maid Darioleta finds Perión's sword, taking it up 'en señal de la jura y promessa que le auía hecho en razón del casamiento de su señora' (I, 19.84–87). To Perión, in this first tryst, it seems that in Elisena resides 'toda la fermosura del mundo' (I, 19.91–92). Thanking God for having brought him to 'tal estado', he leads her to the bed. There aquella que tanto tiempo con tanta fermosura y jouentud, demandada de tantos príncipes y grandes hombres se auía deffendido, quedando con libertad de donzella, en poco más de vn día, quando el su pensamiento más de aquello apartado y desuiado estaua, el qual amor rompiendo aquellas fuertes ataduras de su honesta y sancta vida gela fizo perder, quedando de allí adelante dueña. (I, 19.96–108)

This passage is followed by an extraordinary expression of the ambiguous tension surrounding the complex of individual intention and familial obligation. The principle of female consent is defended, but the moral hazards it presupposes are clearly recognized. Women may be graced with the free will presupposed by the concept of consent, but precisely for that reason they must guard themselves from temptation. The narrator, in an aside to his audience, declares that through Elisena's experience we are given to understand that women are empowered to divert 'sus pensamientos de las mundanales cosas', while disdaining 'la grand fermosura de que la natura les dotó'. and the 'fresca juuentud que en mucho grado la acrescienta'. Thus, women, rejecting the 'vicios y deleytes' assured by the 'sobradas riquezas' of their parents, and motivated by a desire to save their souls, may place themselves 'en las casas pobres encerradas'. In this way freely submitting their 'libres voluntades' to the supervision of others, they watch their lives go by 'sin ninguna fama ni gloria del mundo, como saben que sus hermanas y parientes lo gozan'. In such pious circumstances, even the most devout women must

con mucho cuytado atapar las orejas, cerrar los ojos, escusándose de ver parientes y vezinos, regogiéndose en las deuotas contemplaciones, en las oraciones sanctas, tomándolo por verdaderos deleytes, assí como lo son, porque con las fablas, con las vistas su sancto propósito dañan, do no sea assí como lo fue el desta fermosa infanta Helisena [...] (I, 19–20.109–136)

Earlier Darioleta had declared of Elisena and her lover that both had defended themselves from many, but now found themselves unable to defend themselves against each other (I, 19.76–82). Shortly thereafter, Darioleta is described as having saved her mistress's honour: 'Si no fuera por la discreción de aquella donzella suya, que su honrra con el matrimonio reparar quiso' (I, 20.142–43). Elisena is vulnerable: 'ella de todo punto era

determinada de caer en la peor y más baxa parte de su deshonrra, assí como otras muchas'(I, 20.145–48).

We have seen in the previous chapter that the kindreds mobilized by Amadís and his cousins exist in the here and now of synchronic kinship, and are opposed to the diachronically focused interests of the agnatic descent groups with whom they come into conflict. The opposition naturally centres on the question of marriage because that is the institution which serves as the fulcrum both of individual ambitions and of dynastic objectives. At the same time, the heroes themselves cannot ignore the political functions of marriage as an expression of practical, mobilizable kinship. Thus, the individualist notion of consent and the kin-ordered function of the go-between show an uneasy association in the narratives. King Escariano asks Tirant, 'com a germà seu d'armes', to arrange a marriage with the Queen of Tlemcen. To this request the hero replies: 'jo la'n suplicaré una e moltes voltes que hi consenta, car segons nostra llei lo matrimoni que per força és atorgat no val res' (911).

Affinal alliances such as that proposed by Escariano motivate much of the action in the chivalric romance. Ruiz de Conde has pointed out this aspect in regard to *Zifar*. She describes the marriage arrangements of the widowed Queen of Galapia, in Book 1: 'El matrimonio es por razón de Estado y los consejeros son los que tienen que arreglarlo' (95). We may speak of a 'reason of state', but the state in question is conceived as lying in the domain of kinship. Likewise 'por razón de Estado' is the marriage of Zifar to the Queen of Mentón. The importance of affinal kinship in the political realm is exhibited, in *Amadís*, in the alliance called upon by Lisuarte at the time of his succession to the throne of Britain. He is aided by his father-in-law, the king of Denmark, who provides him with a fleet. Leaving his wife Brisena and his daughter Oriana in Scotland, he enters the kingdom, there encountering 'algunos que lo estoruaron como hazer se suele en semejantes casos'. His kingship is confirmed only 'con gran trabajo' (I, 39.10–30).

At the successful conclusion of a conflict motivated entirely by the desire of Amadís and Oriana to escape her forced marriage to the Roman emperor, the hero himself contrives a political marriage, as he requests of Lisuarte that the latter agree to marry Leonoreta, Oriana's younger sister, to the newly acclaimed emperor of Rome

pues el emperador de Roma no tiene mujer y es en disposición de la hauer, que os plega darle a la infanta Leonoreta vuestra hija; y a él ruego que la reciba porque sus bodas y mías sean juntas y juntos quedemos por vuestros hijos. (IV, 1181.274–80)

The king immediately recognizes the utility of this proposal: 'lo tuuo por bien de lo tomar en su deudo'. The emperor responds with equal enthusiasm: 'la recibió con mucho contentamiento' (IV, 1181.281–85). One of the great incongruities of *Amadís* is that Leonoreta, the younger daughter of Lisuarte, is not consulted, nor is her consent a factor in the marriage to the new Roman emperor arranged for her by Amadís and her father. The hero points out to Lisuarte that the emperor has no wife and is 'en disposición de la hauer'. Lisuarte agrees, and the marriage pact is concluded to the satisfaction of Amadís, Lisuarte, and the emperor (IV, 1181.285). It is apparently assumed that Leonoreta will consent. Presumably this is because the marriage is clearly advantageous, therefore clearly desirable. Amadís, however, is guilty of the very offence committed by his father-in-law, and on account of which so much blood has been shed: he arranges a marriage for entirely political and lineage-oriented purposes ('porque sus bodas y mías sean juntas y juntos quedemos por vuestros fijos') without consulting the bride.

In another significant episode, Amadís commands the giant Balán that he must, in restitution for his slaying of Darioleta's son, release her husband and daughter, while restoring their property and their vessel. In addition, the hero demands something more of his newly conquered foe. Here again the principle of marriage as an alliance of lineages is expressed through Amadís's role as political matchmaker:

y por el hijo que le mataste que le des el tuyo, que sea casado con aquella donzella; que ahunque tú eres gran señor, yo te digo que de linaje y de toda bondad no te deue nada, pues ahún de estado y grandeza no están muy despojados, que demás de sus grandes possessiones y rentas, gouernadores de vno de los reynos de mi padre son. (IV, 1271.393–403)

The narrator of *Amadís* betrays his own obsession with kindred and matrimonial alliance by his declaration of the significance of the marriage between Bravor (the son of Balán) and the daughter of Darioleta. They will have a son, Galeote, destined to take after his mother rather than his father ('no [...] tan grande ni tan desemejado

de talle como lo eran los gigantes'). This Galeote, heir to his
father's kingdom, will marry a daughter of Galvanes and
Madasima. These in turn will have a son of their own, also named
Balán, like his paternal great-grandfather. Thus the Isle of the
Boiling Lake remains in this family until 'aquel valiente y
esforçado don Segurades', a knight of the time of 'Uterpadragón,
padre del rey Artur, y señor de la gran Bretaña'. This Segurades
will leave a son, Bravor el Brun, destined to be killed by Tristan of
Leonís. Bravor will leave behind his son, Galeote el Brun, 'Señor
de las Luengas Ínsolas', and a great friend of Lancelot of the Lake.
Thus is made clear, affirms the narrator, for those who have read
the tales of Tristan and Lancelot, in which figure the tales of these
knights called Brun, 'el fundamento de su linaje' (IV, 1273.493–
555).

Amadís, as we have seen, several times does precisely that
which alienated Lisuarte from his daughter — namely, he arranges
marriages on the basis of political and genealogical advantage.
However the hero does it better, by reconciling the imperatives of
alliance and consent. In expressing his gratitude to brother, cousins,
friends, and vassals of the Ínsula Firme, Amadís tells them:

> no ayáys empacho que vuestra voluntad manifiesta me sea [...] en lo
> que a vuestros amores y desseos toca, si algunas destas señoras
> amáys y por mujeres las quisierdes. IV, 1190–91.322–33)

In yet another case of matchmaking facilitated by chivalric
intervention, Amadís supports Gandalín in the latter's handling of
the affair of a felon knight who has abducted a damsel. The
abductor, declaring himself the helpless victim of love, throws
himself on Gandalín's mercy, even asking for the latter's inter-
cession with the girl's mother: 'Y me sea ayudador, pues que la
hija está de mí contenta, que lo esté la madre y me la dé por
muger.' The young lady reassures Amadís and Gandalín: 'que
ahunque fasta allí auía estado en su poder contra su voluntad, que
viendo el gran amor que la tenía y a lo que por ella se auía puesto,
que ya era otorgado su coraçón de lo querer y amar, y le tomar por
marido'. At this Amadís recommends to Gandalín that the latter
place the two lovers in the hands of the girl's mother: 'y en lo que
pudieres, adereça cómo lo aya por muger, pues que a ella le plaze'
(IV, 1302.1241–62). Here again is a clear expression of the
principle of marital consent, and of the knight as the facilitator of

that principle within society. The episode has a happy ending. Just as the damsel, confronted with the intensity of the knight's love for her, had changed her mind, 'como las mugeres acostumbran fazer', so also the girl's mother changes her mind, 'siendo de la mesma naturaleza que su fija'. Thus, 'a plazer y contentamiento de todos fueron casados en vno' (IV, 1302.1283–94).

Marriage brokerage as a function of chivalric leadership appears in *Tirant* just as it does in *Amadís*. At a feast in honour of the French ambassadors sent by their king to negotiate the marriage of Philip of France to Princess Ricomana of Sicily, the diplomats enumerate the three elements of their mission. The first is that the French king is 'molt content' that his son marry the princess; the second, that if the Sicilian king had a son, 'ell li daria una filla sua per muller ab cent mília escuts'. And the third consists of an invitation to a crusade: 'com ell hagués amprat al Papa e a l'Emperador e a tots los prínceps de la crestiandat li volguessen valer per mar, com ell tingués deliberat d'anar contra infels' (*Tirant* 341–42).

Thus, the hero arranges the marriage between Philip of France and Ricomana of Sicily, as the French king acknowledges: 'segons que per lo virtuós Tirant era estat concordat' (341). It is Tirant who acts as go-between for Philip and Ricomana, finally arranging the marriage in chapter 111, as both the Sicilian King and his daughter entrust him with making the final arrangements (355–56). When Tirant contrives to send Ricomana's servants away, placing the princess and Philip together alone, she angrily refuses to kiss Philip unless her father commands her to do so (356). When the two young men try to force the issue, she screams, causing her maids to rush in: 'e pacificaren-los e donaren-los per bons e per lleals' (357).

For Tirant, then, marriage brokerage is one of the functions of lordship. Its corresponding obligations extend beyond the sphere of battle comradeship. Seeking their co-operation in the furtherance of his amours, he assures the ladies-in-waiting of his beloved Carmesina that he will reward them with riches as he does Estefania. As for the Viuda Reposada, he promises her 'marit que fos duc, comte o marquès, ab tants de béns que ella ne reste contenta e faça rics a tots los seus'. As for all the rest, including Plaerdemavida, he wishes to do the same (654). Later, he feels that

Estefania also looks to him to arrange her marriage, as we see in his promise to see her wed to his cousin Diafebus (the Constable): '¿e no us he jo ja dit que lo dia de nostra partida jo suplicaré al senyor Emperador, present la senyora Emperadriu i la Princesa, e totes seran avisades que sien bones en fer aquest matrimoni? E restarà ací lo Conestable [...] e fareu llavors vostres bodes' (667). In another example of marriage brokerage as a function of noblesse-oblige, the Empress assures the silence and active co-operation of her maid, Eliseu, who has discovered the love affair of her mistress with the young knight Hipòlit: 'tu seràs en ma openió e més favorida de totes les altres, e jo et casaré més altament de totes' (761).

Marriage as the vehicle of political reconciliation and alliance is, then, a factor taken completely for granted in the romances. There is no attempt to reconcile this assumption with the implicit contradiction of viewing love as a personal issue. The political functions of marriage are particularly stressed in *Tirant*. Interestingly, when referring to the pagans, the narrator assumes merely the political function; love is not a factor in the marital equation, as it is so preponderantly in the case of the hero and his cousins. Tirant, in his interrogation of Turkish sailors, hears of the company of the Gran Caramany, a Muslim leader (567). In his party are his daughter, betrothed to the Turkish sultan, together with a number of damsels 'de gran estat', each with a fabulous trousseau, and each bringing along 'son eixovar', for all are destined to be married 'a grans senyors'. In *Tirant*, to take another example, the Sultan's ambassador proposes a truce and a peace treaty to the besieged Greek emperor, along with a marriage proposal, in one diplomatic package:

> e tu com a pare per ell seràs tengut, e tu a ell poràs haver com a fill,
> e si per premi de tal concòrdia li volràs dar a ta filla Carmesina per
> muller [...] A així poríem dar fi a tots los mals. (599)

Marital alliance is, of course, a commonplace of European and world history. What makes the Sultan's proposal significant, in both historical and narrative terms, is the fact that marital alliance is conceived as an exclusively inter-lineal reality. There is no nationalism here: the diplomatic relationship proposed is between families and not nations as we know them. This is revealed by the Sultan's additional offer — 'en premi del dit matrimoni' — of the restoration of 'ciutats, viles, castells', and a cash settlement, 'dos comptes de dobles'. The arrangement is expressed in thoroughly kin-oriented terms, as 'ab tu e ab los teus', and is conceived not merely as a peace treaty but as an active alliance: 'e fer t'ha valença contra tots aquells qui noure't volran' (599).

Just as Amadís facilitates the marriage of Galvanes to Madasima, so too does Tirant arrange the marriage of his cousin Agramunt to the Lady Plaerdemavida. Like Madasima, she is an exile who has lost her inheritance. Fate has ordained, declares Tirant, that she shall be 'reina de dos regnes, sens perdre l'esperança de cobrar les [...] viles e castells, e tot lo [...] heretatge pres e ocupat per infels'. She will be, he assures her, 'col·locada en matrimoni ab rei virtuós e valentíssim cavaller', while becoming 'molt afix en afinitat e grau de parentela, del llinatge de Roca Salada e de la casa de Bretanya'. By means of this matrimonial alliance she will recover, he promises, towns, castles, and the rest of her 'patrimoni'. Tirant concludes his pact with a solemn vow confirming the bond of affinal kinship: 'E jo et promet devaler a aquell així en béns com en persona, e ab totes mes gents [...] e seràs feta parenta mia; jo ame aquell e a tu com germana' (994).

Carmesina, we may note, is also a matchmaker. In her last will and testament, she stipulates that her lands and moveable goods should be sold, and the proceeds used for a significant purpose: 'e los preus que n'eixiran sien repartits en casaments a totes les mies donzelles, segons l'estat e condició de cascuna [...]' (1164). On her death-bed, with her father's body on her right hand and Tirant's on her left, she laments her lover's death, assuring the ladies of her retinue:

> E si ell hagués vixcut, cent donzelles de vosaltres havien d'ésser nóvies ab mi ensems aquell dia que Tirant e jo teníem a celebrar les festes nupcials, e dar a cascuna tants de mos béns fins que fósseu ben contentes. (1166)

After the death of his uncle Tirant, Hipòlit, himself the beneficiary of matchmaking by the hero, employs the arrangement of marriages as an instrument of social control. Grateful for the discreet performance of the Viscount of Branches on the diplomatic mission of returning the hero's body to Brittany, the new Emperor engages in still more redistribution of wealth, giving the

Viscount the County of Benaixí 'en premi de sos treballs'. Hipòlit
is not finished:

> Aprés donà a tots aquells qui s'eren casats ab les criades de
> l'Emperadriu e de la Princesa bones heretats, que en podien molt bé
> viure a llur honor e cascú segons son grau [...] E aprés per temps
> casà totes les altres, així com de bon senyor se pertanyia. (1186)

Hipòlit's career is like that of Zifar: he marries well, inherits a
kingdom, and, after the death of the heiress-ruler who is the
instrument of his ascent, marries another wife who is the mother of
his children. The Empress lives only three years after their
marriage, leaving him free to marry the daughter of the King of
England, 'de grandíssima bellea, honesta, humil e molt virtuosa e
devotíssima crestiana', who gives him three sons and two
daughters. Before his death, Hipòlit 'heretà molt bé a tots sos
parents e criats e servidors' (1187).

In *Tirant* William of Warwick, upon his departure in pilgrimage
to the Holy Land, arranges the marriage of his squire while
bequeathing the latter all his earthly goods: 'donà tots quants diners
li eren restats a l'escuder, perquè l'havia ben servit, e col·locà'l en
matrimoni perquè no es curàs de tornar en Anglaterra' (123). The
fact that his motives are a mix of altruism (he rewards the squire's
service) and pragmatism (he wants the squire to remain in Italy,
spreading the rumour of his master's death) does not diminish the
importance of the marriage-broker function.

Also in *Tirant*, one of the Greek Emperor's chief functions, as
head of a clan, is to arrange marriages. This he does for his niece
Estefania, 'una parenta sua molt acostada'. The elements of the
transfer of various goods, outlined in her declaration, are confirmed
in the friar's speech in chapter 221. To the husband of this niece
the Emperor has already ceded the Duchy once ruled by her father
and stepfather, along with the girl herself and 'tots los béns, joies,
robes que el dit Duc deixat li havia'. In addition to these goods
moveable and immoveable, the Emperor, 'de sos béns propis',
gives to Estefania 'cent mília ducats' (672).

Marriage as alliance, and the matchmaking prerogatives of the
monarch or lord, are likewise seen in *Curial*. At the end of the
story, the King of France, who has honoured the hero at every
opportunity, invites the Marquis of Monferrat and the latter's sister,
Güelfa, who has, the king knows, been estranged from the hero for

some time. The king has in mind 'aportar a effecte que Curial casas ab la sor del Marques'. The latter, for his part, accepts the invitation, expecting, indeed, that the king 'donaria marit a sa sor' (421–22). After many intervening adventures, including the hero's valiant intervention in the defence of the Greek empire against the Turks, it is the king himself who performs the offices of go-between, asking the Marquis, Guëlfa's brother, with 'molta composicio de paraules', that he give 'a Curial la Güelfa per muller' (455).

The meaning of marriage as alliance is thus one of the principal themes of the chivalric romance. The ultimate reconciliation of feud, for example, is shown to be the shared grandchildren of lineages hitherto confronted: those, for example, of Perión of Gaul and Lisuarte of Great Britain. Esplandián, the son of Oriana and Amadís, the grandson of Lisuarte of Great Britain and of Perión of Gaul, thus personifies the alliance of his patrilateral and matri-lateral lineages. Perión expressly states the function of Esplandián in his speech to the hermit Nasciano (who has raised Esplandián as his *criado*): 'parésceme que contándomelo dizen que embió dezir al rey Lisuarte por vn escripto que este donzel pornía mucha paz y concordia entre él y mi hijo Amadís [...]' (IV, 1132.974–78). Later, seeing the obvious love shown by Lisuarte toward the youth Esplandián, Amadís understands the boy's unwitting contribution:

> embermejecióle el rostro, que bien conosció que el rey sabía ya todo el hecho dél y de Oriana, y de cómo el donzel era su hijo. Y tanto le contentó aquel amor que el rey a Esplandián mostró, y assí lo sintió en el coraçón, que le acrecentó su deseo de le seruir mucho más que lo tenía, y esso mismo hizo al rey; que la vista y gracia de aquel moço era tal para su contentamiento que mientra en medio estuuiesse no podría venir cosa que les estoruasse de se querer y amar. (IV, 1165.894–907)

Similarly, the story of *Tirant* focuses on the kindred resulting from the union of Tirant and Carmesina. Ending with the tragic death of the hero, followed by that of his father-in-law the Greek Emperor, it presents the plight of the Empress: ' [...] veure morts marit, filla e gendre! [...] E tanta tribulació venir en un dia!' (1165) Many other calamities and tribulations have beset the Empire, but it is the personal, familial dimension, the plight of two lineages joined as one, that the author emphasizes above all else. The story ends with the return of the hero's body to his homeland in Brittany, where he is honoured in death by the Duke and Duchess and by 'tots los parents e parentes' (1185).

The notion that affinal ties are as conducive to kindred solidarity as those of consanguineal relationships is clearly expressed in *Amadís* by means of Angriote's explanation to the widowed queen of Dacia of don Bruneo's relationship to Amadís (Bruneo, we recall, marries the hero's sister Melicia): 'don Bruneo es en deudo de hermandad por su esposa con Amadís de Gaula' (IV, 1202.35– 37). There is, however, another kind of marital arrangement. Cousinship, as we have seen, serves as the principal focus of mobilizable kindreds in *Amadís*. We recall, for example, that the nucleus of the fighting force to be sent out to rescue Madasima and the twelve captive maidens, held hostage by Lisuarte, is the impromptu action-group composed of cousins of Amadís, as we saw in the list of allies announced by the hero, which included, in addition to Galvanes (the beneficiary, as it were, of the collabora- tive action depicted), his nephew Agrajes, the hero's half-brother Florestán, their cousins Palomir, Dragonís, and Brian de Monjaste, as well as several others affiliated by friendship and vassalage (II, 567.965–77). We note that this mobilization is designed to facilitate the marriage of Galvanes to Madasima, the rights to whose kingdom have been pre-empted by Lisuarte's high-handed attribution of the kingdom to his younger daughter.

Bourdieu's observation that assistance in marriage arrangements is one of the primary purposes of kin mobilization is likewise confirmed in *Tirant*, where, for example, the hero, seeking help in the furtherance of his love affair with Carmesina, appeals to Diafebus to speak to the princess on his behalf, addressing him as 'parent e germà' (408). The intimacy of their relationship is confirmed by the hero's reliance on his cousin for the most delicate and vital of all missions, the arrangement of marriage. The relation- ship is, at the same time, one of extreme respect. Throughout the story, Tirant and Diafebus will address each other as 'cosín germà' or 'Senyor cosín germà', until the very moment of the hero's death in chap. 471 (1151).

The problem of secrecy, then, must be understood in light of the foregoing contradictions. The hero and his beloved seek not to overthrow a system they would themselves employ, given the appropriate circumstances, but to circumvent it for the sake of amorous expediency. There is therefore never any question of the primacy of agnatic interests, only of the best means of upholding them. The romances are about daughters who get their way in the matter of mate selection. But their marital bias in no way precludes their wanting exactly what their fathers want: the perpetuation and prosperity of the lineage.

Oriana's joy on her discovery that the Donzel del Mar is really named Amadís, the son of kings, leads her to confide her secret to the Damsel of Denmark. It is to be kept, declares Oriana, 'como poridad de tal alta donzella como yo soy y del mejor cauallero del mundo' (I, 66–67.36–54). Later, after Amadís has performed such deeds as the restoration of Briolanja's kingdom, the defeat of the forces of Cildadán, and — above all — his successful performance in the ordeal of the Arch of Faithful Lovers, Briolanja tells Oriana, as they coyly speculate as to who might be the hero's beloved (the former suspecting Oriana, the latter seeing the suspicion): 'El bien puede amar [...] pero es lo más encubierto que lo nunca fue cauallero' (II, 497.770–72). Again, the secrecy of the relationship does not invalidate it. Oriana, having confessed to the good father Nasciano the details of her secret love and of the birth of Esplandián, replies to the hermit's criticism: 'ella dixo llorando cómo [...] tenía [de Amadís] palabra como de marido se podía y deuía alcançar' (III, 780.533–38). Nasciano recognizes the secret marriage of Amadís and Oriana, based on mutual consent, as legitimate: 'que vuestro padre sepa lo passado, y que no vos puede dar otro marido sino el que tenéys' (IV, 1121.145–47). Ruiz de Conde notes the significance of the public reaction, at the court of Lisuarte, to the 'discreción de los dos amantes'. So discreet have they been, she comments, 'que nadie se había dado cuenta de la relación que entre ambos existía'. She points out as well that the story clearly understands the significance of secrecy with regard to patriarchal control, through its depiction of Lisuarte's 'conversion' to his daughter's way of thinking (as he finally resigns himself to 'el marido que le plugo tomar') (Ruiz de Conde 1948: 210–11).

Earlier in *Amadís*, Briolanja had mentioned that in his sojourn in her kingdom, when she had unsuccessfully proposed marriage to him, Amadís never so much as mentioned 'ninguna muger [...] como todos los otros caualleros lo hazen' (II, 497.749–53). When the Emperor her father seems on the point of guessing the existence of her secret love for Tirant, Carmesina is dismayed: 'de vergonya, tornà tal com una rosa' (520). When she deduces that her father has not discovered her amour, she confides in the Lady Estefania that her body was all but drained of blood for fear that her secret ('nostre fet') might be discovered. Her crime, however (having given Tirant money), 'és crim meritori [...] e deu ésser pres a la fi perquè es fa, com sia acte de caritat' (522). Both her fear of discovery and her need to rationalize her favours to Tirant are significant. Later she will tell Tirant that she did not speak up and urge him to accept her father's gift to him of the County of Sant Angel: 'de vergonya no tenguí atreviment, per lo vell Emperador que no conegués lo meu mal, car cosa convinent és que la vergonya sia mesclada ab amor' (556).

The need for stealth, a major source of the prurient suspense of the narrative, is repeatedly stressed in *Tirant*. The hero and Diafebus arrange, for example, to sneak into the bedrooms of their respective sweethearts, Carmesina and Estefania. The former's maid, Plaerdemavida, guesses that this must be the case: 'véu que la Princesa no es volia gitar, e li havia dit que se n'anàs a dormir, e aprés sentí perfumar, prestament pensà que s'hi havia de celebrar festivitat de bodes sordes' (559). Later, Plaerdemavida seeks to persuade Princess Carmesina to allow Tirant to sleep with her for but one hour; the princess replies that her maid must be mad, but allows that if, once in her apartments, he refused to leave, she would maintain silence: 'si anar no s'en volia, ans deliberaria de callar que ésser difamada' (699). Carmesina resists the seduction arranged by Plaerdemavida. And the hero himself, observes Ruiz de Conde, hesitates: 'antes morir que ofender'. When Plaerdemavida blackmails the princess into compliance, threatening scandal, Carmesina, finding herself 'entre la espada y la pared', chooses the lesser of two evils, defending herself verbally against Tirant: 'de las dos deshonras, la pública, por traer consecuencias sociales, le parece la peor'. We have already established why the public dimension is the more terrifying: the 'consecuencias sociales' incurred by exposure of her struggle with the hero derive from the most sensitive and vulnerable aspect of the agnatic world, namely, its hold on the right to dispose of marriage, the only possible instrument of lineal continuity (Ruiz de Conde 1948: 135–36).

Narrative tension in the romances derives from the contradictory imperatives of consent and lineage. Neither of the two generations in conflict can ignore the perspective of the other. The strain on familial harmony is exacerbated by the social implications of consent. For consent ultimately implies isolation of the conjugal pair from kin on both sides. It is, consequently, an incentive to monogamous love and a catalyst of the formation of the nuclear family, with all its perils of fragility and isolation.

The romances dramatize the isolation of the couple — and the resultant reciprocal dependency of the lovers — in very clear terms. Oriana assures Amadís that she could not live without him: 'Si yo del mundo he sabor', she declares, 'por vos que en él biuís lo he' (I, 247.236–42). She then states that they will be together come what may, regardless of any danger or disgrace: 'sea antes con desamor de mi padre y de mi madre y de otros' (I, 247.255–61). This isolation of the couple from their respective kin is poignantly highlighted by Oriana's unwillingness to allow Amadís to depart in search of adventure, after they have taken up residence in their kingdom of the Firm Isle. Her appeal is expressed in terms of her separation from kith and kin, and the consequent dependence on her beloved: 'como se viesse en aquella ínsola apartada de su padre y madre y de toda su naturaleza, y otra consolación no tuuiesse ni compañía sino a él para satisfazer su soledad, nunca otorgárgelo quiso' (IV, 1245.49–55).

Postmarital residence, always involving a complex interaction of descent and marriage rules, is complicated by the consensual environment. The fact that several personages marry in to their bride's family, and the fact that when this is not the case alternative residential patterns are dramatically emphasized, must be discussed. The cluster of kin-related practices and prohibitions imposed by Church and State were naturally conducive to the establishment of so-called *neolocal* residence, involving an independent household for the married couple. Such would certainly be the ideal for a couple who married in defiance of their kinsmen. 'Los casados casa quieren.' The wisdom is proverbial, the reality often unattained. Some characters in the romances do in fact found a new household independent from those of the respective families of the spouses. Thus, Roboán settles down, in the closing chapters of *Zifar*, with Princess Seringa in his newly acquired empire of Trigridia (bequeathed to him as the adopted son of that empire's newly deceased ruler). Amadís and Oriana become the King and Queen of the Firm Isle (Book IV). Curial and his beloved Güelfa go to live in the principality of Orange, granted to the hero by the King of France (456). Some personages in the romances, by contrast, establish *uxorilocal* residence (i.e. with the wife's kin). This is the case of Zifar (marrying the princess of Mentón), and of Tirant (marrying Carmesina, the heiress of the Byzantine Empire). In *Amadís*, the uxorilocal marriage of Briolanja and Galaor is almost idealized: 'como assí sus voluntades tan enteramente entonces se juntaron, assí permanesciendo en ello después que a su reyno se fueron, touieron la más graciosa y honrrada vida, y con más amor que se vos no podría enteramente dezir' (IV, 1200.502–09). Such cases of uxorilocality are symptomatic of the so-called epiclerate, which implies the survival of the patrilineage of the wife through recruitment of an 'in-marrying' son-in-law. They do not, therefore, correspond to the matrilineal social structures normally giving rise to uxorilocal arrangements. I shall have much to say concerning this topic in the next chapter.

Only very occasionally do we encounter references to *virilocal* residence (i.e. with the kin of the groom), the norm for patrilineal societies. An example is the passing reference, in *Curial*, to the knight Aznar's behaviour after his marriage: 'ab molta honor e riquesa, lo dit Aznar, per tornar en lo regne don era natural, daquell jorn auant, ab sa muller a aparellar se començà' (262). The fact that, in *Zifar*, Roboán's bride, the princess Seringa, goes to live with him in the Empire of Trigridia (chap. 227) might seem to suggest a virilocal pattern. However since Roboán is the adopted son and heir of a childless emperor, the choice of his adoptive home is functionally equivalent to neolocal residence.[8]

Even as the chivalric heroes struggle against a social order to whose margin they have been relegated, they seek to replicate that order and by so doing achieve legitimation. Neolocal residence in the romances of chivalry is, in other words, a function of lineal

---

[8]   On the implications of post-marital residential patterns, see Leach 1968: 486; for a discussion of the complexities of residence in cognatic kinship systems, see Fox 1967: 156–63, and Barth 1973.

segmentation. The latter phenomenon, mentioned in the previous chapter, characterizes unilineal descent as practised by certain societies, such as the Nuer. In response to political, demographic, economic, or merely familial pressures, a junior member of a lineage will strike off on his own, establishing an independent branch of the original lineage. The new branch is held to be a segment of the old, while the continued relationship between segments is at once antagonistic and complementary. Despite the inevitable conflicts between junior and senior segments, continued solidarity of the lineage with respect to other lineages — and of the tribal aggregate of lineages with respect to other peoples — causes outside groups, it has been suggested, to regard this process as one of 'predatory expansion'.[9]

Quintanilla Raso notes that despite the internal cohesion of aristocratic kindreds, all such groupings carried within them 'un riesgo de disgregación'. A frequent phenomenon among aristocratic families was the tendency for a 'rama de segundones' to become independent from the 'línea primogénita', thus forming 'un nuevo linaje'. In the period immediately following the foundation of such junior branches, we note 'el afán por lograr su propia entidad'. The segmentary process was initiated when 'el segundón heredaba un patrimonio suficiente como para no tener que someterse al cobijo del pariente mayor del linaje, y quedaba refrendado por su establecimiento en otro lugar y por la fundación de su propio mayorazgo'. The goal of ambitious younger sons, in effect, was the establishment of 'sus propios linajes' (Quintanilla Raso 1982: 340).

The centrifugal tendencies intrinsic to a system of primogeniture have been alluded to in relation to the plight of Zifar's younger son Roboán, excluded from inheritance by his brother Garfín's role as heir apparent. Roboán responds to his situation by a statement of purpose which foreshadows his neolocal (i.e. segmentary) behaviour at the end of *Zifar*. 'Punare en trabajar e fazer tanto,' he declares, 'que [Dios] por la su piedat me porna en tan grant onrra commo a mi hermano o por ventura en mayor.' His purpose in

---

[9] See Sahlins 1966: 90–99; see also, for a critique of the segmentary concept, Terry 1972: p. 96 n. 2.

setting forth is to 'prouar las cosas del mundo, por que mas vala' (252).

In *Amadís* the chief expression of this neolocal theme is the winning of the Firm Isle, earned free and clear by Amadís through his accomplishment of the ordeal of the Leales Amantes. The conquest and foundation of the Firm Isle by the Greek exile Apolidón constitutes, in fact, a mythologized justification of neolocality. The age-old custom of the island compels Apolidón, upon his arrival, to do combat with the reigning giant. The death of the latter makes Apolidón the king. Here is the achievement-based ordeal that earns the hero political dominion and an independent (i.e. neolocal) household (III, 820). Having defeated and killed the giant, Apolidón becomes 'libre señor de la misma ínsola'. Because the giant had been so hated and feared, 'Apolidón, después de ser conoscido, muy amado fue' (II, 357–58.100–19). The island's fortifications and isolation allow Apolidón and his wife Grimanesa to live in peace, fearing no one. We note that conquest transfers territory and polity intact, with no political or economic changes implied. The same will hold true for Amadís and Oriana, when they come into the same kingdom through their completion of the ordeal of the Arco de los Leales Amantes. As Oriana passes the final ordeal, magic voices describe her as the 'noble señora que por su gran beldad ha vencido la fermosura de Grimanesa'. She will make, the voices affirm, a suitable consort to 'aquel cavallero que, por ser más valiente y esforçado en armas que aquel Apolidón [...] ganó el señorío desta ínsola' (IV, 1190).

In *Curial*, the neolocal fantasy is expressed through the hero's acquisition of the buried treasure revealed to him by the enamoured Moorish maiden, Camar. Finding the fortune in question in the orchard of the girl's family, the hero reflects: 'ab aquelles dobles [...] poria tornar en millor estat que nulls temps se fos trobat, si fos possible que en terra de christians les poguessen aportar' (389). Later, Curial will augment this treasure with the vast reward ('no lexa en casa sua ne [...] moneda, ne vaxella dor, ne joyells dor, ne pedres precioses, ne perles') sent to him by a grateful Greek emperor, after his heroic leadership of the battle against the invading Turks (438). It is clear that he owes all subsequent success to Camar. The fact that Camar, converted to Christianity, commits suicide, throwing herself headlong from a tower (395), in despair at her separation from Curial (who in any event does not reciprocate her love), adds a note of pathos to his ascent. The same may be said for the manner in which Zifar ascends to the kingship of Mentón, through the death of that kingdom's young queen (chap. 118).

The chivalric founders of autonomous households see themselves as the originators of new lineages created in the image of the clan which excluded them; their enterprise is therefore essentially mimetic — they perpetuate the very agnation they resist so vehemently. What distinguishes the Peninsular chivalric romance from earlier works long recognized as its narrative models is the emphasis on monogamy. Fogelquist, as we have seen, characterizes this thematic transition in terms of a shift in the locus of control over the female. The triangle of the jealous husband (Arthur), his wife (Guinevere) and her lover (Lancelot), gives way to the domineering father (Lisuarte), his daughter (Oriana), and her suitor (Amadís). A similar contrast could be made between the triangle formed by King Mark, Isolde, and Tristan (Mark's brother's son), and that represented by the Greek Emperor, Carmesina, and Tirant.[10] The transition is confirmed by Lida de Malkiel's outline of the plot of *Amadís* in terms of its parallels to the early-thirteenth-century *Prose Lancelot*. Both stories tell the tale of an orphaned youth of unknown parentage. Received at a royal court, he falls in love with his lord's wife or daughter. Later, the hero rescues his beloved from an abductor, only to be unjustly suspected of infidelity. There transpires an interlude of self-imposed exile and near madness. Eventually, after repentance by the jealous lady, the lovers reconcile and take refuge in a marvellous residence, their fortress against the world (Joyeuse Garde in *Lancelot*; Ínsula Firme in *Amadís*).[11]

The point to be made here is that the here-and-now adultery of the Arthurian stories is replaced, in the Spanish chivalric romances,

---

[10] *Cárcel de Amor* offers a love triangle similar to the one we encounter in the chivalric romances. Leriano, son of Duke Guersio, is in love with Laureola, the daughter of king Gaulo of Macedonia (San Pedro 1985: 88–89). For a late medieval Spanish version of the Tristan triangle, see Northup 1928: 122–24 (containing the episodes of Mark's marriage to Isolde, and the wedding-night replacement of the Queen by her handmaiden, called Branjen in this version).

[11] Lida de Malkiel 1959: 415. See also Frappier 1959: 296–302.

by the future-aligned, household-oriented devotion of the monogamous couple. This emphasis on the household reflects a change in
medieval European social reality which was, if anything, even more
subversive of clanic integrity than the segmentation observed in
traditional unilineal societies, or than the self-defeating agnatic
strategies discussed in the previous chapter. Herlihy, for instance,
examines the impact of consensual doctrine in terms of the creation
of independent households, and of the devastating effect of these
on the integrity of traditional kinship networks. With the focus on
individual consent and the foundation of independent households,
families, he observes, could no longer arrange marriages or prevent
them. The father was 'helpless in the face of elopement'. Church
doctrine was thus 'a damaging blow to paternal authority', for it
'assured that the medieval family could never develop into a true
patriarchy'. This, notes Herlihy (1985: 81, 83), occurred precisely
at the time when the patrilineages were seeking to control
European kinship, or, at any rate, 'to preserve the wealth and status
of its male members over time, by limiting the number of claimants
upon its resources' (as seen, for example, in practices which
marginalized and disinherited younger sons and daughters).

As R. Howard Bloch astutely remarks, in a discussion of the
'economics of romance', the conjugal household resulting from the
amorous liaisons which constitute the focus of the romance genre
reflect 'the displacement of the marriage decision away from those
invested with the maintenance of genealogy'. This yielded a
situation in which 'the autonomy of the individual to determine the
biological course of lineage [...] posed the possibility of over-
multiplication and division-fragmentation and diffusion of race as
well as of lands'. This emphasis on the *ménage* as opposed to the
maison (i.e. the lineage) leads to the formation of a 'fundamentally
new *patrimoine*', belonging to 'the newly formed conjugal couple,
definitively separated from the lineage of birth'. The earlier rule, of
'agnatic autonomy of maternal and paternal lines [...] is abrogated
so as to effect the continual cognatic alienation of that which [...]
was considered the inalienable right, the proper, of dynastic succession' (Bloch 1983: 162–64).

In the elopement of Apolidón and Grimanesa (Prologue to Book
II of *Amadís*) we see a combination of several fantasies that
reinforce the association of neolocality and monogamous love. The

couple lives the dream of neolocality and of an independent dominion of one's own — the dream, in short, of segmentation in the strictest sense. The Firm Isle, at the same time, exalts monogamy by its veneration of the Leales Amantes, a magical test devised by Apolidón. Based on true and eternal love, rather than on mere carnal desire or pragmatic association, and characterized by sexual fidelity, 'leal amor', magically verified in the candidate, is the principal criterion for successful completion of the ordeal of the Leales Amantes which entitles Amadís and his beloved to rule the Firm Isle.[12]

The case of Macandón, the aged nephew of King Apolidón, serves as another example of *leal amor* in *Amadís*. Arriving at the court of Lisuarte, he explains that he has been searching everywhere, for sixty years, in hopes of finding a knight and a lady worthy to dub him knight and to hand him a sword. Their worthiness is to be determined by the knight's ability to withdraw a sword from the magic sheath, the lady's by the fact that the dried and wilted flowers of a magic garland will blossom luxuriously. Macandón's father, Ganor, the brother of Apolidón, had exacted an oath from him — since he, the squire, had been engendered 'en gran amor' between Ganor and his wife, the daughter of the King of Canonia, the son should comply with the following condition: 'que no fuesse cauallero sino de mano del más leal amador que en el mundo fuesse, ni tomasse la spada dino de la dueña o donzella que en aquel grado amasse' (II, 470.354–59). Thinking to quickly satisfy these conditions by presenting himself to his uncle Apolidón and the latter's *amiga* Grimanesa, he found his uncle's beloved lady dead. Since he could not be knighted, he could not rule in his father's country (knighthood being a condition of kingship).

Tirant likewise glorifies monogamous love, as we see in the hero's self-righteous rejection of the amorous advances of the Queen of Tunis. Because of his love for 'una donzella de gran estima', a maid 'tan virtuosa' who has behaved toward him with great 'virtut d'honestat', it would be a 'gran defalt' if he committed 'tan gran maldat devers ella' in betraying her love (899). If the queen finds in him a protector, it is only on the basis of the

---

[12] True and loyal love between monogamous lovers is celebrated in book IV of *Amadís* (1285–86).

chivalric altruism shown by the virtuous knight toward all women (902).

Curial is also self-consciously obsessed with monogamy and the implied separation of the spouses from their respective kin. Güelfa is made to suffer a severe penance of self-reproach for her lack of faith in her lover. Heeding the self-serving lies of envious courtiers, she has banished Curial from her sight, while cutting off her pecuniary support. In his poverty, he has taken ship in search of piratical riches. Shipwrecked, like Tirant, on the North African coast, and sold into servitude (359), Curial is presumed dead. Güelfa lapses into self-recriminating despair. Brought to her senses by the feeling of loss, she realizes that she has slain 'aquell que los cauallers no podien matar [...] vençut lo vencedor de tots, donant a exili lo pus virtuos e millor cauallero del mon' (362).

Of the four principal romances analysed by the present study, *Zifar* is most concerned with the familial aspect of monogamy. Where the other tales focus on the vicissitudes of courtship, with little attention paid to the eventual household and family of the lovers, *Zifar*, at least in its first two books, concentrates on the story of a man, his wife, and their two sons: the classic 'nuclear' or 'conjugal' family. After the most rigorously 'nuclear' example of conjugal, neolocal family structures, this kind of family — including the standard Occidental family of the modern world — has been classified as of the 'Eskimo' type. Systems of the Eskimo type usually possess a small class of words for relatives within a narrow range of patrilateral and matrilateral kin: uncle, aunt, nephew, niece, grandma, grandpa. A special terminology is reserved for the members of the nuclear unit (i.e. father, mother, son, daughter, brother, sister). Terms for members of the nuclear family are not used for anyone outside the family. Outside this zone generalized terms such as 'cousin' or 'uncle' are employed for an entire range of kindred. The terminology of descent-oriented societies, by contrast, is far more variegated and precise; the nuclear family receives no particular terminological stress in descent systems. The terminology referred to corresponds, more or less, to kindred-based systems such as those portrayed in the romances.[13]

---

[13] Fox 1967: 258–61 (summarizing a very wide range of studies).

Zifar's concentration on the tale of a nuclear family is not necessarily significant. Most societies assign some degree of importance to the group defined by a man, his wife, and their children. In most societies, however, the nuclear family is not pervasively emphasized over other kinship groupings. Stories about the group formed by a man, his wife, and their children may therefore be expected to exert an emotional appeal in most societies, but a story's concern with the nuclear family does not, however, necessarily bespeak a prevailing emphasis on that particular kinship configuration by the society for whom the story is composed. Nor does narrative emphasis on the nuclear family provide a necessary clue as to the date of composition: the nuclear family has been emphasized — in contrast to prevailing norms centred on other structures — by various communities and segments of societies throughout history. Hence the enduring and multicultural popularity of the many versions of *Apollonius of Tyre*, the many ancient and Byzantine romances having to do with familial separations and reunions, and the innumerable versions, from all regions of Eurasia, of what Gordon Hall Gerould called 'The Man Tried by Fate'. In his analysis of the numerous versions of this tale, in Asian and European tradition from Japan to Iceland, Gerould defines the basic motif:

> A man for some weighty reason, often religious or resulting from religion, departs from home with his family. He loses his sons (usually twins) and his wife by accident or human violence or both. After various adventures and considerable suffering, the several members of the family are at last reunited. (1904: 335)

The family of stories derived from this model has enjoyed an exceedingly wide reception for many centuries, with many versions of these tales about nuclear families separated and united originating in Asian and Near-Eastern societies where extended kinship and unilineal descent were the traditional norm. Narratives vary, often revealing modification for an audience for whom traditional, extended kinship structures of a certain type were still operative. Nonetheless, the nuclear family of husband, wife, and their children remains the narrative core in all versions. The *Life of St Eustace*, considered the proto-typical European version of this story, is the basis of the first two books of *Zifar*.[14]

When we regard the nuclear family as a response to a set of isolating circumstances, as symptomatic of certain social structures and tendencies which may occur in any culture at any time, and which were present in the society and economy of the Peninsula, as we saw in the previous chapter, then the issue of family structure in *Zifar* and the other romances may be placed in the general framework of social transformations in the latter part of the Peninsular Middle Ages. The medieval Hispanic chivalric romances provide numerous indications that the society of their authors and intended audiences had long since departed from traditional patterns of descent. As we saw in the previous chapter, they present a kindred-based system limited to the collaboration of first cousins, as well as uncles and aunts, nieces and nephews, all within one generation of consanguineal relationship. Cousinship as a principle of mobilizable kinship — indeed of political action — is chiefly exercised among a network characterized as much by its members' physical mobility as by the narrow range of their cousinship. Aside from uncles and aunts, who lie within the same narrow limits of relationships as the numerically predominant cousins, active extended kinship of the wide range (to fourth or fifth cousins) described by Phillpotts, is absent from the romances.

Some romances are less kindred-oriented than others. In *Zifar*, for example, there is little mention of extended kin of any kind for the protagonist and his family, in either the ego-centred synchronic sense or the diachronic, agnatic sense. In chap. 8, it is true, we read of how Zifar heard the story of his ancestry ('yo seyendo moço pequeño en casa de mi abuelo, oy dezir que oyera a su padre que venia de linaje de reys', 33). But this, as mentioned previously, corresponds to the status-conscious genealogical concoctions typical of late medieval society. This apparent reference to patriliny does not suffice to demonstrate a descent-oriented society. Such references, in any event, could as well be attributed to cognatic

---

[14] See also, in addition to Gerould, Jordan 1908 and Wagner 1903: 11–30. Contrary to Wagner and others, who assumed a European *Life of St Eustace* as *Zifar*'s main source, Roger M. Walker (1974: 64–70) conjectures that the primary source of the Spanish romance's first two books was an Arabic version, 'The King Who Lost Kingdom and Wife', from the *Thousand and One Nights*. For the Arabic tale, see Burton 1886: I, 319–31.

kindreds (Fox 1967: 153, points out the 'patrilineal tinge' of most cognatic societies), or to the influence of biblical genealogical models.

The one mention of Grima's kin (*Zifar* 104) occurs in the passage in which she leaves the kingdom of Urbin 'para su tierra a ver sus parientes e sus amigos e murir entre ellos'. Similarly, in *Tirant*, Plaerdemavida proclaims her destination when she has a falling out with her mistress Princess Carmesina. In a solemn declaration meant to echo the formula of leave-taking of an estranged vassal from his lord, she exclaims: 'jo em vull partir de vostra altesa e no vull més servir-vos, ans me'n tornaré a casa del Comte, mon pare' (724). Like Zifar's wife, Plaerdemavida seeks to return to her kinfolk. She reiterates this intention to the men sent by the princess to fetch her back ('per força o per grat'): 'ella no em pot forçar que jo la servesca per força, car a casa de mon pare me'n vull anar' (728).

In a descent-oriented society we should be likely to find intervention by relatives — a couple would not be left to its own devices, nor a young unmarried girl overlooked by her kin. The absence of systematic intervention by a wide range of kinfolk is symptomatic of a more loosely-knit kindred orientation. On the other hand, the isolation of Zifar and his family from extended kin could also occur in a story about a conjugal family isolated by circumstance from the extended kinship network, as is the case with the Arabic 'King Who Lost Kingdom and Wife' and many other non-European versions of the 'Man Tried by Fate'. But the Arabic and other Asian versions are about refugee families whose isolation from relatives is entirely accidental. The situation of Zifar and his family seems to reflect an integral characteristic of the society depicted within the work. Zifar and his wife are shown with a household of their own at the beginning of the romance (chaps 2 & 3), indicating a neolocal pattern of marital residence, to be contrasted with the virilocal or uxorilocal patterns typical of lineally oriented societies.[15] The couple's choice of emigration as a solution to their problems (chap. 15) confirms the neolocal pattern: they are described as being ashamed, because of their poverty, of living among their relatives, and as leaving their homeland 'a

---

[15] Fox 1967: 84–85; Scheffler 1974: 774–71; Leach 1973: 53–58.

buscar vida en otro lugar do los non conosciesen' (46). This is the
normal response in a society where the neolocal ideal of marital
residence encourages couples to establish their own household. The
trend persists in modern Spanish society. Julian Pitt-Rivers
observes, citing such proverbs as 'cada uno en su casa' and 'casada
casa quiere', that the neolocal solution is considered the norm. 'To
marry without setting up a separate home is regarded as a make-
shift arrangement'. Recent studies of family and marriage in Spain
reveal that the tendency is not limited to the rural environment
described by Pitt-Rivers. The persistence over many centuries of
these Spanish patterns of kinship has also been recently documented.[16]

Zifar's concern for neolocal residence and the nuclear family is
seen in the dramatic importance assigned to fortuitous or miraculous reunions of family members long separated by misfortune.
This exploitation of one of the ancient clichés of the romance genre
is typified, in Zifar, by sequence of events in which Grima, the
hero's wife, arrives in the kingdom of Mentón. She recognizes her
husband, now married to the reigning queen, but says nothing for
fear of compromising him (chap. 87). Later, in an inn, she chances
to meet their sons (chap. 91). Finally, after a misunderstanding (she
is found in bed with the boys and accused of illicit relations, chap.
94), the boys are recognized by their father (chap. 95). After the
convenient death of the queen (the double marriage is rationalized
by reference to the hero's abstention from sexual relations with this
second wife), Zifar officially recognizes Grima and the boys (chap.
96).

While Zifar is the only romance in our core group that devotes
attention to the hero as a father and husband, the other texts do not
completely neglect the nuclear family. Amadís, like Zifar, contains
several scenes of a nuclear family reunited. In Book I of Amadís,
Elisena reveals that she and Perión are the hero's parents: 'veys
aquí el rey que vos engendró' (I, 85.149–50). Her sin, Elisena

---

[16] Pitt-Rivers 1971: 99; Estudio 1976: 38–45; Lisón Tolosana 1966: 168. The
neolocal residential preference observed in the romances corresponds to the social
and demographic patterns outlined by José Antonio Maravall, who correlates the
trend toward construction of single-family dwellings with increased emphasis on
the nuclear family, with the growth of trade and accelerating urbanization, and
with the rise of a discernible middle class (1978: 256–58).

declares, was not to have loved Perión and conceived a son by him, but rather, through fear of discovery, to have cast the infant adrift 'como mala madre' (I, 85.147–49). When the hero and his brother Galaor arrive at the port of Mostrol, they conceal their identity when sending messengers to queen Elisena. When they come into her presence, she cries out to the Virgin (having not seen Galaor since his abduction by the giant Gandalac years before) and faints dead away. Kissing her hands 'muy humildosamente', they revive her. She takes them into her arms, kissing now one, now the other, speechless with joy, until all three are interrupted by the arrival of the brothers' sister Melicia (III, 685.551–55). Later it will be Amadís's turn to experience joy at the imminent reunion of his own family. When he learns, through a secret letter from his cousin Mabilia, of the clandestine pregnancy of his beloved Oriana and of the imminent birth of his son, Esplandián, the narrator describes his thrill: 'cómo hauía acrecentado en su linaje' (III, 678.26–29).

As in *Zifar*, family reunions in *Amadís* go through a partial phase, with the mother and child meeting first, as in Oriana's encounter with Esplandián (III, 779.420–66). At first she does not know him ('Oriana su madre, que no lo conoscía'). Then, from the account of his rescue and upbringing by the hermit Nasciano, the lad's foster father, Oriana and her confidantes realize that this must be the son thought to have been killed in infancy: 'Quando Oriana y Mabilia y la donzella de Denamarca esto oyeron, miráuanse vnas a otras, y las carnes les temblauan de plazer conosciendo verdaderamente ser aquel niño fijo de Amadís y de Oriana'.[17]

Although Tirant and Carmesina never have the chance to found their own household, *Tirant* portrays the nuclear family as a source of sentimental interest, if not as a focus of heroic exploits. Tangential characters confirm the importance of the nuclear family in the social world of the author and his audience. For example, the wife of William of Warwick laments, when the latter (disguised as the Hermit King) denies their only son exemption from military service:

---

[17] The theme of delayed or tentative reunion of long-separated family members is, of course, a recurrent folkloric motif, one of the most prominently utilized in the *Libro de Apolonio* (Monedero 1987, st. 463–547). For discussion of this and related motifs in the *Apollonius* versions, see Perry 1967: appendix 1; also Kortekaas 1984: 4–7).

E per aquest sol fill que a mi resta jo só dit mare, e si aquest mor en
la batalla, ¿què serà de mi, trista, desaventurada, que hauré perdut
marit e fill e tot quant bé tenia en aquest miserable món? (152)

To be sure, the countess is consoled by 'Dos cavallers qui parents
eren de la mare e del fill'. But the stress is clearly on her relationship with husband and son. The emotional solidarity of which the
countess feels deprived prepares us for the pathos of *Tirant*'s final
scenes, in which the Emperor and Empress and their daughter
mourn the loss of the son-in-law who was to have been the
guarantor of their lineage and realm, and of the husband who was
to have provided earthly happiness. 'Muira jo, e iré als regnes de
Plutó', laments the Emperor, 'de tanta dolor portant ambaixada'
(1153). Carmesina, on hearing of her beloved's death, declares her
intention to wear her wedding gown at Tirant's funeral: 'les mies
robes [...] fetes per fer a la solemnitat de les mies bodes' (1154). At
the hero's bier, she upbraids Fortune: 'Aquest era sustentació de
ma vida, aquest era consolació de tot lo poble e repòs de la vellea
de mon pare' (1155). Her mother the Empress, seeing Carmesina
dying of grief over the corpse of the hero, pleads with the princess:
'¿És aquest lo goig e l'alegria que jo esperava haver de tu?' (1159).
The pathos generated at the end of *Tirant* derives from a
simultaneity of deprivations, all of them defined with respect to the
nuclear family — that of Carmesina and Tirant which is never to
be, that of the Empress and her husband, which she sees obliterated
before her very eyes. 'Pensau la miserable senyora', the narrator
urges, 'quina devia estar: ¡veure morts marit, filla e gendre!'
(1165).

   As we saw in the previous chapter, such historians as Glick,
García de Cortázar, and Guichard postulate a connection between
various economic and demographic trends and the increasing
emphasis in Peninsular society on the nuclear family. Their conjecture concurs with a broader position, represented by a number of
anthropologists and social historians, which holds that the nuclear
family is common among those peoples who, for reasons of
geographic dispersal and economic constraint, place no importance
on unilineal descent groups or on systems of spousal exchange. The
dispersal of kin conducive to the breakdown of extended kinship
may occur within a small population over a large territory
incapable of supporting great numbers or it may be caused by

emigration. Where the nuclear family predominates, marriage is viewed as an establishment of ties only between the natal families of the spouses, although a certain importance is also attributed to the two kindred groups united by marriage. Such systems usually stress the equal importance of the matrilateral and patrilateral kin of ego.[18]

The importance of the nuclear family in the romances, implied by such narrative elements as those we have just discussed, thus reflects social developments in late medieval Spain. But this is only a partial explanation of the function of monogamy, nuclear family, and neolocal residence in these narratives. The social evolution which such themes reveal was itself influenced by what we might be tempted to dismiss as the merely ideological dimension of marital consent. This, as we have seen, was most conspicuously revealed in inter-generational conflict over the arrangement of marriage. Familial dissension on this subject, as we have also seen, is frequent in all societies, despite the traditionally unitary image of clanic solidarity projected by official agnatic interests. What characterizes medieval European marriage is not the notion of consent in itself, but its promotion by the powerful ideological interests represented by Church and State.

The younger generation of the romances, which is the focus of the narratives, invokes the principle of consent as a matter of amorous expediency. Consent is the doctrinal foundation of their independence in the selection of a mate. From this recourse to consent stem the other aspects of chivalric love: monogamy, neolocality, nuclear family, the establishment of a separate household in the guise of an independent branch of the original lineage. Representing as it does a defiance of patriarchal authority, consent transmutes love from a generalized amity into a frantic, individualized surrogation of clanic fellowship. The couple, thrown on their own resources, concentrate their temperamental energies on the reciprocal dependency intensified by isolation from kith and kin.

Hence the emphasis, already noted, on true love as faithful devotion, as 'leal amor'. But familial prerogatives are not the only

---

[18] Fox summarizes these views (1967: 19–20), without necessarily agreeing with their determinist implications.

social dimensions affected by the logic of consent, and love, in these stories, is more than a displacement of agnatic sentiment from the collective to the individual. Love as the emotional correlative of consent empowers the individual in dimensions other than those of lineage, and by so doing further undermines the traditional status quo.

In *Tirant*, Carmesina's mother the Empress, in declaring her feelings to the young Hipòlit, reminds him (echoing a similar statement by Plaerdemavida, 732) that 'amor no accepta noblesa, ni llinatge, ni egualtat, car no fa diferència si és d'alt lloc o de baix' (745). This is a definition self-consciously designed to make love a social equalizer, a cross-cutting principle of status allocation in service of the expedient needs of the socially privileged lover. This use of love in the manipulation of status categories brings us into a broader field of interests than that defined by the issue of consent. The latter issue is the chief concern of the junior generation. From the perspective of the senior — the official — generation, however, consent is but one in a series of problems which must be dealt with if the lineage is to survive and prosper. The problems in question involve complex options: choosing potential in-laws, rejecting would-be in-laws; deciding which children to designate as heirs, to marry off, or to disinherit.

Such intricate questions are functions of what I call the calculus of advantage. This is the topic of the next chapter.

CHAPTER 5

Marriage and the Calculus of Advantage

The manipulation of status categories through amorous relationships, as illustrated by the scene just quoted from *Tirant*, places love and marriage within the extensive repertoire of individualist social strategies in the converging domains of economic, political, and honorific stratification. This strategic concept of love, while not always clearly articulated by the romances, is the foundation of amorous behaviour in their social universe. Conflict arises over an incompatibility of perspectives: both the lineage and its daughters, who are the focus of agnatic aspirations, conceive of marriage as the means of attaining objectives. These are political and economic for the family; personal, emotional, and sexual for the daughter. The complication that makes for the chivalric plot, with its commonplaces of the irate, possessive father (or elder brother), the wilful daughter, and the upstart suitor, arises from a dispute over whose ambition should take precedence.

Tirant presents a spectrum of amorous strategies, all of them centred on the free will of the woman. Lady Estefania explains to Carmesina (406–07) that there are three kinds of love. One is 'virtuosa e honorosa'. It involves a relationship with 'algun gran senyor, infant, duc, comte o marquès, qui serà molt favorit e cavaller molt virtuós'. A lady loved by such a man will be proud that everyone knows he dances, jousts, or goes to war 'per amor d'ella', and that he performs 'fets honorosos de renom e fama'. The second kind of love is 'profitosa'. This occurs when 'algun gentilhom o cavaller d'antic llinatge e molt virtuós, amarà una donzella e ab donatius la induirà a sa voluntat'. A woman will only love such a man 'per son profit'. Such a love, she declares, is displeasing, for as soon as 'lo profit cessa, l'amor defall'. The third kind of love is 'viciosa, com la donzella ama lo gentilhom o cavaller per son delit'.

This amorous typology reflects an individualist and female point of view. Based, ultimately, on a notion of female consent as the defining and regulatory factor in love and marriage, it will inevitably clash with the familial and clanic perspective of an older, controlling generation that feels constrained to control female sexuality for the sake of lineal security. Apart from the peripheral element of adulterous love affairs, portrayed chiefly in *Tirant*, the amorous relationships in the chivalric romances involve planned or actual marriage leading to the intended or eventual foundation of households. In each case, the impediments placed before the couple are prompted by the obsession of the woman's family with the vital importance of its daughters.

Bourdieu's analysis of matrimonial strategy embraces two basic alternatives in the calculus of lineal advantage: alliance or integration. When the clan focuses on the relationship reinforced or established with another clan, the focus is on alliance. When the family aims at augmenting its domestic organization and assets, the objective is integration. The calculus of matrimonial advantage as it refers to internal consolidation of clanic resources focuses on what Bourdieu calls 'symbolic capital'. This can be significantly depreciated by such things as the death or disability of a prominent clan leader. A lineage can, through the loss of symbolic capital represented by key personnel, 'decline' within a few generations from the standing of one which customarily arranges 'male marriages' (i.e. those based on political alliance) to that of one which relies on 'ordinary marriages, generally set up by the women, within their own network of relationships' (Bourdieu 1977: 67–68).

The political aspect of marriage necessarily focuses less on the personal attributes of the son- or daughter-in-law and more on the social and economic standing of the family with whom alliance is proposed. Hence the pattern of the daughter marrying 'up and out' as a source of drama and conflict in both history and literature. There is, of course, no necessary connection between individual personality and social standing. The allure of a son-in-law's family status — the situation amounts to a cultural cliché — is often eclipsed by his lack of talent, character, or personal charm. The affiliative imperative underlying marital alliance, however, minimizes the importance of the in-law's personal attributes; these are inconsequential to the matter at hand. When we speak of the integrative aspect of marriage, on the other hand, we focus on the individual qualities of the spouse to be recruited. When the lineage focuses on this aspect, we may speak of the recruitment of an in-law. In such circumstances, notes Robert Winch, the family has 'a lively interest in the work-related qualifications of a kinsman's prospective mate'. Thus, when selecting a daughter-in-law, a family will focus on such factors as the 'industry and prospective fecundity' of the candidates. To this we may add that in a regime in which female consent must be taken into account, a daughter's personal preferences constitute another factor in the selection of a groom. However, whether the focus is on the alliance assured by the standing of the in-law's family, or on the integrative potential of his or her eventual pragmatic contributions (as defender, provider, or co-worker; as the father or mother of grandchildren), the traditional family feels the urgent need to control the selection of mates: 'In order that their plans should not be thwarted by the passions of the young, the older people institute devices such as early marriage and efficient chaperonage' (Winch 1968: 3).

It would be inaccurate, when speaking of familial control of mate selection as expressed in political marriages, to assume that the denial of filial consent invariably implies an emphasis on the ascribed status of the potential in-law and a consequent lack of concern for his or her individual character. Such indifference may be the case with political, alliance-oriented marriages. However, the personality and character of the in-law matter a great deal to the lineage when the issue is one not of alliance but of integration. What matters to the lineage in that case is not any specific attribute of any particular spouse, but rather the expedient needs of the lineage in a specific moment in its history, and the very issue of control of marriage as a means to fulfilment of those needs. From the viewpoint of the elder generation, the issue of mate selection must be non-negotiable; it is a matter of life and death for the lineage.

In *Tirant*, for instance, the French's king's reaction to his daughter's abduction (in the story of the foundation of the Roca Salada clan, 677–78), is that of a father who places extraordinary importance on his daughter's marriage. His furious response to the arrogant upstart who obtains her hand by a ruse (the young man is the typical heiress-hunting, disenfranchised younger sibling) betrays what might be termed a filiacentric obsession. This is the norm in the chivalric romance.

Daughters are important to their families in all societies, but not all societies assign daughters the same role within the family. The episode from *Tirant*, and crucial episodes throughout the chivalric romances, reveal, in the prominent role accorded to the daughter, what Judith Hallett has termed *filiafocality*. Referring to certain kinship patterns in noble Roman society, Hallett defines this as an 'emphasis on ties of blood and marriage through and to men's female children'. This daughter-focused 'centrality', she argues, 'derives [...] from 'questions of valuation,' e.g. 'what is the image of a given kinship role — and is it culturally elaborated and valued?' The focality of a role can be affective, emphasizing the 'emotions linked with a given role', 'bestowing attention and value', and 'elaborating the [...] role within the family' (Hallett 1984: 64–65).

Roman daughters, excluded from 'kin-related decision making processes', were also barred from 'active participation and leadership in civil life'. Until they had become wives, mothers, or aunts, they continued to be 'symbolically and publicly defined as *daughters*'. The title *pater* served as a 'social metaphor for controlling, responsible male behavior in interactions with individuals other than one's offspring'. In an analogous way, the daughter's role was used metaphorically in 'delineating the relationship between women and male kin other than their fathers'. A Roman woman was either under the legal control (*manus*) of her husband, 'with rights in respect to him of a daughter', or she remained legally under the protection of her father or an agnatic kinsman. Roman daughters could, while still in their father's *potestas*, inherit his estate, a fact rendering them more influential, economically and politically, than their counterparts in some other patrilineal societies. It is probable, affirms Hallett, that traditional Roman society emphasized not only 'bonds between fathers and sons, but [also ...] those between men and their daughters' and sisters' offspring and spouses'. A concurrent emphasis on agnate and filiafocal aspects of kinship 'is possible and logical' (Hallett 1984: 66–67, 90, 205, & 291).

A pattern resembling the filiafocality described by Hallett may be deduced from Harry L. Levy's account of the importance attributed by the Athenian family to a brotherless daughter. 'In fact if not in theory', he affirms, a daughter in such circumstances was 'squarely athwart the sacral line of descent, providing out of her female body a continuator of her father's male ancestral rites'. Allowing for obvious differences in the details of ritual and customary observance, a similar prominence of daughters as a means of maintaining the lineage is clearly seen in medieval Europe. The woman's function as the vector of patrilineal identity and prestige is still stressed in modern rural Greece, notes Ernestine Friedl, just as in ancient Athens. Thus the desire to make good marriages, thereby 'increasing the social prestige of the family'.[1]

The filiafocality exhibited in the romances seems to conform, then, to a general pattern in Mediterranean culture, in which the female is a principal symbol of family reputation. Pitt-Rivers, for instance, has pointed out the importance in Hispanic society of daughters as a conduit of lineal honour and identity. Spanish titles of nobility, for instance, may pass through the female, 'in default of a male heir in the same degree of kinship'. Thus they frequently transfer 'from one patriline to the other'. Daughters, 'in default of sons', bear titles which their husbands assume 'by courtesy', as their wives' consorts. The Spanish high-born woman is traditionally 'able to transmit her patrilineal status to her children' (Pitt-Rivers 1966: 68–69).

This pattern seems to contradict the *Partidas*' insistence (II.xxi.3) that nobility is not transmissible from a noble woman to her children by a non-noble. The contradiction is perhaps only apparent, if we take into account the fact that genealogical confirmation of at least minimal noble status could always be obtained where the need was truly urgent, and that the rights of children to partake to some degree of their mother's status was, as we saw in our discussion of bilateral kinship, a European as well as a Peninsular tendency. The uxorilateral prerogative originates in

---

[1] Levy 1963: 142; Friedl 1963: 128.

the woman's inherent status: 'her power', affirms Pitt-Rivers, 'derives from her rank, not from her sexuality' (Pitt-Rivers 1966: 71).

Filiafocality in the romances is revealed in such cases as that of Oriana, in her relationship to her father Lisuarte (*Amadís*); Princess Seringa, for the governing males of her lineage (Book IV of *Zifar*); the widowed noblewoman Güelfa, jealously guarded by her elder brother, who seeks throughout the story to arrange a suitable second marriage for her; and numerous secondary characters as well.

Tirant, with its central amorous relationship between the Breton adventurer and Princess Carmesina, the cherished heir of her doting father, provides especially clear expression of the filiafocal theme. An extreme example of filiafocality is discerned in the case of the Gran Caramany who, despairing at the imminent capture of his ship by Christians, places all his wealth in a chest. He then dresses his daughter in an 'aljuba de brocat d'or', binds her around the neck with 'una corda d'or e de seda', whose other end he attaches to the treasure chest. He then casts the chest, along with his daughter, into the sea. We are to assume that he prefers this to letting daughter and wealth be captured by Christians. He then likewise throws overboard all the other damsels on the ship (576). This behaviour is clearly portrayed as mad, barbaric. To regard women as patrimonial property, the author seems to imply, is the mark of the savage, the heathen. Tirant, after capturing him, accuses him of acting with 'crueldat e inhumanitat' in the death of his daughter 'e moltes altres mores' (577).

To the Gran Caramany is to be contrasted the far more humane and fatherly Greek Emperor. Lamenting the loss of his elder daughter through marriage, and the fact that his only worldly consolation is the younger daughter, Carmesina, he emphasizes his affection for and dependence on them: 'l'una tinc mig perduda, que no la puc veure ni oir, ço és la muller del rei d'Hongria, e tinc ací tot lo meu bé' (596). The concern for the well-being and future happiness of the daughter involves, as noted in the previous chapter, a sincere concern for her consent to any proposed match. But there is more. The daughter is not merely a pawn in the formation of marital alliances or the perpetuation of the lineage: her relationship with her father is one of affection and mutual respect. Hence his sincere distress at seeing her mysteriously (for he knows nothing of her love for Tirant) suffering and 'quasi morta, d'extrema dolor' (596).

Because she is his pride and joy, his spiritual sustenance, the importance the Emperor assigns to Carmesina is no less than that shown by other, seemingly more fanatical fathers toward their daughters. Filiafocality, an amalgam of tender affection, possessive authority, and matrimonial intrigue, may be perceived in the emotional significance of the daughter's marriage from the viewpoint of Carmesina's parents. This is seen in the Empress's lament, already referred to in connection with *Tirant*'s regard for the nuclear family. Filiafocality pervades the Empress's speech, spoken to the grieving Carmesina over the bier of the fallen hero; the emphasis here is as much on wedding and marriage as on the family that will never be:

> ¿Són aquestes les núpcies que ab tanta consolació ton pare e jo e tot lo poble esperàvem de tu? ¿Són aquests los dies assignats de celebrar núpcies imperials? ¿Són aquests los tàlems que acostumen posar a les donzelles lo dia benaventurat de les sues bodes? ¿Són aquests los cants que s'acostumen de cantar en tals festes? [...] ¿són aquestes aquelles alegres consolacions e benediccions que pare e mare donen a sa filla en aquell dia del seu repòs? (1159)

Filiafocality, with its investiture of agnatic honour in the person of the daughter, necessarily implies a notion of 'the good marriage'. This would correspond, in Bourdieu's terms, to the affiliative — as opposed to the integrative — aspect of marriage. That is to say, that good marriages are those perceived to be in the interest of the lineage, especially with respect to its relations with other lineages. A father is filiafocal in the intensity and complexity of his relationship with his daughters, and in the intricacy of the schemes he must entertain in order to marry them appropriately without alienating them. When the accent, however nuanced, is on the recruitment of a desirable son-in-law in terms of the political, honorific, or economic advantages assured by the standing of the prospective groom's family, we speak of upward-bound or hypergamous marriage for the daughter.

In the Indian context to which the term was first applied, hypergamy involves, as Louis Dumont expresses it, a 'slight status difference, a slight inferiority of the wife's family in relation to the husband's'. As a criterion of spousal recruitment, it 'implies if not an obligation at least a strong recommendation for the girl's parents to find her a superior partner'. The hypergamous marriage corresponds, in the Indian context, to the 'Brahmanic-classical' notion of marriage as a 'gift of the maiden', according to which 'one acquires merit by the gift of goods to the Brahmans', i.e. that one 'exchanges raw materials of no value for spiritual goods'. In the Indo-European world, the bride is viewed as a meritorious gift 'on the condition that no payment is received for the girl'. The bride, in other words, is 'assimilated to a material good', while giving her away is 'accompanied by material gifts and by as lavish receptions as possible'. The bridegroom's family shows itself 'more demanding about the prestations it receives with the girl, as if it would only accept marriage into an inferior family on condition of receiving hard cash'. But this situation corresponds with the notion of the meritorious gift: 'one gives a daughter and goods to a superior in exchange, not [necessarily] for spiritual merits, but for something similar, namely the prestige or consideration which results from intermarriage with him' (Dumont 1980: 116–17).

Dumont notes the repercussions of hypergamy within a caste divided into a number of clans, 'strictly hierarchized in relation to each other [and] dispersed over a wide area'. Marrying an equal is not possible, since the rules of exogamy require marriage outside the clan. Given that a man cannot marry a woman of superior status, hypergamy will be obligatory. Hypergamy strictly observed thus theoretically implies that men are 'supernumerary in the inferior part of the endogamous group'. This is because women 'will have married for preference into a superior group'. At the same time, in the upper regions of the scale, 'women would be supernumerary [...] unless recourse were had to large-scale polygyny'. Since they marry up at each level, women are scarce at the bottom of the scale, while men are lacking at the top (since, marrying down, they leave relatively fewer matches for upper-level women). The first problem, notes Dumont, tends to be solved by 'unions of inferior status with women of other castes', while the second leads to infanticide of daughters at the top of the ladder, collapse of endogamy at the bottom, and 'polygyny among the powerful' (Dumont 1980: 118).

Dumont's account of the Indian marriage system provides a

conceptual apparatus for analyzing the medieval European marriage system which plays so prominent a role in the life of the knight errant. As the remainder of the present essay will demonstrate, the errantry of the knight is largely a function of a marriage market defined by hypergamy as a preferential rule of marriage. This involves, as in the Indian context, scarcity of eligible males at the top of the social scale, with a corresponding scarcity of females at the bottom.

Hypergamy in a broader sense has come to take on a wider meaning which refers to a woman's 'marrying-up' within any stratification system. Sociologists and social historians, explaining this phenomenon in terms of ideological, economic, or demographic conditions, have identified some societies as particularly hypergamic in their marital statistics. Thus, American women have been characterized as tending toward hypergamy. Studies of the female preference for marrying-up suggest that it coincides with a broader tendency in modern Western societies toward 'status heterogamy' (i.e. marriage between partners of unequal status), expressed either through hypergamy (upward marriage for the woman), or its opposite, hypogamy (Rubin 1970: 633–34).

Where the hypergamic regime of traditional societies tends to cement alliances between lineages, hypergamy in the modern context is a vehicle of individualistic female social mobility. The traditional hypergamous match allies two lineages, one of which, that of higher social standing, needs a daughter-in-law who will provide the lineage with grandchildren. The other family, that of inferior status, seeks the political and honorific advantages of a good marriage for their daughter. The situation is complicated in a cognatic system, such as that confirmed for the society of the chivalric romances, by the fact that grandchildren are shared by both sides, and maternal grandparents (and uncles) often enjoy a favoured position.

The *Partidas* discuss status differentials with regard to marriage from what must be considered a modern classist viewpoint. 'Maguer la madre sea villana et el padre fidalgo, fijodalgo es el fijo que dellos nasciere et por fijodalgo se puede contar, mas non por noble'. The son of a *fijadalgo* by a *villano*, on the other hand, is neither hidalgo nor noble. 'Fidalguia', affirm the *Partidas*, is 'nobleza que viene á los hombre por linage'. A thing obtained 'por herencia', it is therefore diminished when he who inherits it 'menguase en lo que los otros acrescentaron casando con villana ó el villano con fijadalgo' (II.xxi.3). As in most 'strata-defensive' theories, the degree of permeability between 'upper' and 'lower', between 'noble' and 'non-noble' is a crucial issue. It is therefore a matter of importance to define the minimal criterion for elite membership. Juan Manuel, a theoretician of status, is accordingly careful to define *infanzón* as the lowest category of *caballero* (at the same time conflating the concepts of *fidalguía* and nobility): 'como quier que los infanzones son caballeros, son mucho más los otros caballeros que non son infanzones, et éste es el postremer estado que ha entre los fijos d'algo' (Juan Manuel 1974: 185).[2]

Literary representations of hypergamy are innumerable. It is a particularly frequent element in the plots of romances. In *Erec et Enide*, for example, it is Enide who marries up. Her father is a vavasour living in a fortified town, whereas Erec is the son and heir apparent of King Lac. The vavasour is poor, as we see from the description of his daughter Enide's clothing, which, though old and shabby, cannot conceal her beauty (Chrétien de Troyes 1968: ll. 405–10). When Erec asks about the family's apparent poverty, Enide's father replies: 'Tant ai esté toz jorz an guerre, / tote en ai perdue ma terre, / et angagiee, et vandue' (515–17). His daughter, he further explains, is the niece of the count who holds the local castle (524). Despite her many suitors among the local nobility, the vavasour continues, he has rejected all proposals, in the hope that eventually a truly honourable match will present itself, through which 'ou roi ou conte [...] l'an maint' (532). Erec declares that his host cannot as yet have realized 'de quel afeire et de quel gent' his guest comes: 'Filz sui d'un riche roi puissant' (648–50). He proposes marriage: 'la li ferai porter corone, / S'iert reïne de dis citez' (664–65), to which his host, recognizing that his guest is 'molt [...] preuz et hardiz', joyfully replies, 'tot a vostre comandemant / ma bele fille vos comant' (673, 675–76). Taking his daughter by the hand, the vavasour declares: 'Tenez [...] je la vos doing' (678). While there is no particular regard shown for a

---

[2]   The two marriages of the protagonist's daughters in the *Poema de Mio Cid* are prominent literary examples of hypergamy. For an extensive discussion of the problems and contradictions arising from the Cid's arrangement of his daughters' marriages, see Harney 1993a: chap. 3.

woman's consent, it is also clear that the damsel, smitten with Erec and delighted at her luck, consents to the match: 'molt estoit joianz et liee / qu'ele li estoit otroiee, / por ce que preuz ert et cortois, / et bien savoit qu'il seroit rois / et ele meïsme enoree, / riche reïne coronee' (685–90).

Bourdieu discusses the mentalities underlying hypergamous practice in terms of the collective sentiment of clanic honour among the men of the agnatic group. His observations, although they refer specifically to the situation of a patrilineal North African people, the Kabyle, are applicable to the circumstances of the lineages portrayed in the romances. 'It is no exaggeration', he remarks, 'to claim that the group's whole matrimonial history is present in the internal transactions over each intended marriage'. The interest of the lineage, which is to say, that of the official lineage represented by the men,

> requires that a man should not be placed in a subordinate position in the family by being married to a girl of markedly higher status (a man, they say, can raise a woman, but not the opposite; you give — a daughter — to a superior or an equal, you take — a daughter — from an inferior). (Bourdieu 1977: 67)

The key terms 'markedly higher' and 'equal' are open to considerable modification according to the personalities of those involved, and such factors as genealogical histories, wealth, or titles. The pressure, affirms Bourdieu, is toward equality between the lineages linked through marriage. The wide array of elements (bridewealth, wedding expenses) whose cost inflates 'in proportion to the prestige of the marriage' tends to discourage the affiliation of groups 'too unequally matched in terms of economic and symbolic capital'. Bourdieu cites a Kabyle proverb: 'Men ally with their equals'. The equality in question, he reminds us, can be based on different forms of capital, both material and symbolic (Bourdieu 1977: 67–58).

The hypergamic model of marriage is thus a key component in the repertoire of agnatic practices against which the knight finds himself in constant reaction. It is the prevalent assumption of hypergamy as a preferential rule of marriage which accounts for the inaccessibility of the hero's beloved. Where daughters are expected to marry up, suitors of inferior condition are assumed to be out of the running. Thus Amadís, finding himself in the month of April in a wood, despairs at the unattainable social superiority of his beloved. The sounds of birds singing and the sight of flowers causes him to lament his state, 'sin linaje y sin bien', hopelessly in love with 'aquella que vale más que las otras todas de bondad y fermosura y linaje' (I, 67.100–11).

When he finds himself smitten with Carmesina, Tirant falls sick: 'menjà poc de la vianda, y begué molt de les sues llàgremes, coneixent ab viva raó que era pujat en més alt grau que no devia' (376). A little later, he exclaims despairingly: '¿Ab quin ànimo ni ab qual llengua parlar poré, que la puga induir e moure a pietat, com sa altesa m'avançça en totes coses, ço és, en riquea, en noblea e en senyoria?' (385). He writes a letter to his beloved, in which he declares his love and his discouragement at the disparity of their stations: 'Lo treball d'açò es pensar quant vós valeu' (729). When Hipòlit, Tirant's nephew, courts the Empress, he humbly declares: 'jo no tinc vassalls, béns ni heretatge que davant la majestat vostra hagués a venir' (735).

The hypergamic regime is what explains the Abbess's reassurance to Güelfa as to Curial's fidelity in his comportment toward Laquesis, the daughter of the Duke of Bavaria: 'al Duch no fallira qui li diga que Curial no es pera fer matrimoni ab sa filla' (78). Later, Laquesis will hear from her mother: 'tu ames home qui no es couinent a la tua noblesa'. This misguided love causes Laquesis to lose 'vn dels pus nobles matrimonis del mon' (234; her mother refers to a proposed match with the Duke of Orleans).

When the envious Carefree Widow, Carmesina's nurse, questions the princess's attraction to Tirant, she invokes the logic of hypergamy. The 'perpetual fama' of Carmesina's 'honesta pudicícia' is endangered, insists the nurse, by her contact with this upstart: 'Molts magnats e grans senyors reis, e fills d'aquells' have asked for her hand in 'lleal matrimoni'. If Carmesina entered into 'lícit matrimoni' with this foreigner, the widow demands to know what credentials entitle him to this honour: 'feu-me gràcia del títol que té, de duc, comte o marquès o de rei' (405–06). Carmesina herself will later upbraid Tirant for his indiscretion in declaring his love for her (409–10).

Hypergamy defines the woman's notion of the suitable match. Thus *Amadís*'s Queen Brisena declares of Mabilia, the confidante of Oriana, that she will not leave her palace 'sino casada como persona de tan alto lugar' (III, 667.621–23). Similarly, the Infanta Celinda's letter to Lisuarte (III, 695.262–69), her one-time paramour and father of her illegitimate son Norandel, reminds him of the time when he, wandering as a knight errant in search of adventure, came to her aid as she resisted the aggression of an unwanted suitor ('por mí desechado en casamiento, por no ser en linaje mi ygual').

Hypergamy provides a powerful instrument of political influence through its commodification of the good marriage. The Empress in *Tirant*, after nearly being caught by her husband *in flagrante delicto* with her lover Hipòlit, commands Eliseu, the lady-in-waiting who had discovered them, to henceforth serve Hipòlit ('més que a la mia persona'). If the lady co-operates, the Empress assures her, there will be ample rewards. It is significant that chief among these is a good match, to be arranged by the Empress: 'tu seràs en ma openió e més favorida de totes les altres, e jo et casaré més altament de totes' (761).

In a lineage-oriented regime, hypergamy often assumes a disregard for the wishes of the woman. This is the reality which underlies the theme of forced marriage which is the central element of *Amadís*'s plot. Marital alliance, which implicitly disregards or demeans the notion of free choice by the daughter to be married, is Galaor's point of reference in the scene in which, having been asked by Lisuarte for advice on the matter of Oriana's marriage of state to Patín, he points out the fallacy of assuming such a marriage's inherent political advantages. Galaor's reasoning betrays the author's commitment to a daughter's rights. 'En esto que dezís de os ayudar dél', he assures the king, 'antes vos sería mengua pensar y creer que aquél os hauía de sacar de necessidades'. 'Según sus maneras soberuiosas', Galaor reminds his lord, 'tornárseos-ya al reués, que siempre recibiríedes por su causa afrentas y gastos muy sin prouecho'. In short, concludes the loyal knight, that which Lisuarte takes 'por gran honrra' will in fact end in 'la mayor deshonrra' (III, 863.516–36).

Lisuarte is clearly shown to be in the wrong. After his daughter's tearful departure for Rome, the king consoles his grieving wife: 'Dueña, no conuiene a vuestra discreción ni virtud mostrar tanta flaqueza [...] quanto más por esto en que tanta honrra y prouecho se recibe' (IV, 1006.62–66). Alliance-motivated hypergamy is the principal motive in the arranged marriage of Lisuarte's daughter Oriana to the Roman emperor. The king justifies his intentions to the hermit Nasciano (who has revealed Oriana's clandestine but valid marriage to the hero):

> mi hija Oriana nunca tuuo marido, ni agora tiene, saluo aquel emperador que le yo daua, porque con él, ahunque de mis reynos apartada fuesse, en mucha más honrra y mayor estado la ponía. Y Dios es testigo que mi voluntad nunca fue de la desheredar por heredar a la otra mi hija. . . sino porque hazía cuenta que este mi reyno junto en tanto amor con el imperio de Roma, la su santa fe católica podía ser mucho ensalçada. [...] (IV, 1124.367–80)

Oriana's mother laments her daughter's forced marriage in much the same way that Camar's mother, in *Curial*, deplores the girl's marriage to the King of Tunis, arranged by Camar's father. Camar declares that she would rather die than consent to such a marriage (269). Even as Faraig reminds her (370) of the immense advantages to her family ('tu auras honor e molt de be, e nosaltres serem per tu honrats e auançats molt', 'tos fills seran Reys'), and of her unique importance to her own lineage ('Tu sabs que yo no he altre be sino tu'), her mother defends Camar's right to reject undesirable suitors. Bourdieu's contrast of masculine, official (i.e. alliance-oriented) kinship and feminine, unofficial kinship (i.e. protective of the personal interests of the wife's offspring) is played out in the scene in which Camar's mother berates her husband for seeking to impose a match without their daughter's consent, calling him a 'traydor' and 'alcauot' (372).

The motives of the arranged marriage of Oriana to Patín, couched in terms of affinal alliance and hypergamous advantage, are clearly enunciated in Guilán the Pensive's report to the Roman emperor on the events leading up to the rescue of Oriana by Amadís and his faction and the defeat of the Roman contingent under Salustanquidio. Guilán begins by describing Lisuarte's intentions:

> él, conoçiendo vuestra virtud y grandeza, ahunque esta infanta fuesse su derecha heredera y la cosa del mundo que él y la reyna su muger más amassen, por vos tomar por fijo y ganar vuestro amor, contra la voluntad de todos los de sus reynos je la dio con aquella compaña y atauíos que a la grandeza de vuestro estado y suyo conuenía. (IV, 1056.62–72)

One of the side-effects of the hypergamous regime is the assumption of their desirability as partners by males of superior status (a significant component of the don Juan legend). This aspect of hypergamy is revealed in Salustanquidio's desire to marry Olinda, the beloved of Agrajes. Lisuarte declares himself delighted with this prospect, 'diziendo que según su discreción y honestidad y gran fermosura, que muy bien merescía ser reyna y señora de gran tierra' (III, 897.453–56). The prevalence of an assumption of social superiority explains the arrogance of the knight, in the first book of *Amadís*, who abducts the daughter of Antebón. 'Amiga', he demands, 'pues que yo soy cauallero y vos mucho amo, ¿por quál razón no me tomaréys en casamiento, teniendo más riqueza y estado que vuestro padre?' (I, 216.312–16). Similarly, when Patín of Rome arrives at the court of Lisuarte, he decides, infatuated with Oriana, to propose a marriage: 'pensó que seyendo él de tan gran guisa y tan bueno en sí y que auría el imperio, que si la demandasse en casamiento, que le no sería negada' (II, 386–87.114–18).

The lord Vilesermes, arrogantly allowing Tirant the opportunity of making amends and thus avoiding their impending duel, declares that the youth must return the brooch given to him by Agnes de Berrí, the beloved of Vilesermes:

> Car tu saps bé que no est digne ne mereixedor de posseir cosa alguna que sia d'una tan alta e tan virtuosa senyora com aquella, per quant lo teu estat, llinatge e condició no és suficient per a descalçar-li lo tapí esquerre. (227)

The arrogant knight, however, may himself be caught in the invidious contradictions of hypergamy. Lady Agnes, recounting how Vilesermes had been enamoured of her for years, describes him as 'home de gran riquesa, e molt valentíssim cavaller, que valia tan com negun altre cavaller pogués valer'. Seven years did this knight woo her, only to be defeated and killed by Tirant:

> ha fetes de singulars cavalleries per amor mia desijant haver-me en sa senyoria per lícit matrimoni, ço que jamés haguera aconseguit per jo ésser de major auctoritat de linatge e de béns de fortuna. (231)

Tirant's cousin Diafebus understands hypergamy; its logic compels him to implore Lady Estefania to let him serve her, despite the difference in their conditions: 'per bé que jo no en sia digne ne mereixedor, atesa la gran bellea, gràcia e dignitat que la mercè vostra posseix'. Love, he reminds her, 'eguala les voluntats, e a l'indigne fa digne d'ésser amat' (487). Carmesina, more pragmatic, assumes that paternal favouritism will assist love's labours. She assures Diafebus that she has considered asking her father to make Tirant a count. An aunt of hers, she informs him, has left her a county: 'e per ço jo vull que Tirant l'haja [...] almenys, si senten o saben jo ame a Tirant, serà gran excusació mia: diran que ame un comte' (490).

When *Tirant*'s Jew of Tlemcen suggests to Escariano a plan for betraying the city, its king, and his heir, the proposed terms of his collaboration require, in exchange for services rendered, the arrangement of a hypergamous marriage: 'açò faré per la senyoria tua ab pacte tal, com jo tinga una filla la qual desige maridar honradament'. The Jew adds an extra incentive: 'e de mos propis béns li daré dotze mília ducats' (868–69). It is all the more significant, in terms of our discussion of both filiafocality and hypergamy, that the Jew offers as collateral his own sons as hostages: 'E per major seguretat tua, jo tinc tres fills los quals posaré en poder teu, que si et vinc a menys de ma promesa, tingues llibertat de dar-los mort adolorida' (868). The sons serve merely as counters in the transaction with Escariano; the daughter is everything, and is the principal beneficiary of the deal which the Jew seeks to conclude with Escariano. The Jew will betray his city and endanger his sons' lives, in exchange for a marriage between his daughter and a young Jewish oil vendor of excellent family (mentioned earlier, in chap. 2, in connection with his explanation of the Hebrews' division into patrilineal clans).

In seeking to arrange this hypergamous match, the Jew has recourse to one of the agnatic toolkit's most potent instruments: the dowry ('de mos propis béns [...] dotze mília ducats'). Often functioning in conjunction with hypergamy, dowry serves as an incentive in recruiting desirable sons-in-law, and as a status-enhancement for the bride's father and lineage in the eyes of the groom's family and before the world. As a prestation, however, it is in reality destined not for the groom but for the bride. Normally, only on the death of the latter may the husband inherit, although he may administer, during the lifetime of the bride, the property transmitted to her. The dowry is often connected to the expectation of further inheritance on the death of one of her parents. In addition, notes Goody, 'dowry varies in kind and quantity according to the wealth and status of the bride and her family, the very poor making only very limited transfers, perhaps none at all'.[3]

Diane Owen Hughes affirms that the Mediterranean world presents a characteristic system of marital prestations within which brideprice (prestations from the groom's family as a symbolic payment for the bride) and dowry do not function as 'opposite or opposed gifts', but rather frequently coexist within a larger pattern of matrimonial endowments and exchanges. Among the Romans, when marriage was with *manus*, dowry originally 'fell totally into the husband's control'. The Greek system, on the other hand, involved a more generous gift by the husband. This was viewed as a 'return gift [exchanged for] dowry'. Roman practice, by contrast, emphasized the betrothal guarantee, the *arra sponsalica*. The general Mediterranean tendency was for the groom and his family to be outdone by the bride and her family in the number and value of prestations. The prospective dowry of the bride is usually a 'weighty and substantial settlement on which prospective bridegrooms might cast greedy eyes' (Hughes 1978: 263–64).

Levy summarizes, in terms similar to those of Hughes, the dotal practice of ancient Athens (1963: 140–41). In the latter context, he notes, dowry functioned as an 'avenue of benefit [to a daughter] from her father's patrimony'. A woman's husband controlled but 'did not become the owner' of his wife's dowry. Rather, 'he held and administered the dowry in trust for sons borne to him by the wife who brought the dowry with her'. The dowry, a 'separately accountable' entity, was either 'vested in the sons of the marriage, or returned to the woman's former *kyrios*' (i.e. her father or the senior agnate of her lineage).

Under Germanic influence, notes Hughes (266), a parallel system emerged in the early Middle Ages, in which the husband's donations to the bride and her family were the more significant matrimonial prestations. Marriage prestations in the Germanic tradition tended to function as a means of bride purchase. The marriage market, in such a system, seems to favour the bride's family. We may speculate, employing a notion of spousal commodification, that a brideprice system implies a scarcity of

---

[3] Goody 1983: 241, also 206 ff.; see also Goody 1970 and 1973a: 1–2 & 17–20.

brides, and consequent high valuation of women. A dowry system, by contrast, suggests a surplus of women, a relative scarcity of eligible males, and thus an inflation in the cost of recruiting husbands.

Germanic marriage customs, like all systems of matrimonial exchange among traditional kin groups, 'wove a web of gifts and settlements'. According to the reciprocal logic of exchange systems, as explicated by Mauss, Lévi-Strauss and others, the gift imposes the obligation of a counter-prestation — a matter, in Hughes's words, of a 'guarded gift'. The significant point of contrast between a system of brideprice and one of dowry is the direction of what we might call 'beholden-ness'. In a dowry system, it is the bride's kin who seek to outdo and impress the groom and his people. In the brideprice system, such as that of Germanic kinship, the groom's gifts are meant to impress the kinfolk of the bride; she, meanwhile, provides only a small token countergift, such as items of weaponry.[4]

Within five centuries of the Germanic invasions, observes Hughes, dowry had reappeared as the dominant practice in the Mediterranean region. The Romance-speaking population, meanwhile, had apparently continued, despite the official predominance of the Germanic model, to maintain the traditional dotal system. The urban society of the later European Middle Ages presents a fully developed dotal regime, in which dowry tended to deplete family economies to such a degree that many called for its abolition, citing as well its corruptive influence among dowry-hunting young men, and ancient examples of its deleterious effects — as well as ancient attempts to eliminate dowry, as in Lycurgus's ban on dowries in Sparta (Hughes 1978: 265).

Two things emerge from Hughes's analysis of European dowry. One is the importance of dowry as an affirmation of status by the

---

[4] Hughes 1978: 266. Anything like an adequate incorporation of Lévi-Strauss's treatment of the principles of reciprocity is impossible in the context of this study. I shall content myself with a judicious citation. A system of prestations does not, Lévi-Strauss insists, simply support or facilitate marriage: 'the system of prestations *results in* marriage'. He goes further: 'Exchanges are peacefully resolved wars, and wars are the result of unsuccessful transactions.' The gift which is the centrepiece of exchange is never merely a commercial transaction, but rather a pretext for the establishment and maintenance of 'the artificial kinship relationship of brothers-in-law' (Lévi-Strauss 1969: 67).

bride's family. The other is the asymmetrical nature of the prestations: it tends to be the bride's family which contributes the largest or perhaps the only prestation. Hughes points out that status stratification shifts the emphasis in matrimonial arrangements and prestations from a bilateral reproduction of two lineages to a unilateral enhancement, on the one hand, of the status of the bride's family, particularly of her father and brothers, and on the other hand, of a perpetuation of the groom's lineage by recruitment of a bride.

More general ethnographic studies support Hughes's observation as to the material asymmetry of the practice. On the other hand, the groom's side may provide various kinds of symbolic capital. 'While dowry-giving households lose daughters and wealth', observe Alice Schlegel and Rohn Eloul, 'they can gain status'. Alliance with a powerful or prestigious clan is frequently obtained by recruitment of 'a high-status son-in-law' (with the concomitant honorific and political advantages). Dowry may also may be employed 'to attract a poorer but presentable son-in-law whose loyalty will be assured through his wife's wealth — in other words, to gain a client son-in-law' (Schlegel & Eloul 1988: 301).

The pattern of 'dowry and consent', even as it spread throughout Europe, was, although abetted by the revival of Roman law, in many ways contradictory to the spirit of that law. Medieval jurists, notes Hughes, 'stressed the relationship between dowry and female inheritance rights'. This assumption of the connection between dowry and female inheritance revealed a tendency toward viewing the dowry as a daughter's 'premortem inheritance' (Goody's phrase) of her share of the paternal estate. Due to this concept of dowry as 'a substitute for a daughter's normal claim' on the paternal estate, one of the frequent effects of medieval dotal practice was the 'denial to dowered daughters [of] further rights in their paternal inheritance'. Concomitant to this 'effective disinheritance' of the daughter was a 'preference for cash dowries throughout the western Mediterranean'.[5]

The *Partidas*, in contrast to the asymmetry implied by hypergamy and dowry, accentuate the inherent reciprocity of marital prestations, which they class as 'dote' and 'arras'. The dowry

---

[5]   Hughes 1978: 278, 279–80, & 281.

(*dote*), they acknowledge, is, while given by the wife to the husband 'con entendimiento de se mantener et ayudar el matrimonio', nonetheless to be regarded 'como propio patrimonio de la muger'. The man's donation to the bride at marriage, the Latin *donatio propter nuptias*, affirms this law, is called in Spanish *arras*, although, it is noted, 'las leyes de los sabios antiguos' considered this term to refer to the pledge (*peño*) guaranteeing the fulfilment of the marriage contract. Donations should be 'fechas egualmiente, fueras ende si fuese costumbre usada de luengo tiempo en algunos logares de las facer dotra manera' (IV.xi.1).

The *Partidas* observe the Latin distinction between *adventitia* (prestations from bride to groom derived from property or wealth accruing to her personally from sources other than the patrimonial estate) and *profectitia*, defined as property which 'sale de los bienes del padre, ó del abuelo ó de los otros parientes que suben por liña derecha'. The *Partidas* insist that if a father owes a debt to his daughter, and pays this debt, at her request, to her husband as part of the dowry, that this should be considered — 'maguer pagase el padre [...] de sus bienes propios' — not *profectitia* but *adventitia*. The father who thus discharges a debt 'non gelo da asi como padre, mas asi como gelo darie otro extraño' (IV.xi.2). The patrimonial nature of the dowry is reaffirmed in other laws under the same title, such as that which stipulates that the husband may acquire his wife's dowry outright only through contractual agreement, or by reason of the wife's adultery, or 'por costumbre' (23). This last qualification represents a concession to local, traditional usage. In the case of the wife's death in a childless marriage, dowry given as *profectitia* reverts to her father (30); if she has children, they inherit the dowry (31). The dowry, then, is a thing over which the husband has control and usufruct, including whatever increased profit it realizes (18 & 25). It is, however, transmitted from the woman's paternal kin to her children.

The *Fuero viejo* likewise accentuates both the reciprocal nature of the prestations which accompany marriage, and the woman's rights in controlling those payments which come from her side. This code provides, for instance, that a *fijodalgo* give 'el tercio del eredamiento' to his wife, 'en arras'. She, having lived 'una buena vida', is entitled to keep this on his death. If her husband's heirs wish to deny her this, they must indemnify her to the amount of 'quinientos sueldos'. The woman is also entitled to the husband's 'mula ensellada o enfrenada', as well as the furniture and clothing she brought into the marriage, as well as 'la meitat de todas las ganancias que ganaron en uno' (v.i.294). The *donadio* given by a hidalgo 'a la ora del casamiento, ante que sean jurados', could consist of a 'piel de abortones' long enough to allow 'un cauallero armado entrar por la una manga e salir por la otra', as well as, among other things, a saddled and harnessed mule, a silver plate, a Moorish slave woman, or simply a cash payment to the 'quantia de mil maravedis' (v.ii). The *donadio* could be taken from the amount set aside in trust before the marriage, with half of the total destined for the wife, half for the husband (v.xiv).

Dowry, as a special prestation assigned to the wife by her family, for the purposes outlined by Goody, Hughes, and others, is not present in the *Fuero viejo*. The *Fuero viejo* distinguishes *arras*, a kind of prenuptial good-faith insurance paid by the husband, from what the wife brings into her marriage, namely her trousseau: 'el mueble que [la muger] trajo consigo en casamiento'. This last, according to Joan Corominas, was not to be called *ajuar* until the fourteenth century, and not as common usage until the sixteenth (Corominas & Pascual 1980–91: s.v.). The term *arras* means, he says, 'lo que se da como prenda en algún contrato', as well as 'donación dotal'. The *Fuero viejo*'s reference to the third of a man's estate consigned to his wife's usufruct or possible inheritance, and to the *donadio* to be stipulated 'a la ora del casamiento', fall under this conceptual rubric. They are not dowry in the strict sense. In the *Poema de Mio Cid*, however, the term *axuvar*, notes Corominas, signifies 'heredad que la esposa recibe de sus ascendientes' — in other words, the asymmetrical prestation called dowry in modern ethnographic parlance (*PMC*, ll. 1650 & 2571).

In cases where it amounted to outright disinheritance of daughters, dowry was a patriarchal stratagem that defied traditions and laws protective of women's rights. In addition, dowry inevitably conflicted with the consensual model of marriage. The dotal regime, argues Hughes, 'drew attention away from the conjugal bond to focus it instead on the relations between the couple and the wife's kinsmen'. The emphasis on consent as a definitive factor in marriage, as propounded by Gratian, Peter Lombard, and many other authorities, and as adopted officially by the Church, appeared on the scene 'at precisely the time when the net of dotal marriage was catching daughters ever more firmly in the marital schemes of their kinsmen', for medieval dowry was 'almost from its beginnings [...] part of a status, rather than an inheritance system'. Dowry, in other words, was a way of using rights over daughters 'as a way of asserting status or competing for it'. This aspect of dowry, moreover, suggests that, rather than an aspect of bilateral inheritance in the system of cognatic kindreds, it is 'a form of disinheritance within a social group whose organization had become significantly *less* bilateral'. Dowry was, therefore, another item in the repertoire of political strategies — many of them discussed in the previous chapter — designed to promote the interests of the agnatic lineage at the expense of all but designated primary heirs (Hughes 1978: 284 & 290).

The dotal patterns reported by Hughes coincide with the agnatic tendencies already detected in the romances as the status quo against which the knight and his beloved react. The dotal system tends toward a systematic disinheritance of designated daughters, accompanied by obvious marital schemes implemented by the father or male kin of the hero's beloved. Meanwhile, because marriage in the consensual regime becomes a subset of amorous relations in general, the binding reciprocity of the gift, which underlies the logic of traditional marital prestations, now serves not the woman's lineage but herself alone: the gift of the maiden is exclusively controlled by the maiden herself.

Conflict in the romances arises when fathers seek to marry daughters 'up-and-out', to husbands of superior status and political influence. Oriana and Güelfa, as well as several secondary characters, find themselves in the predicament of daughters who seek to wrest control of the maiden's gift — the focus, as it were, of filiafocality — away from overseeing males, whether fathers or brothers. While defending daughters' rights to inheritance and to choice in the selection of a mate, the romances do not, however, simply endorse women's will as the determining factor. The texts subscribe to a countervailing matrimonial ideology, one based on reciprocity in marriage prestations. This prestational symmetry does not necessarily involve literal equivalence in the types of payment. In this, the chivalric texts resort to the ancient tradition of marriage transactions as a varied array of reciprocal prestations, services, and considerations. The romances invoke the tenets of this tradition in support of individual liberation, but they also portray the resulting pact as a mutual benefit to the lineages of both partners.

Tirant consciously accentuates the 'personalizing' transformation of the marriage prestation between lineages into an amorous prestation between individuals. The Empress, having embarked upon an adulterous relationship with the young knight Hipòlit, admonishes him, as she seeks to persuade him, through an enunciation of the principle of binding reciprocity, to accept the gift of a many-jewelled necklace: 'no refuses jamés res que ta enamorada te done, car regla comuna és: qui és major en dignitat, la primera vegada que prenen amistat, deu donar a l'altre, qui no ho deu refusar' (763).

In *Tirant*, Lady Estefania, in her letter of intent in which she pronounces her 'paraules de present', making herself the effective wife of Diafebus, engages as well to bring both property and moveable goods into her marriage:

> e port-vos en contemplació de matrimoni lo sobre dit ducat de Macedònia ab tots los drets a ell pertanyents; més, vos porte cent deu mília ducats venecians, e més tres mília marcs d'argent obrat, joies e robes per la majestat del senyor Emperador ab los des son sacre consell estimades uitanta-tres mília ducats; e més, vos porte la mia persona, que estime més. (494)

She concludes by renouncing her rights and all claims, 'renunciant en aquella llei que féu aquell gloriós emperador Július Cèsar, la qual se nomena llei de més valer, la qual és en favor de donzelles, viudes e pubiles' (494).

While endorsing the principle of female consent, the romances nonetheless remain aware that nuptial prestations, including prenuptial gifts and dowry itself, are elements in the greater system of reciprocities that bind lineages in affinal alliance. In *Amadís*, we recall the rich 'atavíos' brought along with Oriana in her marital voyage to Rome (IV, 1056). *Tirant* lavishes much attention on the detail of such bridal wealth. Thus, the narrative's depiction of how the hero raises the stakes in his efforts at brokering the marriage between Prince Philip of France and Ricomana of Sicily by reminding her of her father's intentions with regard to the disposition of the family estate and thus of her potential dowry:

'vos vol dotar de totes les terres del ducat de Calàbria ensems ab dos-cents mília ducats' (310).

In *Tirant*, upon the confirmation of Ricomana's betrothal to his son Philip, the King of France sends 'a la nora quatre peces de brocat molt belles e tres mília marts gebelins e un collar d'or obrat en París molt bell e de gran estima, perquè ha havia en ell engastades moltes pedres fines qui eren de gran vàlua'. The French queen, meanwhile, does not omit her own gifts, as she sends 'moltes peces de drap de seda e de brocat e molts cortinatges de seda e de ras molt especials, e moltes altres coses' (342). The attention paid to these details reveals the affinal significance of these prestations, as well as their function as an ostentatious affirmation of status.

The gift-giving, as *Tirant* demonstrates, continues after the marriage takes place. The King of France, arriving in Sicily, is met by his daughter-in-law: 'e la nora fon a la vora de la mar, e aquí se feren molt gran festa sogre e nora'. The French monarch, we are told, 'li donà de grans donatius, e tot lo dia la portava per la mà que no la's deixava partir'. Every day of her father-in-law's sojourn in Sicily, the princess awoke to find 'un ric present, l'un dia de brocats, altre sedes, cadenes d'or, fermalls e altres joies de molta estima'. Nor are prestations unilateral, as regards the two families. The King of Sicily 'festejà molt bé al rei de França, e presentà-li cent cavalls molt bells e molt singulars'. Ricomana is commanded by her father, moreover, to personally attend to the provisioning of the French ships. The visit concludes with the French king's departure. He is accompanied by the Prince of Sicily, to whom, upon their arrival in France, the king gives 'una filla sua per muller' (364–65).

The question of the various and contradictory motives of marriage prestations normally hovers in the background of the romances, which relish the surface detail but avoid an analysis of motives. *Curial*, however, is overtly attentive to the psychological reciprocities of marital prestations, as well as to the legal, affinal, political, and honorific nuances attached to them. In a description of the noble Lady Yoland's marriage to Lord Aznar we are told that the bride, the sister of Guillalmes de la Tor, is 'de molt noble linatge', and that she is 'molt ben heretada'. Her status merits the intervention of the king himself: 'volent mostrar en molt grant singularitat la sua reyal magnificencia [...] moltes joyes e cinch milia escuts dor al dit Aznar dona'. Yoland's relatives, on the other hand, not wishing the patrimonial property contained in the dowry to be taken away by this son-in-law, buy him out: 'per raho que lo dit Aznar sen pogues portar la dot de sa muller, la heretat li compraren' (262).

Dowry must be understood in the context of the marriage market. A daughter must be wisely invested, not merely spent, in that market. This is particularly true in the case of the father with more than one daughter and no sons (the case of several personages in the romances, including *Amadís*'s Lisuarte and *Tirant*'s Greek Emperor). Daughters may be distinguished, in this crucial aspect of the calculus of lineal advantage, by any number of criteria, but the chief among these is age. When and in what order to marry daughters is an issue that presides over much of the action in the chivalric romance.

It is from this perspective that we must approach the primary conflict in the narrative of *Amadís de Gaula*. The point of contention — between the hero and his allies and King Lisuarte and his faction — is the arranged marriage between the hero's beloved, Oriana, eldest daughter of Lisuarte, and Patín, the brother of the Emperor of Rome. This hypergamous marriage is perceived by the bride's father exclusively in terms of prestige and political advantage. At the same time, even as Lisuarte disinherits his elder daughter, surrendering her, as it were, to another lineage, he intends to name his younger daughter Leonoreta his principal heir (III, 862.465–67). Oriana's impending marriage with Patín, a match arranged by her father without her consent, elicits a very negative public opinion:

> todos le dezían que lo no hiziesse, que era cosa en que mucho contra Dios erraría quitando su hija aquel señorío de que eredera auía de ser y ponerla en sujeción de hombre estraño de condición liuiana y muy mudable, que así como por el presente aquello mucho desseaua, assí a poco espacio de tiempo otra cosa se le antojaría.
> (III, 871–72.328–38)

We are clearly expected to side with Oriana, as she invokes both the solidarity of the kindred and the chivalric ideal of service to women, in her desperate appeal to her cousin King Arbán of North Wales:

¡O rey de Norgales, mi buen cormano! pues que mi gran desuentura
me ha sido tan cruel que os y aquellos que por socorrer las tristes y
cuytadas donzellas muchos peligros hauéys passado, ¿no me podéys
con las armas socorrer? Acorredme siquiera con vuestra palabra,
consejad al rey mi padre no me faga tanto mal. (III, 894.241–50)

The above passage is yet another expression of the essential
contradiction at the heart of *Amadís*. On the one hand, Oriana
appeals to traditional sentiments of kinship loyalty: she invokes the
solidarity of cousinship. On the other, her plea is in defiance of the
kin-based notion of marriage as an alliance between lineages.
Lineage-oriented marriage is shown in *Amadís* in terms of the
unnatural separation of a daughter from her home and family (as
well as the unlawful disinheritance which she suffers at Lisuarte's
hands). Oriana tearfully confronts her father: 'Mi señor, vuestra
voluntad es de me embiar al emperador de Roma y partirme de os y
de la reyna mi madre y desta tierra donde Dios natural me fizo' (III,
895.288–92). Oriana, in order to avoid marriage with the hated
Emperor Patín, even seeks to play the card of her traditional rights
by offering to renounce her inheritance and enter a convent:

Y porque todo esto sea escusado y Dios sea de nosotros seruido, yo
quiero ponerme en orden y allí biuir, dexándoos libre para que de
vuestros reynos y señoríos dispongáys a vuestra voluntad; y yo
renunciaré todo el derecho que Dios me dio en ellos a Leonoreta mi
hermana, o a otro, qual vos más quisierdes. (III, 895.300–10)

The motives of fathers like Lisuarte may be analysed with
reference to John Hajnal's concept of the 'Mediterranean Marriage
Pattern' (MMP). This configuration shows a relatively late age at
marriage for males, a much younger age for brides. Hajnal argues
that the general European pattern, especially since the eighteenth
century, has been one of late marriage for both husband and wife,
with significant numbers of both sexes never marrying. The ancient
and medieval world showed a far greater range in both age at
marriage and individual matrimonial history (in regard to divorce
and remarriage, as well as spinsterhood). Hajnal suggests as a
possible explanation of the modern trend a correlation with the
economic basis of the prevailing kinship system. The rise of the so-
called 'stem-family', in which 'land descends to a single heir, the
other sons going elsewhere' (essentially the agnatic pattern of

primogeniture), is naturally conducive to deferred marriage for the suitor who seeks to 'establish an independent livelihood adequate to support a family' (Hajnal 1965: 101, 120–25, 127–30, & 133).

Delayed marriage is a recurrent phenomenon in the history of European marriage. Heers documents, for the cities of northern Italy, the difficulty of marrying off a daughter if one had insufficient dowry. He cites the institution of Florence's *Monte delle doti* (from 1425), a kind of insurance depository guaranteeing interest on deposits, to be redeemed on the marriage of a family's daughter or daughters. Men delayed marriage for reasons of money as often as did women (Heers 1977: 60–61). The protagonists of the chivalric romance, disregarding the presumed social norm of the later Middle Ages, refuse to delay marriage, despite both the domination of agnatic interests and the lack of dowry. We may characterize the romances as conforming to Hajnal's modern marriage pattern, in the sense that they portray family influence in terms of a stem-family formation that leaves couples who disregard family approval with no choice but to establish neolocal residence.

Marriage takes place, argues Bourdieu, as a function of a lineage's 'products on the matrimonial market'. These are largely determined by such 'secondary characteristics' as matrimonial status, age, and sex. Thus, a man's market value will have a variable effect on the kinds of marriage arranged for him, according to his status as an optimally marriageable bachelor, an over-age bachelor, 'an already married man looking for a co-wife, or a widower or divorcee wanting to remarry'. Women are similarly classified, except that the 'depreciation entailed by previous marriages is infinitely greater'. A man, if willing to accept the possibility of marrying a social inferior or a previously married woman, may bide his time, since men are generally more likely to find a spouse. A father with daughters, by contrast, 'can play with time so as to prolong the conjunctural advantage he derives from his position as the receiver of offers [...] only up to a certain point'. The father who waits too long 'will see his products devalued because they are thought to be unsaleable, or simply because they are past their prime' (Bourdieu 1977: 68).

An only son, notes Bourdieu, is 'married young so that he can continue the lineage as quickly as possible'. At the same time, the marriages of siblings are never treated as if 'each marriage [were] an isolated unit'. The time and manner of each marriage is largely determined by 'the marrying of all the others, and thus varies as a function of each child's *position* (defined mainly by sibling order, sex, and relationship to the head of the family), within the particular *configuration* of the whole set of children to be married, itself characterized by their number and sex'. Although primogeniture is not observed as systematically as in the medieval European context, among the Kabyle the eldest male sibling tends to be favoured 'to the detriment of his younger brothers'. The eldest boy is, moreover, likely to be married 'first and as well as possible', and, more tellingly from the comparative viewpoint which, I hope, will help us to comprehend the patterns I am about to analyse in the romances, 'outside rather than inside the lineage'. Younger brothers, meanwhile, are 'destined for *production* rather than the *exchanges* of the market or assembly, for work on the land rather than the house's external politics'.

A son's function in matrimonial strategies is influenced, therefore, by the number and sex of his siblings. The eldest of several sons will be deployed differently from one who is the only son or the only male, with sisters. A family with numerous daughters and few or no sons is 'in an unfavourable position and finds itself forced to incur debts toward the families which receive its women'. A family 'rich in men', on the other hand, can 'invest' its sons in a variety of ways, showing a more flexible response to economic and political conditions (Bourdieu 1977: 68–70).

David Rheubottom, referring to northern Italian evidence as the basis of a 'comparative historical ethnography', studies marriage in townships in Ragusa between 1400 and 1520. He begins by citing David Herlihy and Christiane Klapisch-Zuber on Florentine marriage. Husbands there tended to be older than their brides; many men never married, while few women remained unmarried. Florentine demography, according to Herlihy & Klapisch-Zuber, was such that there were more women aged 15 to 20 years than men 25 to 30. Contesting the hypothesis of Herlihy and Klapisch-Zuber, that the urban, wealthy classes delayed marriage for men because of the masculine obligation to found and support a household (a hypothesis supported by Hajnal), Rheubottom points out that the majority of young grooms reveal not a *neolocal* pattern of marital residence, but rather bring 'their brides into the paternal or fraternal *phase* of the household's developmental cycle'. More-over, it is the younger men in Ragusa who receive the largest dowries (Rheubottom 1988: 360–61).[6]

A scarcity of desirable male suitors (assuming hypergamy) leads to competition for their attentions on the part of prospective brides' families. Thus the characteristic asymmetry of the dotal system. Within this restrictive marriage market, the younger the marriage-able age of the daughter, affirms Rheubottom, the 'greater the number of potential husbands'. Her family, in such circumstances, has 'more choice and a longer period of time in which to exercise it'. Betrothal, Rheubottom notes, 'deducts' the bride and groom from 'the pool of eligible partners'. The average age of grooms and brides was 33 for the former, 18 for the latter. Often the groom did not 'actually remove the bride to his own home and consummate the marriage until later'. The interval between betrothal and con-summation averaged three years; when it was over five years this was usually because the bride was underage (361, 362, & 365).

Rheubottom confirms the prevalence of a 'sisters-first' policy in the society of Ragusa. This naturally tended to increase the marriage age of brothers. The 'direction of causality', he argues (i.e. between the 'sisters-first' pattern or the age differential of brides and grooms), must lie on the side of the practice of sisters-first marriage. Moreover, siblings of the same sex, as in the romances, marry in order (365–66). In Ragusa, brothers were thus obligated to see their sisters married first. However this policy accounts only for a four-year gap in age between brides and grooms. How, Rheubottom asks, may we account for the fifteen-year gap observed in the records? Large sibling groups, he argues, mean larger male-female age differentials at marriage. A pattern of sisters-first, moreover, tends to yield a constant marriage age for women, but a fluctuant age for men. In 'closed marriage systems', he points out, the pool of marital candidates is small. To this factor are conjoined the usual European church-imposed consanguineal restrictions. It is thus not surprising that the brides of younger men 'bring larger dowries' into the marriage, given that a younger man, with all the personal and lineal advantages that youth implies, will be perceived as a better match in the restricted pool of candidates.

---

[6] See Herlihy and Klapisch-Zuber 1985: 202–31.

Rheubottom's evidence shows no clear trend toward either hypergamy or hypogamy. As in dotal systems everywhere, he suggests, the 'emphasis is on "matching like for like"'. Where there are status differences between the spouses, the slight tendency is toward hypergamy.[7]

Alliance and the relationship between lineages, notes Rheubottom, tend to overshadow the bride-groom relationship in the network of interlocking kinship relations. 'Contracts', he observes, 'can be read as if marriage was a relationship between father-in-law and son-in-law in which the bride was a third party'. The *pacta matrimonialia*, concludes Rheubottom, established a complex and 'economically and socially consequential' alliance between individual men and their families. Betrothal, moreover, constituted a 'prior transferral of honor obligations from father to husband'. While making a girl the responsibility of her intended spouse, betrothal of sisters also permitted brothers to arrange their own marriages. Finally, wife-taking 'confers respect and deference' to a lineage (Rheubottom 1988: 370).

Oriana's arranged marriage to the vainglorious Patín, Emperor of Rome, is the core of the dramatic conflict in *Amadís*. It illustrates the principles of matrimonial calculation described by Bourdieu with reference to the father who has daughters in an agnatic regime, and the dynamics of sibling differentiation outlined by Rheubottom. Differing marriage patterns of siblings according to age is seen in Lisuarte's change of attitude toward his daughter's suitor after the death of the latter's elder brother. When Patín is merely the younger brother of the reigning emperor, Lisuarte is unreceptive ('la voluntad del rey muy apartada de tal juntamiento era'). Then, as Patín inherits the Roman imperial throne on the death of his elder brother, he renews his petition for Oriana's hand, 'creyendo con el mayor estado en que puesto era más ligeramente la cobrar' (III, 790.625–28). Lisuarte and Patín establish a relationship based on the latter's marriage to Oriana, and in which Patín, in response to Oriana's rescue/abduction by the men of the Firm Isle, acts as the more interested party; she has, in line with the customs detailed by Rheubottom, passed into her betrothed's sphere of responsibility.

---

[7]   Rheubottom 1988: 367–69. See also Goody 1976: 106.

Lisuarte explains the affinal logic of the match, and the strategic significance of designating the younger sister as heir, to his trusted counsellor Galaor:

> Ya sabéys el gran poder y alteza del emperador de Roma, que a mi fija embía a pedir para emperatriz. Y yo entiendo en ello dos cosas mucho de mi pro: la vna, casar a mi fija tan honrradamente, syendo señora de vn tan alto poderío, y tener aquel emperador para mi ayuda cada que menester ouiesse; y la otra, que mi hija Leonoreta quedará señora y heredera de la Gran Bretaña. (III, 862.456–67).

Elder daughters, in the regime portrayed in *Amadís*, are married off first, in hypergamous fashion and with dowry, for political purposes. The elder daughter is 'spent' first on the matrimonial market — used, as it were, as a counter in the alliance game, rather than for perpetuation of her lineage — because elder daughters are harder to marry than younger, in a system where all families are looking for maximum reproductive potential (including in the sense of the greater number of possible grandchildren). Fathers therefore make the best match possible for elder daughters, while holding back the youngest as the focus of agnatic continuity. Elder daughters — again to employ the distinction proposed by Bourdieu — serve a political purpose, while younger daughters fulfil an integrative function.

The pattern is very clear in *Tirant*, in which the hero, after asking the Greek emperor why he persists in calling Carmesina 'Infanta', reminds the ruler of the arrangement that left the Princess in her present situation:

> Per bé, senyor, que vostra altesa tinga altra filla, muller del rei d'Hongria e de major edat, e per lo gran dot que la majestat vostra li donà en contemplació del matrimoni, ella renuncià a tots los drets a l'exce·lent Carmesina. (388)

Because Carmesina is now, as Tirant reminds the Emperor, the 'heretera del Regne', she merits the title Princess (388). The elder daughter, meanwhile, had been married off, with dowry. The Emperor declares that his only worldly consolation is the remaining daughter, Carmesina: 'No tenia', he explains to Tirant, 'sinó dues filles, l'una tinc mig perduda, que no la puc veure ni oir, ço és la muller del rei d'Hongria, e tinc ací tot lo meu bé' (596). The Emperor's original situation is essentially the same as that of King

Lisuarte, in *Amadís*. Lisuarte seeks to marry off his elder daughter Oriana, giving her a substantial dowry, while reserving the succession to the throne for his younger daughter Leonoreta.

We see the same pattern — the elder daughter disinherited and married to a husband of superior status, the younger daughter appointed principal heir — in *Curial*. There the Duke of Bavaria's daughter, the elder of the two daughters of the Duke mentioned in the text, has been married to the Duke of Austria; the younger sister remains, it is clear from context, as the heiress (42–43). Immediately after Curial's successful defence of the Duchess of Austria against a charge of adultery, we witness a scene in which the Duke of Bavaria, the father of the vindicated duchess, seeks to show his gratitude by offering his daughter Laquesis (a younger sister of the Duchess of Austria) in marriage:

> lo Duch de Bauiera, volent dauant tots vsar de la sua magnificencia, hauent vna molt bella filla donzella, de edat per ventura de quinze anys (e era la pus bella, per fama e per fet, que en aquell temps en limperi d Alamanya se trobas), presa aquella per la ma, sen vench dauant Curial, e dix li: 'Curial, car amich meu: nom se en quina manera retribuir te pusca la honor que lo jorn de vuy mas feta, sino donant te aquesta mia filla per muller, e que prengues la meytat de la mia terra, e, apres de mos dies, de tota sies senyor'. (44)

The strategy of designating the younger sister as heiress of the family fortune makes her the functional equivalent of an elder brother in the system of primogeniture; it is as if she were the elder or only brother of the sisters married before her. An only son — we recall Bourdieu's remark — is 'married young so that he can continue the lineage as quickly as possible' (Bourdieu 1977: 68). The father with several daughters trades his older daughters in the marriage market, while retaining the youngest for the purpose of recruiting a son-in-law who will beget grandchildren belonging to her lineage. A younger daughter is a more suitable heiress for a number of reasons, not the least of which is her greater number of potential child-bearing years.

Hypergamy, a frequent concomitant of dowry and of strategic differentiation of siblings for deployment on the marriage market, is viewed in a very dim light by the romances. The disadvantages of the practice are discussed a number of times in *Amadís*. Galaor, for example, responds to Lisuarte's request for advice on the matter

of the arranged marriage between Oriana and the Emperor of
Rome:

> en lo que dezís que casaréys vuestra fija muy honrradamente y con
> gran señorío, esto me pareçe muy al contrario, porque syendo ella
> vuestra sucessora heredera destos reynos después de vuestros días,
> no le podéys fazer mayor mal que quitárselos y ponerla en sujeción
> de hombre estraño donde mando ni poder terná. Y puesto caso que
> alcançe aquello que es el cabo de semejantes señoras, que son los
> fijos, y éstos vea casados, luego será puesta en mayor sujeción y
> pobreza que ante, viendo mandar otra emperatriz. (III, 863.501–16)

Argamonte, another of Lisuarte's counsellors, points out that an
imperial son-in-law could decide to take possession of the ancestral
estates of his wife. 'Como es poderoso', warns Argamonte, 'no con
mucho trabajo los podría tomar'. Thus, through the disinheritance
of one daughter, both daughters could end by being deprived of
their inheritance: 'assí que entrambas seyendo deseredadas, sería
esta tierra [...] sujeta a los emperadores de Roma' (III, 873.412–25).

Amadís's Briolanja, like the Lady of Galapia and the Princess of
Mentón in Book 1 of *Zifar*, is a sole surviving heir. The narrator
makes clear the legitimacy of her claim by the defensive posture of
her uncle, the usurper Abiseos ('gran vergüença ouo, considerando
el tuerto que le tenía hecho'), and the reaction of 'los naturales del
reyno', who are shown to feel 'gran piedad [...] en sus coraçones en
la ver tan injustamente desheredada', and silently pray that God
grant an end to 'vna trayción tan grande' (I, 335.352–66). Oriana,
by contrast, is the elder daughter of two. *Amadís*, in its depiction of
the hypergamous marriage which effectively disinherits her in
favour of her younger sister, questions not only the underlying
motives of the policy, but rather its pragmatic efficacy as a marital
strategy calculated to bring maximum advantage to the lineage.
Thus Galaor's misgivings represent a consensus of the king's
subjects:

> heredar a vuestra fija Leonoreta en la Gran Bretaña, éste es vn muy
> mayor yerro [...] Quitar os, señor, este señorío a vna tal hija en el
> mundo señalada, viniéndole de derecho, y darlo a quien no lo deue
> hauer, nunca Dios plega que tal consejo yo diesse; y no digo a
> vuestra hija, mas a la más pobre mujer del mundo no sería en qu'el
> suyo se le quitasse. (III, 863.537–49)

It is often hinted in the chivalric romances that marriage is an avenue to economic prosperity and political power for the ambitious male. *Amadís* prudishly refrains from an overt emphasis of this theme, preferring to exalt the prowess of its hero, and the propitious opportunity, presented by the Firm Isle, of escaping the humiliation of being the kept lover or the son-in-law moving in. *Tirant* shows no such squeamishness, frankly depicting any number of men who take advantage of marriage in the furtherance of ambition. The narrator of *Tirant* informs us that Lady Estefania was not the daughter of the present Duke of Macedonia (an intriguer and coward who seeks the ruination of Tirant). Rather, her real father was a 'gloriós príncep e valentíssim cavaller molt ric', the 'cosí germà de l'Emperador'. That nobleman's only daughter, she was bequeathed the duchy upon her father's death ('deixà-li lo ducat'), and was to take possession of her inheritance on her thirteenth birthday. Her mother, 'dona poderosa', shared with the Emperor the functions of 'tudora e curadora' of the young girl. The mother, meanwhile, 'per haver fills', married the Count of Albí, who thereupon assumed the title of Duke of Macedonia (495).

The theme of the kept man is a recurrent one in the two Catalonian romances. At times *Tirant* is almost gleeful in its frank depiction of the impecunious chivalric gold-digger. After giving him fabulous gifts, the Empress teases her young lover Hipòlit: 'poca admiració serà que jo no et faça, ans de molts anys, corona real portar' (762). Even as he accepts her generosity, the young man is cheerfully aware of the disparity in rank: 'Conegut tinc que ab gran desegualtat só amat de vostra altesa' (763). We see that it is not only an ethic of noblesse oblige which governs the need for generosity on the part of the high-born lady who takes a lover of lower station. There is also the pragmatic dimension of opportunity and the establishment of a shared residence conducive to the desired proximity. The empress in *Tirant* is chided by her maid Eliseu:

> ¿E la majestat vostra no basta per a sostenir-lo e dar-li de vostres béns tant e tan abundantment que no s'haja amprar de negú? Jo, qui só una pobra donzella, me tendria per desaventurada, que si tingués enamorat jo li ajudaria tant com me seria possible, encara que en sabés empenyorar la gonella per socórrer-lo; quant més l'altesa vostra qui sou tan gran senyora e tan riquíssima. (765)

The Empress commands Eliseu to be the go-between in trans-
mitting material assistance to the young man (765). Hipòlit allows
his life to be completely changed by the generosity of his mistress,
as she buys him clothes and jewellery, assigns him an entourage of
three hundred servants, and presents him as well with a treasure
chest (766–67).

This situation amounts to a subversion of traditional patrilocality
and the traditional maintenance of the wife by her husband. Similarly, in contrast to the apparently normative virilocal independence
of *Curial*'s Lord Aznar, referred to earlier, we find the situation of
the worthy but indigent hero aided by Güelfa, through the agency
of the go-between Melchior de Pandor. She declares to the latter:
'yom he mes en lo cap de fer aquest home, per ço quem par que ho
meresca' (14). Throughout the story, until the period of her
maximum ire, and that only for a time, Güelfa generously assists
her lover in his wanderings and in maintaining a style of life
befitting the man she wants him to be:

> vna fonch la sentencia e conclusio del parlament, e en aquella
> safermaren: que la Güelfa continuament trametes e donas a Curial,
> no solament les coses necessaries a son despens, ans encar les
> voluntaries, per ço que, per pobretat, no hagues a perdonar a voler
> qui li vengues. E axi fonch mes en obra; car tantost fonch manat a
> Melchior que donas a Curial totes les coses que volgues, sens
> contradiccio alguna. (222)

The relationship between the Empress and Hipòlit is essentially
the same, in economic terms, as that between Curial and Güelfa.
Both Hipòlit and Curial are kept men. The heroes of the other
romances are also materially indebted to women, but the dependence is shown in less conspicuous terms. Zifar, for example, owes
everything to the Queen of Mentón, who bequeaths him both
political sovereignty and the riches of a prosperous kingdom (book
II). While Amadís and Tirant are not shown to be overtly dependent
on their beloved to the same degree as Curial, Hipòlit, and Zifar,
we know from the description of their respective backgrounds that
they are as poor as their counterparts in the other works. Amadís, at
first a penniless youth of unknown parentage, then a wandering
knight with no kingdom of his own, is objectively destitute in
comparison with Oriana, a fabulously wealthy princess-heiress.
Tirant, a wandering noble youth, which is to say a soldier of

fortune, relies completely on the expectation of eventual inheritance through his wife. Like Güelfa, Carmesina provides her lover with the means to shine in society, as we see in her deathbed confession to having taken money from her father's treasury to give to her lover, so that he could appear generous before other knights (chap. 676).

The situation of the lover kept by his rich mistress or aided by his rich wife makes for a kind of uxorilocal residence. The frequency of this sort of uxorilocal residence in the romances does not necessarily imply outright matriliny. In her analysis of residential variations in matrilineal groups, Kathleen Gough chooses as the criterion of comparison what she calls a 'residential unit'. This she defines as 'that localized group of kin whose members regularly coöperate in production and/or the distribution of products'. The actual composition of such units differs considerably from society to society. She groups the units into five types, noting that residential comparisons (based on a common hearth, shared dwelling, or homestead) 'proved less fruitful'. Units comprised in her typology include 'The elementary or [...] compound polygynous unit [...] centering about one man with his wife or wives and their unmarried dependents — often, but not necessarily their children'. This entity, corresponding more or less to the standard definition of the nuclear family of husband, wife, and their children, does not figure prominently in her list of surveyable analogues: only one in fifteen of the societies studied (the Tonga) present this configuration as the 'relatively self-sufficient coöperating unit (the homestead)' (Gough 1961e: 545–48).

Residential focus varies considerably within this group. It may be matrilocal, involving 'an older married couple, their daughters, daughters' husbands, and daughters' children'. It may consist of 'matrilocal extended kinship', with a 'sororilocally resident male head'. This consists of 'an older group of sisters, their husbands, unmarried sons, daughters, daughters' husbands, daughters' children, and sometimes granddaughters' husbands and children'. The 'sororilocal male head' is usually the eldest man (either brother or son) of the central group of sisters; he 'either lives permanently with the group or visits frequently to manage its affairs'. Yet another variation is the 'avunculocal extended kinship unit', comprising the 'adult men of a matrilineal descent group, together with their wives and unmarried children'. Significantly, the only residential type emphasizing the nuclear family to any degree, the Tonga, presents a residential pattern of free movement between hamlets (Gough 1961e: 546–47).

A study of the circumstances conducive to matrilocal residence suggests that neither division of labour (in favour of women vs men) nor status differentials between the spouses necessarily allows prediction of one residential pattern over the other. The authors did find, however, that there was a correlation between warfare and residence. Matrilocal societies tend to engage only in external warfare, i.e. with other peoples, as opposed to internal warfare (i.e. feud), which appears often to characterize patrilocal residence (Ember & Ember 1971: 580–92).

We have seen, in conjunction with our previous discussion of kindreds, bilateral descent, and matrilocal patterns of residence, that the domestic configuration characterized by Raymond Smith as 'matrifocal' is indeed 'mother-focused', with an emphasis on maternal child-rearing as the central activity of the domestic domain (Smith 1973: 139–40).[8] However, the matrifocal elements adduced by Smith — a focus on mothers and maternal roles, economic conditions which cause males to be absent from the home, the exclusion of men from child-rearing practices, even an apparent depreciation of conjugal solidarity — do not necessarily constitute evidence of matriliny in the strict sense (let alone of matriarchy).

These and the other residential patterns analysed by Gough are quite different from the configuration of the in-marrying male in the chivalric romances. At the same time, questions of post-marital residence are relevant to the analysis of a narrative's concepts of lineal descent. These concepts, in turn, help to explain the motivations of the characters. The heroes of the chivalric romance are poor and politically impotent. Their ladies are high-born, their rivals sovereign. The knight, in pursuit of his goals — in essence, economic independence and social prominence — is often shown to be materially beholden to his beloved. How are we to reconcile

---

[8] See also Smith's further discussion of what he calls the 'matrifocal bias' in his study of kinship and social class in Jamaica and Guyana (1988: 126–27 & 158–60).

the apparent ignominy of the gold-digger with the professed heroism of the knight errant?

The machinations of the lovers in these works constitute, we have seen, a scheme for achieving legitimacy in the face of 'the ostensible and dominant legality' (Peter Brooks's phrase) of agnatic biopolitics. Hypergamy and dowry are primary political implements in the agnatic toolkit. It is by appraisal of another such implement, the integrative aspect of agnatic marital policy, that we reconcile uxorilocal residence with both patrilineal and chivalric honour.

The marriage patterns described by Rheubottom, and before him by Hajnal, Herlihy & Klapisch-Zuber, and others, typify not only royal dynasties but propertied families in general. The natural concomitant of the calculus of advantage, they function as components of a single system, along with hypergamy and dowry. Two other factors come into play when we discuss the special status of the daughter who, as youngest of several sisters or as only child, is designated the familial heir. The first factor is the testamentary role of the heiress functioning as if she were the only son or eldest son within a system of primogeniture. The second factor is the tendency, when this system is employed, toward hypogamy, i.e. a marrying-down from the bride's viewpoint, a marrying-up from that of the groom.

Marriage to an heiress whose inheritance functions as an incentive for recruiting desirable sons-in-law is common in many societies. Genealogical literature is most instructive in this regard. Focusing on a treatise by Lambert de Wattrelos, Fernand Verkauteren notes that the author stresses the prestige of the maternal line. While confirming the bilateral nature of the implied kinship system, Lambert's account also hints at the prevalence within it of heiress-hunting and upward-bound marriage for ambitious males. Frequent references to male ancestors' marriages into houses more prestigious than their own confirm that the acquisition of fiefs through such advantageous matches was the principal means, in Lambert's family, of building up the family fortune (Verkauteren 1978: 96–97).

In some societies, the in-marrying son-in-law is considered a kind of adopted child, or is in fact adopted into his bride's family, as in the case of the Japanese *mukoyoshi*, the 'groom-foster-son', described by Pitt-Rivers as the 'adopted [...] husband for the daughter when there is no son or no suitable son to whom the patrimony can be entrusted' (Pitt-Rivers 1968: 408–09). Goody observes that this practice has usually been associated with what he calls 'filiacentric union', in which the man makes an uxorilocal marriage in a predominantly virilocal system. The in-marrying spouse is, in a sense, recruited for a bride who is the only child. In general, the husband is viewed as begetting children for the wife's lineage; the heiress is considered, in a sense, the 'appointed father', acting as a social male who produces children for her natal group, rather than for the husband's patrilineage (in patrilineal systems) or for both lineages (in bilateral systems). The practice tends to characterize communities where landed property and primogeniture are the rule, and where men, particularly disinherited younger brothers, are often obliged to marry an heiress in order to obtain land of their own. Generally, the bride does not inherit until after the death of the father, and the son-in-law, after administering his wife's domain during her lifetime, inherits upon her death. In Ireland the practice is called *cliamhan isteak* ('son-in-law marrying in'); in Modern Greece, *soghambros*; in France *faire le gendre*. It often implies, notes Goody, an upwardly mobile marriage for the man.[9]

The pattern of a male marrying in to a lineage without sons of its own has been named for the ancient Greek institution known as the *epiclerate*, in which the inheriting daughter was the transmitter of property and of lineal identity. Michael Gagarin remarks: 'The term *epikleros*, usually translated "heiress," applies only to a woman who in the absence of male heirs is temporarily "attached to the estate (*kleros*)" until some man, normally a relative of hers, marries her and takes control of the property, which will eventually pass to their offspring' (Gagarin 1986: 67 n. 72). Hallett distinguishes the Greek practice from Roman patterns of female inheritance. The Athenian heiress, "included in the paternal estate', was, at her father's death, expected to marry her father's *anchisteus*, i.e. his 'closest living male relative'. An heiress so defined

---

[9] Goody 1973a: 17–18 and 1973c: 12. Winch notes the tendency, within traditionally patrilineal Chinese society, of fathers without sons to seek young men of lower social rank who marry the older man's daughter, take his name, and adopt matrilocal residence (1968: 7).

was often obliged to divorce her present husband in order to marry the *anchisteus*. The male offspring of the new marriage so arranged 'would then inherit the dead man's estate'.[10]

The *epikleros*, then, could be demanded in marriage, along with the estate, by her nearest agnate. If the latter were already married, he divorced his previous wife to marry the heiress. His marriage to her converted him, as Levy phrases it, into the 'fiduciary custodian and usufructuary of the estate until the majority [...] of a son whom she might bear him'. The offspring of such a union 'would be regarded as continuing their maternal grandfather's *oikos*, despite the actual break in the lineal male succession'. If the heiress's nearest male relative did not wish to marry her himself, 'it was his duty to marry her off with the estate as her marriage portion' (Levy 1963: 139).

Raphael Sealey points out that the Athenian *epikleros* may be translated as 'heiress' only if we bear in mind that the daughter in question 'had no power to dispose of the property but was transferred with it' (1990: 29). In this, and in the stipulation that the appropriate spouse for the *epikleros* was the nearest male relative of her deceased father, the Athenian case differs from the more indiscriminate recruitment of sons-in-law in other patrilineal societies. The societies mentioned by Pitt-Rivers, Goody, Winch, and others (Greek, French, Irish, Japanese, Chinese), while differing among themselves, reveal, however, analogous practices that constitute what Goody calls a coherent 'strategy of heirship' (1973c: 3–7). Adjusting for diversity in social practice from culture to culture the term *epiclerate*, expanded and modified from its original ancient Greek context, is applicable to the circumstances of any context involving a fictive patrilineal continuity contrived through marrying-off the daughter 'with the estate as her marriage portion'.

The story of Zifar's rise from landless, kinless knight to king of Mentón, and of his relationship to his second wife and her family, corresponds precisely to the pattern of the son-in-law marrying in

---

[10] Hallett 1984: 74. See also Harrison 1968: 9–12 & 23 (cited by Hallett, 74 n. 17). Hallett summarizes David M. Schaps (1979: 39–42): 'the intention of the epiclerate was to ensure that fatherless and brotherless daughters were married, and hence guarantee that their father's *anchisteus* who became their *kyrios* not seek to profit from the estate by keeping them unwed' (74 n. 17).

to a family without male heirs. Zifar is, in effect, the champion in a tournament whose prize is the hand in marriage of the heiress of Mentón, and the eventual succession to the throne of her kingdom. The match corresponds, in socio-historical terms, to the medieval European pattern of upwardly mobile marriage by aristocratic males. The motives on both sides of the potential marital alliance are set forth in chap. 54, where the Ribaldo tells of the plight of the kingdom of Mentón and of the reward offered to the man who can be its saviour:

> 'Çertas', dixo el ribaldo, 'sepas que ayer pregonauan en aquella villa que de aqui paresçe, de commo el rey de Ester tene çercado en vna çibdad al rey de Mentón, que ha nonbre Grades... E este rey de Mentón enbio dezir e pregonar por toda su tierra que qualquier quel desçercase, quel daria su fija por muger e el regno despues de sus dias; ca non auia otro fijo'. (117)

The goal of the old king in *Zifar* is not simply to attract a protector, a deliverer from the immediate predicament. Such a purpose could have been served by the offer of many things — wealth, lands, title — short of marital alliance with the royal family. But the problem of the siege, however serious, is a short-term issue. The real danger to the kingdom is conveyed in the ribaldo's last sentence: 'ca non auia otro fijo'. The lineage of Mentón, in danger of extinction, is in desperate need of a son-in-law. While male heirs (i.e. brothers of the princess) would have been more desirable transmitters of lineal continuity, a good husband for the brotherless daughter will also serve.

In *Tirant*, the alliance of the French and Sicilian royal families reveals the potential benefit of all such marriages, and yet another instance — albeit deferred — of the phenomenon of a son-in-law 'marrying in' to a kingdom. The narrator digresses, amid other matters relating to Tirant's conflict with the treacherous Duke of Macedonia, to recall (519) that the King of Sicily had married his eldest son to a French princess. Because the young Sicilian prince was so 'discret e virtuós' the French king loved him and would not let him leave his side. Then the Sicilian prince sickened and died. Heartbroken at this news, the King of Sicily is dismayed to learn that the surviving, youngest son 'no volgué lleixar la religió per ésser rei aprés la mort del pare'. The old king, soon on his death bed, 'lleixà hereua la filla, muller de Felip'. The consequence of this turn of events is that Philip, the younger son of the French royal family, now 'se véu rei'.

The Greek empire in *Tirant*, like kingdoms in *Zifar*, *Amadís*, and *Curial*, is endangered both by the aggression of exterior enemies and by the recent loss of the heir to the throne. The Emperor reports, in his letter to the King of Sicily, that not only have the Infidels deprived him of 'ciutats, viles e castells'; he has also lost 'lo major bé que tenia en aquest món, ço és, lo meu fill primogènit' (366). Later he asks Carmesina, his daughter: '¿no sabeu vos que [...] des que lo meu fill és mort, no em resta més bé en aqueste miserable de món sinó a vós, qui sou consolació de la mia amarga e trista vida?' (387). The epiclerate is clearly implied in the scene in which Tirant explains to his imperial host that 'cosa és molt impròpia [...] que la filla qui és succeïdora en l'Imperi sia nomenada Infanta'. Why, demands Tirant, does the emperor 'li furta lo seu propi nom de Princesa?' For this reason, concludes the hero, 'li deu ésser mudat lo nom, com no pertanga sinó a filla de rei dir-li Infanta, si doncs no havia ésser heretera del Regne, que també la nomenarien Princesa' (388).

Still later, both ecclesiastical and clanic notions of the function of marriage are invoked by Plaerdemavida to pressure Carmesina into feeling guilty about her aloof treatment of Tirant. The specific aspect of lineage orientation alluded to by the handmaiden is the epiclerate. The princess is the sole heiress, the repository of lineal identity. Plaerdemavida demands of her mistress how she has responded to the opportunity presented by the death of her elder brother, which made her 'senyora de l'Imperi'. Amid this 'singular dignitat mundanal', has she taken a husband? Has she left behind sons 'perquè puguen defendre la fe catòlica e aumentar la crestiandat?' (742). The imperial clan plays a leading part in the struggle to defend Christendom. But the lineage is, as it were, the principal beneficiary of the religious perspective's legitimating aura. To defend the faith, one must assure the survival of the line. Christian ideology thus subsidizes clanic integrity.

The implications of the epiclerate are clearly set forth in the Emperor's enumeration of the conditions and incentives commensurate with Tirant's assumption of the title of Captain of the Empire. It is significant that this investiture precedes any knowledge by the Emperor of Tirant's liaison with Princess

Carmesina. The language of the declaration is that of kinship, as if Tirant were already an imperial affine. The Emperor's attitude reveals the fundamental motivation of spousal recruitment of a male of lower status, such as a knight errant, by a titled family without male heirs. Declaring that he has lost a son ('per haver perdut un tal cavaller e capità com era lo meu fill') and cannot, due to age, 'portar armes', he thanks Divine Providence for having seen fit to send Tirant, on whom rest all the hopes of the Empire ('en qui tota la nostra esperança resposa'). The surrogative role of the son-in-law as adopted son is made clear: the Emperor requires of the Breton hero that he exercise all possible 'saber i esforç' in furtherance both of the Emperor's personal honour and that of 'l'imperial patrimoni, e de tota la cosa pública'. All dukes, counts, marquises, and any others are henceforth to obey Tirant as they would the Emperor himself (425). The narrative makes it very clear that the marriage to Carmesina assures Tirant's eventual succession to the throne: after her declaration of love and of marital consent (782–3), the hero responds with 'goig inefable' to the news that he is surely 'en camí per poder posseir la corona de l'Imperi grec per mijà de les novelles esposalles' (784).

Plaerdemavida's exhortation to Tirant assumes that marriage, inheritance, and political succession are aspects of one operation. The notion of 'empire' implies a proprietary sense of the polity referred to; the Greek Empire is the patrimony of Carmesina's agnatic lineage. In addition to confirming the gravity of consent as an intrusion on the lineal principle, Plaerdemavida points out to the hero, in her tirade, the decisive political significance of his marriage to Carmesina:

> ¿E no est tu aquell príncep del llinatge de Roca Salada que estrist en batalla aquella plasent nit dins lo castell de Malveí, ab aquella sereníssima Princesa, la bella Carmesina? E [...] par-me que he oït dir, volent sa altesa suplir als teus graciosos precs e supliacions, volent ofendre a pare e a mare menyspreant la sua honestíssima castedat, consentí a tu a hora menyscabada, dins la sua cambra entrar, e posar-te la corona de son pare, la qual és de l'Imperi grec, en lo teu cap e pendre't per universal senyor. [...] (967)

Later, in her speech to Tirant's friend, the newly converted King Escariano, Plaerdemavida reiterates the hero's status: 'la tua senyoria ignora lo que jo sé en ell, com ell sia en sobiran grau

acostat a l'Imperi grec' (970). To be Carmesina's husband, in other words, is to enjoy the status of imperial heir. Plaerdemavida's speech in chap. 229 reveals much concerning the age of the princess, the concept within the community of the relationship established between a son-in-law and his bride's lineage, and the notion of incentives conducive to spousal recruitment:

> ¡Oh Déu, quina cosa és tenir la donzella tendra en sos braços, tota nua, d'edat de catorze anys! ¡Oh Déu, quina cosa és tenir pare emperador! ¡Oh Déu, quina cosa és tenir l'enamorada rica e lliberal, quítia de tota infàmia! (692)

Plaerdemavida clearly uses 'pare', father, to refer to the Emperor; 'father' is in other words a synonym for father-in-law in a case like Tirant's. The son-in-law marrying in, he becomes, in effect, a surrogate son, replacing the dead prince mentioned earlier. Later, the Emperor addresses him as 'Tirant fill' (1065). Tirant's expectation of ascending the throne of Constantinople through marriage to Carmesina is confirmed by her: 'Possessió e domini de tot l'Imperi', she announces, will fall to him as his 'patrimoni', since her father must abdicate: 'per ço com la sua edat [...] no és sufficient per a regir l'Imperi' (1115).

In another episode in *Tirant*, the narrator attributes motives to his Muslim characters that reveal his own notions of the nature of matrimonial strategy. We read of King Escariano, whose land borders on the Kingdom of Tlemcen. This king, we are told, wanted the daughter of the latter's kingdom's ruler: 'volia que li donàs sa filla per muller ab tot lo tresor que tenia, e aprés son obte li donàs tot lo regne' (848). The King of Tlemcen informs him that

> tenia esposada sa filla ab lo fill del Cabdillo sobre los cabdillos, e que ell no devia voler dona qui d'altri fos posseïda, e encara que la tenia prenyada, per què li consellava que en sa casa no volgués tenir ni criar fill d'altri; emperò que si ho feia per cobdícia del tresor ajustat que tenia, ell era content de partir ab ell perquè el lleixàs estar en pau a ell e a sos fills. (848–89)

To this King Escariano replies that he will accept nothing less than 'sa filla ab lo tresor' (849), claiming the validity of a verbal contract between himself and the King of Tlemcen: 'no ha gran temps que és estat tractat per algunes nobles persones matrimoni, ab deliberat consell de cascuna de les parts, de sa filla ab mi, e ferma, segura e donada jornada de dar compliment al matrimoni' (863).

In the conflict arising from Escariano's desire for the Princess of Tlemcen and her inheritance, the Cabdillo sobre los cabdillos ('Chief of chiefs'), exhorts his son, who is betrothed to the princess: 'Tu deus ésser més desijós de la mort que no ésser desposseït de l'esposada, la qual ve de tan gran e alta sang' (849). Here are depicted both the epiclerate and a very clear instance of the calculus of advantage. The princess and all she represents constitute the prize sought by the Cabdillo. He even hints that she matters more than his own son, as we see in the promises he makes to Tirant in order to encourage the hero to intervene: 'Si tu a mi feies aqueix tan gran servir, e ma nora ab son esposat que jo els tingués a ma volentat, de tots mos béns te faria senyor' (855).

The most calculating example of the epiclerate (allowing for an extension of that term to the case of a remarrying widow) is perhaps that of Tirant's nephew Hipòlit, the lover of the Greek Empress. The narrator describes his reaction to the deaths of the Emperor, Princess Carmesina, and the hero:

> E no us penseu que en aquell cas Hipòlit tingués gran dolor; car de continent que Tirant fon mort, llevà son compte que ell seria emperador, e molt més aprés la mort de l'Emperador e de sa filla, car tenia confiança de la molta amor que l'Emperadriu li portava que, tota vergonya a part posada, lo pendria per marit e per fill. [...] (1171)

The epiclerate, holding out the prospect of an advantageous situation for the successful suitor, represents the jackpot for both disinherited younger sons and impatient heirs-apparent. In *Amadís*, the epiclerate underlies Galvanes Sin Tierra's fervent desire to marry Madasima, the heiress of the Isle of Mongaça. Their union provokes the fateful war between the forces of Amadís, who support Galvanes in his marital aspirations, and those of Lisuarte, who seeks to retain the island as an inheritance of his younger daughter Leonoreta. When the fleet sent forth from the Ínsula Firme comes to her rescue, a grateful Madasima presents Galvanes to her subjects, telling them to kiss his hand:

> Besadlas a mi señor y mi marido don Galuanes, que después de Dios él me libró de la muerte, y me ha hecho cobrar a vosotros que soys mis naturales, y contra toda razón vos tenía perdidos, y a él

tomad por señor si a mí amáys. (III, 676.1243–49)

The epiclerate is portrayed as a reward for services rendered. We may thus speak of the siege of Mentón — or the rescues of other damsels similarly besieged, including Oriana in *Amadís* — as tests of spousal candidates. Whoever shows himself heroic enough to perform the appointed task will be doubly useful: in the short term as deliverer of the kingdom; in the long term as saviour of the lineage.

In chap. 77 of *Zifar* the king of Mentón asks his daughter if the newcomer deserves the prize destined for the saviour of the kingdom, namely her hand in marriage. The deeds of the valiant newcomer, she exclaims, seem superhuman ('non de ome terrenal'). The man declared to be responsible for rescuing the city, the king reminds her, is to be her husband: 'en juyzio abremos a entrar para saber quien desçerco esta villa, e aquel vos abremos a dar por marido.' Of this, she cries, there can be no doubt: 'todos estos buenos fechos el Cauallero de Dios los fizo; e sy non por el, que quiso Dios que lo acabase, non podieramos ser desçercados tan ayna' (159–60).

The suitor in such cases is the saviour of the lineage in to which he marries. In *Tirant* this soteric element (functioning in the religious and political as well as familial dimensions) is clearly expressed in Carmesina's prayer in chapter 278. She prays to Jesus Christ, redeemer of 'l'humanal linatge':

> Que plàcia a la sacratíssima majestat vostra de voler deixar posseir aquesta corona a mon senyor Tirant, qui ací present és, ab títol e senyor de tot l'Imperi grec aprés obte de mon pare, puix la divina bondat vostra li ha feta gràcia d'haver-lo cobrat e de poder d'infels lliberat. (792)

Later the utility of the epiclerate will be accentuated still further, as the Emperor makes official what Tirant and Carmesina have already accomplished secretly: 'vos volem', exclaims the Emperor, 'dar nostra filla Carmesina per muller'. Offering to 'fer donació de tot l'Imperi', he informs Tirant that since he, the Emperor, can no longer defend his Empire, he must rely on Tirant's 'virtut e cavalleria'. Confident that the Breton will be for him 'més que fill' (1117), the Emperor commands his daughter to take him as her 'marit e senyor' (1118).

The Emperor, as if to assure the whole world of the stability of both his Empire and his line, orders a proclamation of the significance of this betrothal: 'cridar féu per tota la ciutat [...] que tots tinguessen a Tirant per primogònit seu e Cèsar de l'Imperi'. It is furthermore to be sworn by all subjects of the Emperor that, 'aprés son òbit, lo tinguessen per Emperador e senyor llur' (1119–20). The proclamation announces to the people that the Emperor had thought to abdicate, handing over the reins of power in his lifetime: 'havia deliberat la imperial bondat e lliberal senyoria, de vida sua, renunciar al sobredit famós Capità e magnànim cavaller l'Imperi e deguda senyoria'. This the great Captain, moved by 'la sua presència e estuciosa cavalleria', had not permitted, declaring himself content with 'sols la successió [...] e l'esposalici' with the Princess. This arrangement, the crier proclaims, is for the 'prosperitat i glòria' of all the subjects of the empire (1120).

The practice of son-in-law marrying in can apply, as we have seen, to widows as well as unmarried heiresses. Both are shown to be the frequent object of amorous attentions. The Empress in *Tirant*, for example, is at first an adulterous wife, later a widow who marries her lover Hipòlit in a marriage of state. Güelfa, the widowed younger sister of Curial's patron, is described as 'joue, tendra, rica e cobeiada per molts', a condition that provokes her brother the Duke of Monferrata, the head of their lineage, to order her return to Monferrata, for fear of scandal (7).

The function of marriage as an all-purpose instrument of political control and property transmission is clearly shown in the scene coming soon after Hipòlit's secretly happy reaction to Tirant's death. Pointing out to the assembled kings and barons the need to resolve the Empress's situation ('Si bé la sua edat és avançada, algun gran senyor se casarà ab ella de bona voluntat'), he suggests that one among them be named the new emperor, 'e aquest tal heretaria molt bé a tots los altres' (1173). To this Hipòlit's kinsman Diafebus, Duke of Macedonia, replies (1173) that their choice is clear, since Tirant, their 'bon parent e senyor', expressed in his will the desire to bequeath 'tots los drets que ha guanyats en l'Imperi grec e tots los que per l'Emperador li són estats atorgats' to his nephew Hipòlit. Furthermore, he observes, Princess Carmesina assigned all her rights to her mother. Their course, therefore, is obvious:

que atesa l'amistat antiga que tots sabem que Hipòlit té ab
l'Emperadriu, que la prenga per muller, e alçar-lo hem emperador, e
farem justícia. E aquest, per sa bondat e virtut, nos conservarà cascú
en son heretatge, car és de la nostra sang. (1174)

The romances are preoccupied with circumvention, in furtherance of spousal recruitment, of the hypergamic principle. Sometimes this avoidance of hypergamy suits the bride, sometimes her
family. Occasionally all parties are satisfied. This circumvention of
hypergamy presupposes the absence of dowry. The latter
phenomenon, as we have seen, is frequently mentioned in the
chivalric romances. However, it is not mentioned in connection
with the marriage of the hero to his beloved. Moreover, the heroes
of the romances, and many other male characters in the texts,
contribute nothing in the way of material prestations to their brides'
lineages. The absence of such transactions, as has been frequently
noted by ethnographic researchers, is as significant as their
presence. Dowry, generally linked with hypergamy, constitutes a
disbursement that effectively dissociates the bride from the patrimony of her family of origin. Patterns of post-marital residence in
the romances (but not necessarily those of the hero and his
beloved) confirm the asymmetrical political and economic relationships implied by hypergamy. For example, we note that virilocality
(residence with the husband's kin) is assumed in *Amadís* to go with
hypergamous marriage. This is seen both in the wedding plans and
in the intended post-nuptial residence contemplated by Patín when
he sends for Oriana (III, p. 76).

The chivalric marrying-up portrayed in the romances involves
none of the principal types of groom-initiated marriage prestation
(e.g. bridewealth, *Morgangabe*). This, we might suppose, accepting
the hypothesis of Hughes, is because the dotal regime, implying
such things as asymmetrical prestations, complex social stratification, and hypergamy, had completely taken over by the time of
composition.[11] The protagonists — indeed, most male characters —
are heiress hunters who have nothing material to furnish, and feel
no obligation to provide conventional wedding prestations. But
may we speak of a complete absence of prestations in the case of
the chivalric hero? Although none of the characters contributes, for

---

[11] Hughes's concept is endorsed by Goody 1983: 255–56.

example, anything like bridewealth, and while the predominant tendency seems to be toward hypergamy and its concomitant, dowry — as typified by the case of Oriana, and numerous secondary personages — we may consider the symbolic capital which the impecunious knight could bring to the hypogamous match.

In their cross-cultural study of marriage transactions, Schlegel and Eloul note that 'bride service [consisting of] the transfer of labor rather than goods', is contributed 'by the groom to the bride's family'. For this reason it is often grouped with bridewealth as a kind of marital prestation. The groom may work 'for the bride's father for a period of time to earn the right to remove his wife' (the case of the biblical Jacob's marriage to Leah and Rachel). Another possibility is that 'brideservice elides into matrilocal residence [in which] it is difficult to tell whether the groom is earning the bride or simply working as a member of his parents-in-laws' household, which is also his own' (Schlegel & Eloul 1988: 293).

It is in light of the concept of bride service as a prestation offered by the knight that we must evaluate the resolution of the conflict between Lisuarte and Amadís. The former considers the significance of the death of the emperor, his intended son-in-law, in terms of the virtues of the man who prevented that marriage, namely his daughter's beloved:

> y que si con él y con su deudo ganaua honrra, que mucho más con el deudo de Amadís la ternía, assí como por la esperiencia muchas vezes lo hauía visto, y con esto, demás de recebir descanso, assí en su persona como en su reyno, creçería en tanta honrra que ninguno en el mundo su ygual fuesse. [...] (IV, 1126.543–51)

Hypogamous marriage, portrayed as advantageous to both the bride and her family, occurs frequently in the romances. Like many other social phenomena already discussed, such as cousinship, it is an assumed feature of the social landscape. Thus, among many casual examples of hypogamous spousal recruitment accompanied by epiclerate, we mention the one recounted by the governor of the Isle of the Infante, in *Amadís*. The governor explains the island's history to the hero, describing how King Cildadán of Ireland once ruled over it:

> era infante qu'el señorío della tenía sin tener otro heredamiento alguno. Y más por su gran esfuerço y buenas maneras que por su estado embió por todo el reyno de Yrlanda para lo casar con la fija

del rey Abies, que aquel reyno heredó al tiempo que lo mató
Amadís de Gaula [...] (IV, 1254.149–57).

The theme of the humble knight's superiority, by virtue of his
personal abilities, over the inherited, ascribed status of royalty or
nobles, pervades the chivalric romance. The marriage of Galaor to
Briolanja is, strictly speaking, hypogamous since he is the younger
son of a king, while she is a queen and heiress to a throne. Yet his
personal traits entitle him to consideration as a suitor: 'su gran
valor, así en armas como en todas las otras buenas maneras que el
mejor cauallero del mundo deuía tener'. Galaor's individual
qualities cause her to transfer to him the love and devotion she has
hitherto felt toward his brother Amadís: 'todo el grande amor que a
su hermano Amadís tenía puso con este cauallero que ya por
marido tenía' (IV, 1200.487–502).

In a comparable passage in *Tirant*, Estefania exhorts Carmesina
to appreciate the superiority of Tirant as a suitor (450): '¿qui és
aquell qui mereix ésser digne de portar corona d'emperador sinó
Tirant? ¿Qui és aquell qui és mereixedor d'ésser vostre marit sinó
Tirant?' Her tirade continues, as she assures the princess that she
will someday regret her foolish scruples and hesitations. Tirant, she
declares, does not love Carmesina 'per los béns ne per la dignitat',
but rather for her 'virtuts'. In all the world, affirms Estefania,
Carmesina will not find 'cavaller qui ab ell se puga egualar'.
Tirant, in short, is perfect: 'valentíssim en les armes, lliberal,
animós, savi e destre en totes coses més que tot altre'.

Curial is the son of a 'gentil hom', 'senyor duna casa baxa' (4).
His father having died, and seeing that his mother could offer him
no hope of escaping poverty ('li feu auorrir aquella vida'), the lad
makes his way — 'pobrement e a peu' to the court of the Marquis
of Monferrat (4–5). He thus begins his climb with more handicaps
than any of the knights in the other texts. Soon his inherent worth
makes Güelfa begin to fall in love with him. She recounts to him
'diuerses nouelles, com los homens per diuerses accidents, moltes
vegades, de pobre estat venen a esser grans homens' (10–11). After
Curial has defended the Duchess of Austria in judicial combat
against a charge of adultery, the Emperor, who has presided over
the combat, declares to Curial that the Duke of Bavaria would not
be doing badly, considering the honour that Curial has done him (in

defending the Duke's daughter), if he gave to Curial the half of his duchy (42–43).

Families of high social standing require minimal status qualifications of an in-marrying spouse in order to exercise the option of implementing the epiclerate. Curial satisfies these prerequisites. Although poor, he is of good family. Güelfa's rival Laquesis, also in love with Curial, justifies her love for this young man (dismissed by her mother, we have seen, as not 'couinent'): 'Curial, cert es a tots [...] esser fill de gentil home e de gentil linage, e com vos e yo'. Furthermore, she notes, he has earned the respect of the world (through his chivalric accomplishments and his acceptance at various royal courts): 'lo veem en gentil e fort noble estat; lo coneguem fauorit per l'Emperador' (236). Laquesis, in effect, consciously exalts both the utility of her patrimony (deployed as a dowry) in attracting a spouse, and the importance of achieved status in selecting a mate. Seeing him already 'forts rich e tots temps en real estat', she declares, he lacks only one thing:

> fall li, donchs, la heretat: mon pare lay ha proferta, e com lay hage donada, tant valdra e mes que ell. E, si mon pare no hauia heretat ¿valdria tant com Curial? Certes, no, car Curial, sens heretat, val molt. Donchs, com haura heretat, mes valdra que altre, que en ma fe ja ho val. (237–38)

The theme of the knight's inherent personal superiority, exalting achieved over ascribed status, facilitates the related practices of epiclerate and spousal recruitment. The chivalric romances' depiction of these practices correlates with Duby's model of the medieval European marriage market. Enforced celibacy among younger sons, and the general tendency to marry off daughters as soon as possible, increased the chances — for those lineages which sought a good match for an elder or only son. 'Ainsi se renforce encore', argues Duby, 'cette structure des sociétés nobles, où généralement l'épouse sort d'une parenté plus riche et plus glorieuse que celle de son mari' (Duby 1977a: 30).

Duby explained the shortage of men in the marriage market of the earlier French context in terms of the demographics of the medieval youth culture, which included disinheritance of younger sons, and attrition resulting from the chronic violence of tournaments, vendettas, and feudal warfare (1973a: 215–21 and 1973c: 270–82). Herlihy and Klapisch-Zuber, describing the Florentine and Tuscan society of two to three centuries later, report a similar imbalance in the ratio of potential grooms to brides, with a coinciding tendency toward hypogamous marriages and resulting positive social mobility for males so married. The dearth of husbands is aggravated not by violent life-style, as in the earlier feudal setting analysed by Duby, but by a pervasive tendency among men to postpone marriage and its attendant obligations. So drastic was the shortage of husbands, that dowries were generally used not to engineer advantageous alliances for the bride's family of origin (as in the ideal dotal system outlined earlier in this chapter), but rather to engage in competitive recruitment of husbands (Herlihy & Klapisch-Zuber 1985: 226–28). A ruinous escalation in the size of dowries (often representing a surrender of more than ten per cent of the family's property) prompted families to marry off daughters at the youngest possible age, 'out of anxiety to settle their fate' (223).[12]

Because of the pyramidal nature of status hierarchies, the number of lower-level heiresses (from the viewpoint of any given heiress hunter) will be greater than the number of higher-level ones. Populations grow more rarefied as one approaches the top of the status pyramid. Higher-level groups restrict membership because to do otherwise is to debase the coinage of status honour. *Infanzones*, therefore, must outnumber *ricos ombres*. This fact, in conjunction with the realities of dowry and hypergamy as a preferential rule of marriage, paradoxically insures the frequency of hypogamic marriages. For at the same time that there are disinherited sons of the lesser nobility on the lookout for brides of superior status, there is also a corresponding scarcity of suitable males in the status group of any given heiress, owing to hypergamy. If the males in her group tend to marry both down and up, the higher-status heiress (whether youngest daughter or only child) has a greater likelihood of herself marrying down, given that there

---

[12] The diverse workings of dowry in various regions of the Peninsula are confirmed by Carmen Orcastegui Gros (1984: 15–17). Milagros Rivera Garretas substantiates the correlation of dowry and effective female disinheritance (1984: 20–22), as well as its close connection to inter-lineal alliance (24). María Asenjo González points out the tendency toward extravagant dowries in the higher and middle nobility, as well as the dowry's attendant disinheritance of the bride (1984: 112–13).

are always more candidates in the inferior strata. And the more prestigious the family, the more likely this will be.

It is the value of the daughter in the marriage market that determines her father's perception of the utility of her spouse's status. As we have seen, daughters differ in marriage-market value according to their age, their order of birth among siblings, or their lack of siblings, particularly brothers. There is, then, no such thing, from the viewpoint of agnatic strategy, as absolute status in a suitor. A suitor's status depends on the functions assigned to the daughter intended for him. In the case of a daughter assigned the function of hypergamic enhancement of lineal influence and prestige, the groom's inherent social status is pivotal. By contrast, a daughter's designation as the *epikleros* makes a groom's status a secondary consideration. A suitor's high status can even, in some circumstances, be perceived as a hazard to a bride's lineage.

The findings of Duby with regard to the French nobility, of Herlihy/Klapisch-Zuber, and Rheubottom with respect to Florentine and northern Italian society, show that families felt impelled to marry off daughters as expeditiously as possible, while arranging the best possible match under the circumstances. Daughters were preferably married 'up-and-out', in keeping with the notions of marriage as a political and economic relationship between lineages, and of filiafocality as a guiding principle in the maintenance of family honour. Conditions favouring the selection of a suitor on the basis of personal qualities and achievement, rather than on the ascribed status of his lineage, were reinforced by the Church's 'pro-choice' approach to marriage. Summarizing a family chronicle and genealogical treatise on the origins of the lords of Ardres, Duby describes a 'mythical ancestress [portrayed] as a virgin, an orphan, alone, desolate and destitute'. When the Count of Guines, the overlord of her land, seeks to arrange an unwanted marriage, she takes refuge with her uncle, a bishop. He arranges a good marriage, finding her 'a good knight', a man 'equal to the task of protecting the land' (Duby 1978: 99).[13]

The contrast between inherited rank and standing attained through personal aptitude is repeatedly stressed in the romances.

---

[13]　Asenjo González discusses for the Castilian context — although in less explicit terms than those employed by Duby — the recruitment of spouses into lineage for purposes of internal consolidation (1984: 110–11).

Informed by his grandfather that their family is of a 'linaje de reys', the young Zifar asks how their line had fallen from such heights, to which the old man replies that a certain evil ancestor, 'por maldad e por malas obras', was deposed and replaced by 'vn cauallero sinple, pero que era muy buen ome e de buen seso natural e amador de justiçia e conplido de todas buenas costunbres' (33). *Zifar* expresses in fairy-tale form a principle of meritorious promotion which underlies the romances' concept of courtship and marriage.

Amadís, arriving in Constantinople after his defeat of the dreaded Endriago, is greeted by the Emperor himself. Acknowledging the hero's superiority, the Emperor clearly distinguishes between achievement and ascription:

> comoquiera que Dios me aya fecho tan grande hombre y venga del linaje de aquellos que este señorío tan grande tuuieron, más merescéys vos la honrra que la yo merezco, que vos la ganastes por vuestro gran esfuerço, passando tan grandes peligros qual nunca otro passó; y yo tengo la que me vino durmiendo y sin merescimiento mío. (III, 812.293–303)

The Queen of Tunis, offering herself and her kingdom to Tirant, explains that her attraction to him is based entirely on his abilities. Even the gift of her love, she states, cannot suffice to reward him for what he is worth and what he deserves ('suficient premi al que tu tant vals e merites'). She implores him to take her as his wife, becoming the lord of her country and of her person, in compensation for his labours. This reward is all the more appropriate, given Tirant's evident superiority to all other men: 'verdaderament est mereixedor de molt de bé i honor, molt més que tots los reis e prínceps qui hui porten corona' (898).

Appreciation of the hero's exploits is often expressed by the character of the highest ascribed status. Thus, the Emperor in *Curial* expresses admiration for the hero in terms reminiscent of those employed by the Emperor in *Amadís* and *Tirant*'s Tunisian queen: 'Çertes, yo anch no viu pera liça e pera cambra, sino aquest; e, per ma fe, es gran dan de tot lo mon, que aquest non es senyor. A, malayta sia la ffortuna, que aquest caualler no ha mes en pus noble estat!' (46). In another significant passage in *Curial*, the King of France debates with the two jealous old courtiers, the nemeses of Curial since his arrival in the court of Monferrat. Seeking to influence him against their hated enemy, they emphasize

his ascriptive limitations: 'es fill de vn pobre gentil home, quaix
que anaue a les almoynes'. This upstart, they explain, has had the
temerity to court the sister of his lord, the Marquis, 'en manera que
ell li roba [...] la honor e fama' (267). The king, seeing through
their malice, replies that Güelfa 'te lo millor e pus valeros seruidor
que sia en lo mon'. If Güelfa has freely provided Curial with her
riches, 'ell los mereix molt be'. Among the knights known to him,
the king declares, Curial has no equal:

> car aquest es caualler en parlar e en obrar, en en plaça e en cambra,
> e en liça e en tot loch. Daltra part, es molt abte e virtuos, saui e de
> gran e notable consell [...] E veig que son fet ira de be en millor, car
> es tan diligent, que no pert temps; car, com armes se fan en
> qualseuol manera, ell es dels primers e sen porta la honor. (269)

In his enumeration of the aspects of what we would call Curial's
achieved status, the king does not neglect the hero's abilities 'en
cambra cantar, dançar e solaçar curialment', nor his scholarly
knowledge ('tracta tan reuerencialment los libres'), nor his physical
beauty ('bell e la persona, e gracios'). In short, concludes the king,
only 'malicia o enueia' could prevent the old courtiers from seeing
the 'valor e moltes virtuts de que Deus copiosament la fet rich', or
induce them to suggest that 'Güelfa pert per ell matrimoni'. Curial,
he points out, could obtain the wife of his choice. Therefore, he
affirms, they should recall that 'la costuma de la cualleria e de la
sciencia es tal, que auancen los homens de pobre estat, els fan
grans seynors' (269–70).

Later, the faith of the king in Curial (as well, the narrator clearly
shows, as that of Güelfa) will be justified by the hero's valiant
defence of the Byzantine empire, his appointment by the Greek
emperor himself as Imperial Constable (426), and eventually as
'Duch e capita de moltes gents' as well. Curial becomes the
respected collaborator of the Emperor, and of 'tots los Reys e
Princeps, Duchs, Senyors e grans Barons' (428). The exaltation of
achieved status is made complete by the response of that same
Marquis of Monferrat, Güelfa's brother, who had once been
Curial's lord. A witness to Curial's triumph, he hesitates to come
forward: 'Torbas tot, e viu que ell no era res, en esguart de Curial,
e menys seria si a ell se mostras' (428). Eventually, after the
betrothal of Curial and Güelfa, sponsored and presided over the by
French king himself, the hero will receive from the monarch 'lo

Principat dOrenge'. This triumph, the narrator assures us, is the
well earned reward of a knight who, 'nat en pobre casa, fauorit de
la Ffortuna apres de infinits infortunis, per les sues virtuts', and
despite 'los assalts secrets de la iniqua e porfidiosa Enueia',
deserved at last to obtain 'Principat e muller' (456).

The status implications of the epiclerate and of hypogamy are
frequently expressed in *Amadís*. An old retainer of the slain knight
Antebón tells Galaor how Antebón came to the land 'y por su
bondad' (i.e. his courage and worthiness as a mate) was married to
the lady of the castle (I, 216.283–87). Amadís enjoins Grovenesa to
concede the boon she had earlier promised (not knowing his
identity), demanding that she wed Angriote de Estravaus: 'que
caséys con tal hombre qual deue casar dueña fermosa y de gran
guisa como lo vos soys' (I, 255–56.409–12). King Lisuarte points
out to Grovenesa: 'si vos soys muy rica de auer, él lo es de bondad
y virtud, assí en armas como en todas las otras buenas maneras que
buen cauellero deue hauer' (I, 256.450–4). The Irish princess
already mentioned, the daughter of Abies, marries after his death
the impoverished but worthy young knight Cildadán (possessed of
'gran esfuerço y buenas maneras'), as the result of a kingdom-wide
search 'por todo el reyno de Yrlanda para lo casar con la fija del
rey Abies, que aquel reyno heredó al tiempo que lo mató Amadís
de Gaula [...]' (IV, 1254.154–57).

Hypogamy as a matrimonial option allows the woman latitude in
judging the personal attainments of potential spouses. Pondering
the physical beauty and martial prowess of the Knight of the Green
Sword (Amadís), the Bohemian princess Grasinda (a widow, like
the Lady of Galapia in *Zifar*, and like Güelfa) reflects:

> Y comoquiera que ella tan fermosa y tan rica fuesse, y de tal linaje
> como sobrina del rey Tafinor de Bohemia y casada con vn gran
> cauallero, con el qual no biuió sino vn año sin dexar fijo alguno,
> determinó de lo auer por marido, ahunque dél otra cosa no veya
> sino ser vn cauallero andante. (III, 787.356–65)

Reckoning advantage according to a subtler criterion than mere
status, Plaerdemavida entreats the Emperor to give his daughter
Carmesina to Tirant, pointing out the practical virtues of so valiant
a knight: '¿Què em valria a mi que fos ajustada al linatge de David,
e per falta de bon cavaller perdre lo que tinc? E tu, senyor, hages
desig d'armar l'ànima [...] e no tingues esperança de dar a ta filla

altre marit [... que] al virtuós de Tirant. Hages aquesta consolació en ta vida' (694). She then points out to the princess herself that the latter has no time to spare, if she would not lose so impressive a match as Tirant. Plaerdemavida here invokes the notion of Church-sanctioned individual consent. What differentiates her notion of consent from a strictly ecclesiastic concept is the nuance of 'last resort' that underlies her appeal:

> Tu, qui est d'alta sang eixida, pren marit tost e ben tost; e si ton pare no te'n dóna, si no jo te'n daré; e no et daré sinó a Tirant, car gran cosa és, marit e cavaller, qui el pot haver en sa vida. Aquest, de proesa passa a tots los altres, car moltes voltes s'és seguit que per un sol cavaller són estats fets molts actes singulars, e portades a fi moltes conquestes qui de principi anaven a total destrucció. (694)

In *Zifar* and the other romances the ordeals and vicissitudes of the hero test not only the suitor but the ruler-to-be as well. The emphasis is on the son-in-law's contributions to the host lineage. At the same time, the reciprocal benefits of such matches are not forgotten. *Zifar*'s marriage to the princess of Mentón provides the mechanism by which the hero comes into a kingdom, thus regaining the prominence once enjoyed by his line. At the same time, his succession assures political stability in his adopted realm, and a fictive continuity for the lineage into which he marries.

The elements of *Zifar*'s story — epiclerate, bride service, and hypogamous marriage — are common folkloric themes. Thus, in one of the continental versions of *Bueves de Hantone*, yet another in the great family of texts centred on the theme of 'The Man Tried by Fate' (which includes the first two books of *Zifar*), we see the presence of the epiclerate in the marriage proposal of the princess of Sevilla. 'Li besoins [...] de boin mari', she declares, compels her to her declaration. If she can have him 'a per et a mari', she will be delivered from the predicament that has made her throw herself at him: 'Par vous seront destruit mi anemi' (ll. 9581–85). The queen concludes her offer by stating the two factors calculated to attract the prospective husband: 'Mon cors vous doins et le roialme ausi' (9595) (Stimming 1911–20: I).

The motif of the endangered princess saved by a heroic future husband is the medieval chivalric expression of the folkloric commonplace of 'testing the suitors'. In Bourdieu's terms, this traditional theme dramatizes the conflict between alliance and integration, while favouring the latter. Stith Thompson's *Motif-Index of Folk Literature* shows numerous items under the heading 'Marriage Tests' (H300–499). Under the sub-heading 'Suitor tests' (H310–59) he lists such items as the requirement of suitors to present themselves publicly (H311); physical and mental requirements of the groom (H312); long terms of service imposed as a condition of marriage (H317); the suitor's skills, cleverness, learning, and endurance (H326–28). A significant entry under this heading is that type of suitor test involving a contest as condition of the bride's hand in marriage, such as a horse or foot race, the climbing of a glass mountain, etc. (H331). The offer of the kingdom (or portion of the kingdom) serves as the incentive for the accomplishment of many kinds of task in folk literature; the rescue of an endangered or missing princess (Q112) is only one sub-category of this type.

A prominent medieval Spanish expression of the theme occurs in the tale the Count of Provence's selection of a son-in-law, in *enxemplo* 25 of *El conde Lucanor*. Saladín's advice to the Count is to seek out someone who is above all — regardless of lineage, wealth, or power — a man. For, as Saladín declares, 'más de preçiar [es] el omne por las sus obras que non por su riqueza, nin por nobleza de su linaje' (150–52). Having been chosen over many prominent rivals, the young man, not content to benefit from what amounts to the ascribed status of his selection as most appropriate suitor, decides to rescue his father-in-law from the polite captivity in which he is held by the Saracen lord. The young man is determined to show that 'pues Saladín lo escogiera por omne, et le fiziera allegar a tan gran onra, que non sería él omne si non fiziesse en este fecho lo que pertenesçía' (Juan Manuel 1985: 152). Patronio summarizes the underlying principle, stating that unless a son-in-law is 'buen omne en sí' a daughter cannot be well married 'por onra, nin por riqueza, nin por fidalguía que aya'. Moreover, he concludes, 'el omne con vondad acreçenta la onra et alça su linage et acreçenta las riquezas' (156).

The conspicuous filiafocality of this theme does not justify classifying the society represented in any given story as matrilineal or matriarchal. Cristina González, for example, interprets the chivalric hero's tendency to marry a princess-heiress, in *Zifar*, *Amadís*, and other romances, as a sign of 'vestigial matriarchy'.

Basing her interpretation on the matriarchist theories of Bachofen and Frazer, she describes the folkloric pattern of female succession to the throne. The husband of the queen, she argues, 'pasaba a ser el nuevo rey, matando con frecuencia al viejo'. The hero, submitting to tests of his worthiness, does not always kill the old king, 'sino que muchas veces se sustituye por una cesión pacífica del trono o por una muerte natural o una muerte en la guerra'. At other times, she affirms, we have a 'mixed regime', with the old represented by the 'traspaso del poder de suegro a yerno', and the new by a 'traspaso del poder de padre a hijo'. As the present essay has demonstrated, the inheritance patterns she mentions (father-in-law to son-in-law, father-to-son) are equally explicable with reference to the various stratagems employed by agnatic lineages (González 1984: 122–23).[14]

The meaning of folk motifs such as that of the suitor's test varies according to audience. The suitor's test may mean one thing for a tribal, kin-ordered society, another for a society on its way toward state-stratification. In the romances, the dilemma, from the viewpoint of the heiress's father and family, involves more than finding her a husband. It involves finding a worthy husband, one chosen above all for his personal qualities and prowess, rather than for the ascribed status of his lineage. In that sense, hypogamy was an escape from the tyranny of arranged marriages, which traditionally and by their very nature pay little heed to the inherent worth of the groom, concentrating instead on the political and honorific advantages of the match, in terms of the quality of affinal alliance ensuing between the lineages of bride and groom.

The theme of the heiress besieged — as expressed, for example, in *Tirant* — does not, therefore, reflect the 'primitivism' of the romances. The precarious situation of the heiress and the widow seems a thoroughly contemporary topic to every generation. Thus, the Greek Empress herself becomes the potential victim of the hostile attentions of aggressive suitors, after the deaths of her

---

[14] See chap. 3, n. 5 for commentary on the matriarchalist theory. The author of *Zifar* reworked a number of themes present in his sources, some of which were of ancient or non-European provenance. These themes included the hero's second marriage to an heiress-princess. However, the *Zifar* author modified his material so as to conform to social practices intelligible to his audience (see Harney 1989–90: 580–88).

husband, her daughter, and her son-in-law. Hipòlit, in his speech to the assembled kings and barons, points this out: 'Si bé la sua edat és avançada, algun gran senyor se casarà ab ella de bona voluntat, e ho tendrà a gràcia per ésser emperador' (1173).

The theme of the suitor's test is adaptable to any stratified society in which matrimonial arrangement is a familial necessity. A parallel theme is that of rejection of the fatuous suitor of high status but scant personal charm. This theme is implicit throughout *Tirant*. A humorous instance is found in the passage in which Princess Ricomana toys with the idea of falling in love with Tirant's companion, Prince Philip of France. However, she finds the young man somewhat coarse and a little gauche, despite his impeccable social credentials. She replies to Tirant's praises of his friend by an insistence on a woman's right to seek a perfect match:

> si naturalment li ve d'ésser grosser de sa pròpia natura, ¿quin plaer, quina consolació pot ésser a una donzella que tothom se riga d'ell, e li donen sus i mat en la darrera casa? Por amor de mi digau tal raó, car per mon delit volria home qui fos entès e comportaria ans en estat i en llinatge e que no fos grosser ni avar. (309)

Lineage and social standing are factors in her choice. But so are the personal attributes of the suitor. Hence her misgivings concerning the prince. 'L'experiència me manifesta que és', she declares, 'aquell que jo contemple, d'ésser grosser e avar, les quals dos malalties són incurables' (310). She takes essentially the same attitude about choosing a husband as that recommended by Saladín to the Count of Provence, save that she has a more practical and less heroic criterion. Hence her subsequent intention to test the young prince by observing his table manners at a feast she arranges 'per provar a Felip e veure en son menjar quin comport feia' (315).

Ricomana, observes Ruiz de Conde, 'tiene ya en su mente un tipo de enamorado cuyas cualidades desea encontrar en Felipe. Esta siciliana idealista no se resigna a hacer concesiones en punto al carácter de su futuro esposo' (Ruiz de Conde 1948: 131). Ricomana's dread of the marriage which might end in a lifetime of 'mala companyia' compels her to further test Philip (chap. 110). When a philosopher, having observed Philip, confirms her judgement ('porta 'l'escrit en lo front de molt ignorant home e avar'), she declares: 'més estime ésser monja o muller de sabater que haver aquest per marit, encara que fos rei de França' (352).

The suitor cannot assume any sort of pre-emptive advantage based on his background; he must win her approval. Ricomana thus accepts the prince only after contriving a pretext for testing his choice of beds. When he selects a fine bed over a plain one (353–54), the princess joyfully concludes that she was wrong: 'és-se gitat en lo millor per mostrar que és fill de rei e li pertany, com la sua generació sia molt noble, excel·lent e molt antiga' (354).

Despite its tolerance of, or preference for, inferior social status in the groom, the epiclerate does not of itself favour the bride's preferences. Accommodation of her amorous predilections comes when consent is added to the matchmaking equation. We see just such a fusion of the epiclerate with consensual liberation of the female in *Amadís*, in the relationship between Ardán Canileo and Madasima, the daughter and heiress of the slain Famongomadán. Ardán promises to bring her back the head of Amadís, the slayer of her father, for which he expects her love in return. Although she wants to see avenged the deaths of her father and her brother Basagante, also slain by Amadís, Madasima scorns this bargain: 'no auía cosa en el mundo por que a Ardán Canileo se viesse junta'. Her reasons are significant: she is 'fermosa y noble', while he is 'feo y muy desemejado y esquiuo'. Her mother, the widow of Famongomadán, has other ideas. She receives Ardán as her daughter's suitor 'para defensa de su tierra'. What is more, if he avenges the deaths of her husband and son, she intends to marry him to Madasima 'y dexarle toda la tierra' (II, 524.298–320). Both mother and daughter are testing the suitor, each from a different perspective.

The hero himself, in his relationship to his beloved, is the most prominent example of the epiclerate in *Amadís*. This is seen in the very language put into Amadís's mouth when he joyfully accepts the plan of the hermit Nasciano to publicly reveal 'el secreto de sus amores'. Amadís replies to the hermit: 'si el rey Lisuarte desse propósito está, y por su hijo me quiere, yo le tomaré por señor y padre, para le seruir en todo lo que su honrra sea' (IV, 1130–31.927–31). Here he is clearly the son-in-law marrying in. However, the marriage of Amadís and Oriana presents a significant departure from the uxorilocal pattern described by Goody and others as typical. Through his acquisition of the Firm Isle — a fantasy, as we have seen, of lineal segmentation — Amadís and his bride maintain neolocal rather than uxorilocal residence. The epiclerate in *Amadís* is further complicated by Oriana's younger sister, who, as we have seen, is elevated by Lisuarte to the status of surrogate male heir — she, in effect, is the designated *epikleros*. However, Oriana's status as her father's legitimate heir is the motive for the war fought by Amadís on her behalf. Her marriage to the hero supports the underlying logic of the epiclerate — that of the recruitment of surrogate sons. This is evident in Lisuarte's final acceptance of Amadís as his effective son and heir. We see this in the hero's response to his father-in-law's speech of reconciliation (IV, 1180.191–96):

> según las mercedes y honrras que yo y mi linaje de vos recebimos, a mucho mayores seruicios éramos obligados. Y por esto, señor, no vos quiero dar gracias ningunas; pero por lo postrimero, no digo de la herencia de vuestros grandes señoríos, mas darme por su voluntad a la infanta Oriana, os seruiré todos los días que biua con la mayor obediencia y acatamiento que nunca hijo a padre ni seruidor a señor lo hizo. (IV, 1180.208–19)

The epiclerate, as we have seen, tolerates a de-emphasis of ascribed status in prospective suitors. Secondarily, there may be some consideration of the son-in-law's personal qualities. These are evaluated with reference to the internal needs of the bride's family — integration takes precedence over alliance. Among the domestic requirements deriving from the imperative of familial integration is that of keeping the daughter-heiress happy. The achievements and personal magnetism of the prospective groom thus invite hypogamy on the one hand, covert romance and secret marriage on the other. Daughters could represent the latter activities as a pre-emptive evaluation of their suitors' inherent worth as potential spouses and defenders of the lineage. The latter aspect would justify the former. In conjunction with an ideology of individual consent, the calculus of lineal advantage expressed as a recruitment of viable sons-in-law thus implicitly underwrites the amorous preferences of daughters in general. Not that all daughters play the role of the *epikleros*, but that all those who do present a highly visible example of potential female sovereignty to sisters, cousins, and neighbours.

There is, consequently, more to the drama of marital consent and female empowerment than the assessment of familial interest and the utilitarian appraisal of prospective husbands. When Amadís's mother Elisena falls madly in love with Perión, appraising him as an eventual mate, father, and facilitator of lineal continuity is the last thing on her mind. The same may be said, allowing for incidental differences in each case, for Oriana, Güelfa, Carmesina, and even the princess-heiress who selects Zifar to be her consort. Abetted by the judicial efficacy of consent, daughters were encouraged to think that their opinion held weight in the selection of a husband. Given the need for female approval of partners, it was a logical assumption that dalliance with attractive males could be construed as a forgivable, even licit, preliminary to betrothal. In cases in which betrothal and marriage did not ensue, this could be interpreted as allowable rejection of an unsuitable partner. The romances, of course, show an idealized representation of desire. Love affairs are rendered not in any consistently realistic sense, but as they would presumably have been wistfully envisioned by a large segment of the female audience. The romances' depiction of the woman's amorous regard as an indispensable and generally accurate test of sexual, social, and — implicitly — familial suitability in partners is the core element of this wish-fulfilment fantasy.[15]

The calculus of personal and amorous advantage with regard to evaluating a prospective husband is depicted in Grasinda's account of her perception of the dashing knight whom she later discovers to have been Amadís. She declares to Oriana, Sardamira, Briolanja, and the other great ladies keeping company with the hero's beloved on Ínsula Firme how the hero's exploits and character made her love him:

> Yo fue tan pagada dél y de sus grandes hechos que comoquiera que yo fuesse para en aquella tierra asaz rica y grand señora, y él anduuiesse como vn pobre cauallero, sin que dél más noticia ouiesse sino lo dicho, touiera por bien de lo tomar en casamiento y pensara yo que en tener su persona ninguna reyna de todo el mundo me fuera ygual. (IV, 1037–38.846–56)

---

[15] Brundage documents the prevalence of sexual activity in what he calls a 'heroic age of lechery', as well as the widespread assumption, among a great variety of observers and ethical theorists, that sexuality was an inescapable condition of human nature (417–32).

Lisuarte's speech of gratitude and recognition of the hero's services may be taken as a vindication of the principle of achieved status. Pondering the meaning and utility of Oriana's secret marriage to Amadís, he discovers the advantages of hypogamy from the perspective of a patriarch obliged by the force of events to focus on integration instead of alliance. The desirability of Amadís as a son-in-law, the services rendered by the hero and his lineage, and the beauty and character of his grandson become apparent:

> y el amor que él siempre tuuo a don Galaor, y los seruicios que él y todo su linaje le hizieron, y quántas vezes, después de Dios, fue por ellos socorrido en tiempo que otra cosa sino la muerte y destruyción de todo su estado esperaua; y sobre todo ser su nieto aquel muy hermoso donzel Esplandián, en quien tanta esperança tenía. [...] (IV, 1126.525–35).

Alliance, the thing he sought all along in trying to impose the marriage to Patín on his daughter, is, at the same time, ironically obtained by honouring the principle of consent, i.e. by conceding the legitimacy of the hero's secret marriage to Princess Oriana: 'assí como por voluntad ellos dos son juntos en matrimonio sin lo yo saber, assí sabiéndolo, queriéndolo, queden por mis hijos successores herederos de mis reynos' (IV, 1180.191–96). All that Amadís has achieved — both his deeds in service to third parties, and especially his aid rendered to Lisuarte himself — may now be understood as a test of the suitor. Public recognition of his marriage to Oriana is thus revealed as the ceremonially confirmed establishment of affinal alliance attained through consent and hypogamous marriage.

The integrative component of agnatic strategy is accomplished through hypogamy and the epiclerate; hypergamy and dowry fortify the social and political condition of the lineage. Primogeniture favours eldest sons not because of their sex, but rather because of their tactical utility to the lineage. The epiclerate favours the youngest of several brotherless daughters for the same reason. Hypogamy is thus the mirror image of hypergamy. The political advantages of hypergamous marriage, which require the bride's family to contribute dowry as an inducement both to the groom's kin and to the bride herself (in recompense for the essential disinheritance which her marriage implies), are disadvantages when the integration of the lineage is at stake. In the latter case, it is precisely the absence of material and symbolic capital — of economic and political clout — that makes the accomplished suitor of relatively humble background attractive to the parents and kin of an heiress. The outsider, coming from outside the network of mutual obligations, seduces by virtue of his independence. Allowing the bride and her family to focus on the personal attributes of the son-in-law-to-be, it permits them to emphasize the salutary benefits of new blood. In the contest of individual consent vs familial imperatives, the trump card of the knight errant — in addition to his achieved status and personal qualities — is his very lack of political encumbrances.

In *Amadís*, Lisuarte's marriage to Brisena is an ironic example of the kind of love match he objects to in his own daughter's case. His marriage to Brisena takes place before his elevation to the kingship on the death of his brother Falangriz. Brisena had been wooed by 'muchos altos príncipes'. Her father hesitated to decide among this host of suitors: 'con temor de vnos no la osaua dar a ninguno dellos'. The daughter, seeing the personal attributes of Lisuarte — 'buenas maneras y grande esfuerço' — rejects all the suitors and marries the young man 'que por amores la seruía' (I, 38.363–75). Like the eventual marriage of Amadís and Oriana, this hypogamous union is between a propertyless (although high-born) knight and a bride 'que por su gran beldad y sobrada virtud muy preciada y demandada de muchos príncipes y grandes hombres era' (II, 540.203–07).

The potential political dangers of hypergamy are seen in the predicament of the lady in distress who comes to Elisena for aid, in book IV of *Amadís*. The woman declares that her daughter's arranged marriage to the Duke of Sweden has brought to her lineage 'muy grandes llantos y dolores':

> como este duque sea mancebo codicioso de señorear comoquiera que le auer pudiesse, y el rey, mi marido, fuesse entrado en días, fizo cuenta que matando a él y tomando a los dos mis hijos, que son moçuelos [...] prestamente podría por parte de su muger ser rey del reyno. (IV, 1197.287–96).

The lower echelons of the nobility thus constitute a pool of suitably unencumbered amorous and spousal candidates. The Lady Estefania observes, in witty conversation with princess Carmesina, that married women, 'si s'enamoren de negú no volen haver amistat ab home qui sia millor que son marit ni egual, ans nos baixam a més vils que ells no són' (407). *Tirant*, while underscoring the vulnerability of the male in the hypergamous system, reveals the utility of a suitor of inferior condition. Hipòlit, who courts the empress, declares his lack of bargaining power: 'jo no tinc vassalls, béns ni heretatge que devant la majestat vostra hagués a venir' (735). 'Amor', the Empress reminds Hipòlit, 'no accepta noblesa, ni llinatge, ni egualtat, car no fa diferència si és d'alt lloc o de baix' (745). Social responsibilities, moreover, constitute an impediment to personal fulfilment and happiness: 'son benaventurades', declares the Empress, 'aquelles que no tenen marit per poder-se mills dispondre en ben amar' (747). The knight's lack of political and honorific advantages is irrelevant — and may in fact constitute the principal charm of one who is the social inferior of his lady.

The hypogamous marriage between Hipòlit and the Empress reveals the public and private dimensions of the reciprocal calculus of advantage. The public dimension is one of communal service, the private, one of personal gratification. Hipòlit declares to the Empress (1176), as he responds to the barons' decision to ratify their marriage, that he is not worthy of being her 'marit ni encara servidor'. But, confident in her 'molta amor e virtut', he promises to remain ever her servant and protector: 'car no desigí jamés res tant com és que lo meu servir vos fos accepte'. She replies, addressing him as 'Mon fill', by assuring him of her love and devotion:

> que encara que jo sia vella, no trobaràs jamés qui tant t'ame. E per mi te serà feta molta honor, e seràs molt prosperat, car la molta virtut e gentilea que sempre he coneguda en tu, m'aconhort, per posseir a tu, de totes les altres coses. (1176)

King Escariano, Tirant's brother-at-arms, and chosen by the hero's kinsmen and comrades as their ambassador, explains in more straightforward terms the advantages to be gained from the proposed match. Here too the issue of female consent is fundamental. There is in Escariano's speech (1178) the additional element of a thinly veiled threat concerning the need to manage the knights of the Empire, now that their Emperor and their Captain are both dead. The match, he asserts, is to alleviate her 'treballs', and to give 'repòs e delit' to her 'afligida persona'. Seeing that she will be faced with 'tals coses e tan grans', and 'sens companyia', they propose to arrange her marriage to 'cavaller tal e de tan singular virtut e bondat' that she cannot fail to be 'servida e venerada'. In addition, the Empire owes its salvation to Tirant, who has made Hipòlit, 'nebot seu', his heir. Without a husband, observes Escariano, she will be unable to 'regir ne senyorear tants barons e grans senyors com són en l'Imperi, ne defendre aquells dels enemics infels qui són circumveïns de l'Imperi'. For all these reasons, concludes the Ethiopian king, she should be glad to accept Hipòlit as her 'marit e senyor'.

The Empress replies that, while it is 'difícil refusar o acceptar la [...] demanda', she has not intended to remarry and begs them not to insist: 'com la mia disposició no és per a pendre marit, com sia en tal edat constiuïda que no só per haver infants' (1179). To this Agramunt responds by reminding her that, although 'senyora e regidora de tot l'Imperi grec', she cannot rule alone: 'no és possible poder-lo vós regir ne conservar, ans de necessitat s'iria a perdre, o teniu a pendre marit'. He and the others, Agramunt goes on, will provide her 'tal marit [...] e tal cavaller que sabrà defendre la terra e serà parent del gloriós Tirant'. The relationship of her future husband to the hero ('que sia parent et criat de Tirant') will provoke general rejoicing among her subjects (1179).

The romances, we have seen, express the purpose of marriage in multifarious terms: as a reproduction of lineage, as a vicarious perpetuation of the self, as a fulfilment of social ambition, as an expression of amorous passion. The bilateral nature of consent, the varied nature and multiple functions of inheritance, the place of marriage within the network of present relations and future generations, the linkage of kith and kin: all these are encompassed within the social purview of this historically important genre. The romances dramatize, in ways largely consonant with social history, the choices confronting a family with regard to inheritance and marriage. While conceding lineal benefit as the primary criterion of marital choice, they champion a notion of 'daughters know best' in the determination of which precise spouse will yield this benefit. While admitting the importance of maintaining intact the agnatic patrimony, they dispute the idea that an eldest or only son is the sole appropriate heir. While challenging the validity of hypergamy as a preferential rule of marriage, and recognizing the epiclerate's implicit approbation of achieved status and hypogamous marriage, they contest the conventional designation of youngest daughters as sole heirs and vectors of patrilineal continuity. At the same time, hypogamy is often represented as de facto hypergamy in the honorific, if not the political and economic sense (i.e. as a marriage to the disinherited son of a prestigious family or the impoverished scion of a once-prestigious lineage). Outright hypergamy is shown as incompatible with a daughter's consensual rights, while threatening her patrimony with absorption into that of the groom's more powerful lineage. Hypogamy is advantageous because no dowry is required and because the son of humbler background than the bride's will be less likely to have familial or political associations interfering with his assumption of the role of surrogate male heir. A younger man is preferable to an older because he represents to the host lineage more years as a potential provider of grandchildren.

The official kinship of tradition — of group praxis as it is tinkered together within customary guidelines by the elders of each generation — represents the lineage as a corporate entity before the world. Empowered by social, economic, and political prerogatives, traditional kinship, in the public-relations dimension, presents to the world the picture, both genealogically and dramaturgically (i.e. as a collective enactment of inter-dependent roles), of clanic identity. Official kinship in the traditional connotation is more nuanced, more multifarious, more improvisational than the statutory kinship of law codes or the theoretical constructs of ethnographic studies. The victory of the kinship system of law codes over that of tradition marks the triumph of the state. The knight and his lady, in the romances, do not obey the written law as regards marital consent; they invoke it only for strategic purposes, while seeking, ultimately, the foundation of a household and a family of their own. One of the ironies of social history, as reflected in the romances, is that young persons desirous of independence employed one kinship ideology to resist another, and in so doing, collaborated with the forces destined to undermine the very system they sought to buy into as self-governing shareholders. The possibility that the knight and his lady would someday themselves feel the need to control the marriages of their own offspring does not enter into the narrative equation — a clear indication of the romances' youth orientation.

Rigorously pragmatic in its multifarious response to the unpredictable complexities of the social and physical environment, tradi-tional kinship, particularly in its matchmaking mode, is pictured unsympathetically by the romances. It is portrayed as entailing the selective exploitation of daughters as counters in a strategic game of lineal alliances, with a tendency toward disinheritance of elder daughters in favour of younger. Such practices are dramatized not as beneficial to the agnatic lineage, but rather as an arbitrary disregard for the strictly legalistic sense of primogeniture as inheritance by an eldest sibling. The romances do not regard hyper-gamy and dowry on the one hand, the epiclerate and hypogamy on the other, as optional strategies exercised at the discretion of a protean patriarchy. They see autocratic fathers and arrogant magnates whose tyranny is evinced by their desire to impose marriages on unwilling brides, or to thwart the latters' involvement with partners of their choosing. Girls, meanwhile, are all too often the beloved of an impecunious or marginalized youth. Again, the youthful personages of the romances, both male and female, invoke — expressly or implicitly, and only in those aspects of it which suit them — the letter of the law with regard to succession, inheritance, and marital consent. They use it as a strategy of legitimation in their conflict with the representatives of traditional, official, lineal ideology. They engage, in other words, in biopolitics, using the only means available to them, which happen to be those afforded by the universalizing agencies of statist and ecclesiastical law. This is the principal fact underlying the prurient secrecy of most love relationships in the chivalric romances.

At the same time, there is an enormous contradiction in the hero-knight's courtship of a princess. The hero aims at a goal that will, effectively, transform him into the adversary: he aims at becoming, like his own father, like his father-in-law, like the superintending male kin of his beloved, the head of a household, a link in the patrilineal projection into the future, and thus a player in that very game of agnatic biopolitics from which he is, as a youth, excluded, and by that exclusion defined as a knight-errant. The romances end with marriage and accession to the status of householder (or kingship, its political analogue) because, pandering to a youthful audience, they choose not to imagine life after the threshold between marginalized adolescence and unthinkable maturity.

There are, to be sure, differences in the way the concluding marriage is portrayed in each of the works we have studied. In *Amadís*, it is the hero and several of his companions who are married. After Curial's many vicissitudes and his successes against the Turks and in the great tourney, he and Güelfa are at last sumptuously wed. Although *Zifar*, in contrast to both *Amadís* and *Curial e Güelfa*, shows not the eponymous hero but rather his son Roboán joyously married at the end of the story, it is still clear that a wedding is a proper end to the knight's career and to his story. Only *Tirant*, alone among our four romances to have an unhappy ending, concludes with the death of the hero. But, while thus not portraying a triumphant public marriage as its finale, the narrative, in showing the victorious hero on his way to a magnificent marriage when death overtakes him (1146), plainly understands marriage to be a plausible end to the knight's tale and, by implication, a fitting termination to youth as a phase of life.

It must also be pointed out that the relationship between the hero-knights and their eventual or prospective in-laws is not always straightforwardly adversarial. While in *Amadís* the main plot does indeed revolve around the hero's secret marriage to his beloved and the resistance to this match by her father, *Zifar*'s second son Roboán maintains a tentative and protracted courtship with Seringa that is very above-board. A somewhat reluctant suitor, Roboán waits until he has established himself as emperor before sending for his bride. Tirant and Curial are similar to Amadís in their clandestine and hypogamous courtship of desirable females. In the Catalan romances, however, opposition from the men of the girls' lineages is less straightforward, with plot complications arising not so much from direct confrontation between suitor and future in-laws as from an assumption of the impropriety of hypogamy in particular and of consensual relationships in general.

What all these characters share, despite their differences, is the tendency toward postponement of marriage. They are literary personifications of the later-marrying males described by Duby and by Herlihy and Klapisch-Zuber. Delayed marriage resulted, in medieval social and economic history, where grooms bided their time either searching for the best possible match, or obtaining the maximum livelihood in support of a match already arranged by mutual consent of the couple. In the case of the urban bourgeoisie and artisan class — important elements of the readership of the romances in late-medieval and early-modern times — men waited until they had secured the means of sustaining a household before assuming the responsibilities of marriage. In this sense, the stories appealed to their readers by virtue of their protagonists' exemplary fulfilment of conventional aspirations.

CHAPTER 6

Conclusion

R eaders of my *Kinship and Polity in the 'Poema de Mio Cid'* (Harney 1993a) will note that the terminology utilized and the ethnography and social history works cited — in so far as they apply to literary representations of kinship, marriage, and related concerns — are largely the same in that study and in the present one. There are, at the same time, numerous differences between the society envisioned by the *Poema de Mio Cid* and the one pictured in the chivalric romances. The epic poet sees the social universe as open and competitive. The epic hero is an opportunistic striver, a first-among-equals in a world of man-to-man relationships. There is social stratification in the Cid's world, but the boundaries between strata are permeable. This is a system of classes rather than castes. Deference is not granted on the sole basis of ascribed status. The romance world is, by contrast, highly deferential. Its categories are fixed. It is a universe of rivalry rather than of competition. By this I mean that the 'may-the-best-man-win' spirit of the epic, as in the *Poema*'s scenes of battlefield confrontation and judicial combat, is replaced by an ambience of 'might-makes-right'. The chivalric hero's unbeatable physical prowess stems from his inherently superior status, while the Cid's superiority is earned by his heroic performance. The Cid's is a world of contention between unequal parties (the Infantes de Carrión are morally inferior to the hero and his band). These parties want different things (the Cid wants victory in his campaigns, exoneration as a vassal, triumph as a litigant; the Infantes desire money to pursue dreams of a life of leisure and marriage into prominent families). Rivalry in the romances, on the other hand, is between equals. The knight is one among many knights, all equally chivalric in their status, who want precisely the same thing: the hand of a princess, the inheritance of a kingdom.

Competition is about outcomes; rivalry is about preconditions. The Cid becomes what he is by doing what he does. All that he possesses, he earns, as we see in the famous lines: 'Echado fu de tierra, é tollida la onor, / con grand afán gané lo que he yo' (Michael 1978: ll. 1934–35). The success of Zifar, Amadís, and the others, by contrast, is shown not as an earning of something new, but rather as a recovery of a predestined birthright. Where the result of the Cid's struggle is portrayed as something that must be proved, the triumph of the romance heroes — beginning with that of the earliest in the group, Zifar, the 'caballero de Dios' — is shown to be a foregone conclusion.

So dissimilar are the societies of the two genres that we have to think in terms of a historical discontinuity between the *Poema* and the later chivalric texts. The romance authors may have known of the historical Cid, but they owe nothing to the epic poem or its generic congeners. The notion of a transition between epic and romance — as discussed, for example, by Eugène Vinaver (1971: 2–22), or between epic and novel, as envisioned by Mikhail Bakhtin (1981: 3–4) — is, therefore, a construct of literary history that does not reflect the actual practice of the authors of romances. There was no transition, in the sense of a purposeful adaptation, by later authors of the works of an earlier form.

The *Poema de mio Cid* and the chivalric romances discussed here present, despite their many differences, certain analogies that arise from the somewhat comparable social circumstances of the epic Cid on the one hand, the hero-knights of the romances on the other. Like the protagonists of the chivalric romances, the Cid of the epic, proving his worth by great martial deeds, triumphs against both military adversaries abroad and personal enemies at home. The epic Cid, like the heroes of the chivalric romances, feuds with traitorous courtiers. His adventures lead to exoneration for himself and degradation for his enemies. Also, like the romance heroes, the Cid gathers around his person a considerable following. His leadership is meritorious, as is that of the later knights-errant. The political charisma of the protagonists supports, both in the epic and the romances, the establishment of a separate power base. The

Cid's Valencia is thus somewhat analogous to Roboán's Empire of Trigridia, Amadís's Ínsula Firme, and the lands and titles acquired by Tirant and Curial.

The *Poema* and the chivalric romances glorify heroic social mobility achieved through martial valour and charismatic leadership. However, the Cid is a more constant and inclusive recruiter of collaborators, admitting to the ranks of his followers all those who would escape poverty:

> Por Aragón e por Navarra   pregón mandó echar,
> a tierras de Castiella   enbió sus mensaies:
> quien quiere perder cueta   e venir a rritad,
> viniesse a Mio Çid   que á sabor de cavalgar,
> çercar quiere a Valençia   por a christianos la dar (1187–91)

The heroes of both genres rely on the cooperation of kinsmen. The poetic Cid is the uncle of a number of nephews in his entourage. At the same time, he shows neither clanic nor status-defined partiality in the recruitment of vassals. We see this in such passages as that in which all members of the army receive 'casas [...] e heredades' (1246), and are all, at the same time, sternly forbidden to depart without formally taking leave by kissing their lord's hand (1251–54). The chivalric protagonist's team of collaborators, by contrast, is more restricted in membership than the much larger following of the egalitarian Cid. The heroes of the romances prefer to collaborate with fellow knights, especially those who are their cousins in a system of affiliated kindreds. The heroes of the romances, we might say, are clannish, while the Cid is ecumenical.

Defined as knights-errant (in contrast to the Cid's temporary status of exiled vassal), wandering through many lands and kingdoms and involved in many undertakings, the heroes of the romances are beset by numerous distractions and detours. The Cid, on the other hand, ranges over a more narrowly delineated territory. He has limited objectives — renewal of his vassalage, exoneration of his good name, vengeance against his enemies — and is much more straightforward in his pursuit of them. To be sure, Zifar and Tirant reveal something of the Cid's sense of mission, focussing as they do on the defence of a particular kingdom (Mentón in the case of Zifar, Constantinople in that of Tirant). But while the Cid is a notorious besieger of cities, Tirant and Zifar, like Roboán, Amadís, and Curial, are famous defenders of towns and kingdoms (Harney 1995: 180–88).

Aside from their monogamous devotion to the women in their lives, and a commitment to eventual marriage, the chivalric heroes pursue at most a loosely focused program of social climbing. The Cid, on the other hand, secures his independent kingdom by purposeful military conquest. Whatever independent wealth or property the chivalric heroes acquire is earned chiefly by luck or magic (Amadís's Ínsula Firme, Roboán's Empire of Trigridia, Curial's buried treasure). Otherwise, the knights of the romances attain power and property through service to others (the case of Zifar and Tirant). The romance heroes, in other words, are subservient, while the Cid is an entrepreneur. This contrast between the protagonists of epic and romance reflects the social history of knights as an essentially servile class (Duby 1973b: 327–32; Bumke 1982: 28–39 & 72–80; Nerlich 1987: I, 14).

The Cid, we could say, stalks Alfonso, seeking reconciliation. Refusing to take no for an answer, the Cid woos his lord with gifts, demonstrating steadfast deference. The estranged knight of the romances, by contrast, does not chase his beloved; he pines, he fawns, he languishes. Reconciliation occurs through some fortuitous happenstance or revelation that convinces the beloved to relent. The Cid seeks to shore up an existing relationship in the manly network of feudalism. The knight seeks to establish an amorous, and eventually matrimonial, relationship with a beloved who holds all the cards that matter. The knight seeks the foundation of a household, where the Cid seeks the restoration of an alliance. The knight's objective is, we might say, akin to that of the emulous, down-and-out *segundón*, while the Cid's agenda coincides with that of the independent bandit chieftain. The knight implicitly aims at economic security, the Cid to heal a political disability.

The Cid is what Julio Caro Baroja calls a 'founder hero' (1969: 358–59; 1986: 93 & 139–40). This is seen in his egalitarian treatment of all those who participate in the conquest of Valencia: 'El amor de Mio Çid ya lo ivan provando, / los que fueron con él e los de después todos son pagados' (1247b-48). The leader's steadfast insistence on treating all his followers as equally his men — whether latecomers or original recruits — is a recurrent motif in legends and folklore about founder-heroes (Harney 1992: 78–92).

The predatory economy of the Reconquest period, as Michael Nerlich observes, sustained the positive social mobility of real-world warriors and knights far longer in Spain than in other European countries. During the fourteenth and fifteenth centuries, however, the expansion of police power and judiciary authority among emerging nation-states, as well as the development of international trade and capitalist economy, conspired to render the *hidalgo* class expendable, while terminating the age of the 'pillaging adventure, once commonly practiced as a means of livelihood'. This period of decline for Peninsular *hidalguía* coincided, paradoxically, with the growing popularity of the chivalric romance (1987: I, 27 & 29).

The same period saw a depreciation of the achievement ethic that governs the mobility striving of the Reconquest period, and that inspires the epic adventures of the Cid. In modern sociological terms, ascription came to prevail over achievement as the criterion of status attribution. A study of Castilian *cartas de privilegio* (patents of ennoblement) in the early modern era reveals a tendency among applicants to 'conceal the stigma of venality and *arrivisme*'. In documenting claims to nobility, applicants disregard any notion of 'personal as against inherited merit', a contrastive theme that continued to be invoked by such Golden Age authors as Cervantes, Lope, and Calderón. The standards by which *hidalguía* was measured were those of genealogy, public service, and communal recognition (Thompson 1985: 380–81). The fundamental criterion was appropriate ancestry; what mattered most was 'evidence not of life-style but of inheritance'. Service to crown and country as a justification for ennoblement was characterized by the petitioner as a 'secular treasury of merits built up by his ancestors and relatives'. Outstanding service substantiated inherent nobility rather than personal virtue (382).

The *Poema*, frankly acknowledging the Cid's status as *infanzón*, makes scant allusion to his lineage. In addition, the plot of the *Poema* comprises only a limited segment of the protagonist's total life span. In contrast, the romances glorify the lineage of their heroes, and recount much of their heroes' lives. As noted in the introduction, the chivalric romance tended to take the form of a fictitious biography. The latter is a correlative literary form of social environments in which aspirants to higher status must demonstrate appropriate background and life-style. Authors writing with their audiences in mind, and who themselves participated in the same status anxieties as their readers, naturally constructed plots that expressed the themes of social service, ethical integrity, munificent idealism, and genealogical prestige.

The epic Cid, in contrast to the chivalric heroes, is a mature family man. Save for Zifar, the heroes of the romances are young and unmarried. For them, chivalric adventure is a prelude to, a platform for, advantageous matrimony. Unlike the Cid, who conquers a kingdom rather than a bride, and dies a happy man having seen his daughters well married, the chivalric heroes see their aspirations consummated by winning the hand of a princess. Even Zifar, the most Cidian of the knights-errant, nonetheless performs, during his wandering phase, as do the other chivalric adventurers. His heiress-hunting is a more frankly depicted version of the amorous involvements of his son Roboán, and of Amadís, Curial, and Tirant. The possibility that passion could have been understood as a pretext for acquiring the property of heiresses, and that chivalric amour could be defined as a sublimated cupidity, did not lessen the romantic appeal of the theme.

The romances portray a society in which parents feel constrained to control their daughters' sexuality, while arranging the most advantageous match, from the viewpoint of the family. Both fictional fathers and their real-world equivalents were, as we have seen, constantly subverted in their agnatic schemes by the Church's matrimonial theory, which increasingly tended, as F. L. Critchlow points out, toward the elimination from betrothal and marriage of 'any taint of barter' (1904–05: 499). Here again, we discern a point of contrast between the romances and the *Poema de Mio Cid*. The Cid is quite willing to engage in bargaining (as seen in his guileful negotiations with the moneylenders), and is a crafty and pugnacious litigator. The heroes of the romances, unlike their epic predecessor, prefer hand-to-hand combat to legal proceedings. They generally circumvent their adversaries (as in the case of a sweetheart's parents and family), or they overpower them.

The younger generation, that of the heroes and their sweethearts, feels compelled to dodge parental control and surveillance. This is true whether or not the father or other males of a daughter's lineage show overt inclination to control her marital choices. In the case of the King of Mentón, concerned to obtain his daughter's consent in the marriage to Zifar, or in that of Carmesina's essentially complaisant father and somewhat negligent mother, we see outright parental indulgence. In the case of Lisuarte with regard to Oriana, or of Güelfa and her brother, the male clanic intervention is more evident. In all cases, however, the woman is shown to be in the right; indulgence of her will is proper, opposition to it, improper. The machinations of daughters and their lovers are shown to be a legitimate resistance, where necessary, to parental supremacy.

The Cid of the *Poema* — like Lisuarte in *Amadís*, and other fathers of daughters in the romances — assumes that marriage functions not to promote the sexual gratification, personal happiness, or spiritual fulfilment of the couple, but to advance the social and political interests of extended families. The *Poema*, unlike the romances, shows no awareness of the concept of individual marital consent. The Cid's daughters willingly marry the husbands assigned to them. The *Poema* assumes that dowry is an appropriate matchmaking procedure, and that hypergamy, from the perspective of a bride's family, is the preferred outcome of matrimonial alliances. The Cid, unlike fathers in the romances, does not differentiate between his daughters in matrimonial arrangements, but rather seeks to procure equally good matches for both (Harney 1993a: chap. 3, *passim*).

The *Poema*'s storyline follows the course of the feud between the hero and his political enemies. The marriage of the Cid's daughters to members of the opposing faction is intertwined with the inter-clanic dispute. The Infantes de Carrión, in the *Poema*, are understood to be bad precisely because they are self-centred wastrels who regard marriage solely as a vehicle of private aggrandizement. The plots of the chivalric romances, turning on the issue of marital consent, centre on the conflicts arising from the couple's usurpation of familial control over marriage. Even when this arrogation of matrimonial decision-making is presented in highly attenuated form, as in the case of Roboán's pre-nuptial negotiations with Seringa, what has been said of medieval French courtly romance can also be said of the Spanish genre which was so influenced by it: '[its] principal subject [...] is heterosexual love and its relationship to the social convention of marriage' (Evans 1981: 129). Focusing on this theme, Critchlow's survey of French

romans d'aventure yields a summary of the primary plot that
typified that genre:

> The wishes of a woman about to be married, and for whom a
> marriage is being arranged, are seldom respected or consulted. In
> order to elude her father, therefore, she connives with her lover,
> who has been thrust aside by her unwilling parent for another, to
> defeat her lord's purposes by a resort to ruse. (1904–05: 502)

The lovers in the chivalric romances are assisted in their passionate intrigues by a varied personnel of sympathetic collaborators
— cousins, ladies-in-waiting, dwarves, and otherwise serviceable
courtiers — all conspiring with the sweethearts in their evasion of
familial supervision. Rafael Beltrán observes that the courtly
ambience of the chivalric romances is analogous, in this aspect, to
the situation in *Celestina*, in the sense of an environment of
complicity between the central couple and various accomplices,
including other, similarly transgressive couples (1991: 116–17).
Although not all the lovers in the Peninsular romances resort to
outright subterfuge in coping with parental or familial authority, all
these narratives assume a daughter's rights in the selection of her
suitors and the making of her marriage. Taking as axiomatic that a
daughter's sweetheart is justified in encouraging her circumvention
of parental control, the romances support the notion of love and
marriage as avenues to personal gratification. Securing the hand of
a socially prominent female is an appropriate goal for a young man;
selecting a lover on the basis of his sex appeal, personal charm, and
martial renown is acceptable for a young woman.

In their amorous motivation, the heroes of the romances have
more in common with the *Poema*'s Infantes de Carrión than they
do with the Cid. It is true that the knights in the romances marry up,
and the Infantes marry down. But the Infantes reveal their notion of
ideal marriage as they devise their revenge against the Cid and his
daughters:

> Averes levaremos grandes   que valen grant valor,
> escarniremos   las fijas del Canpeador.
> D'aquestos averes   siempre seremos rricos omnes,
> podremos casar con fijas   de rreyes o de enperadores,
> ca de natura somos   de condes de Carrión. (2550–54)

The Infantes' speech contains the essential elements of the chivalric matrimonial agenda: a need for money and property as the basis for social standing, the preference for brides of superior station, the emphasis on inherited familial status as the grounds for such aspirations. The knights of the romances, consequently, have in common with the Infantes of the Cidian epic an opportunistic craving for wealth and a fixation with socially prominent heiresses. In order to remedy their material destitution and to provide for marriage to more suitable brides, the Infantes use their social prominence to leverage a temporary and spurious marriage to women of lesser status but greater affluence. The knights of the romances, personifying the daydreams of the Infantes' real-world analogues, secure material advantage by means of personal magnetism and accomplishment. The romances transform the covetous, ambitious suitors of reality into glamorous superheroes whose aspirations are justified by fantastic deeds and garnished with amorous sincerity. Honorific achievement and amorous fidelity warrant the chivalric hero's eventual recovery of a social eminence portrayed as rightfully his. The hypogamous match is understood to be a kind of entitlement. In keeping with the ascriptive mentalities of the day, the social mobility engaged in by the knight is couched in terms of a vindication of the status enjoyed by the candidate as a member of an honourable lineage. The epic, taking the viewpoint of family men, dramatizes, rather, the predicament of fathers who must defend their lineage against rapacious nobles who use ascribed status to promote their matrimonial schemes.

In the romances, both generations are bound by the rules of antithetically opposed games. The lovers live for the moment; the parents live for the future. Where the pretext of clandestine marriage is consent, the pretext of family-controlled marriage is honour. Considered an enhancement of the family's standing in the social hierarchy, and traditionally perceived as an obligation of parents toward their daughters, the arranged marriage was a multipurpose formality involving many parties on both sides of the match. Good marriages for daughters saved face for the whole family, including extended kin; to arrange one's own match, particularly in defiance of parental wishes, was a momentous subversion of the traditional social order.

The jurisdictional conflict between Church and clan, which focussed on the clash of family honour and individual happiness, would presumably have been far from lovers' minds when, as in the case of Elisena and Perión, knights and sweethearts are thinking more about sex than marriage. Intended marriage, however, could always be alleged as a rationale for libidinous gratification. Although clandestine marriage could be viewed as an afterthought designed (by authors, by their characters, by real-life persons) to justify sexual relations, the abatement of family control over women's sexuality — or the decline in the general acceptance of the legitimacy of such control, at least by many women and most young people among the readers of the romances — was a tangible condition in the social world of the day.

The romances, while not endorsing unequivocally the urgency of young love, dramatize erotic peril from the viewpoint of the younger generation. The youth of the day would presumably have been diverted by portrayals of fictional parents, especially fathers, as obdurate despots. The circumvention or outright defeat of authoritarian patriarchy would have been the genre's most appealing theme. An attenuated variation on the motif may be discerned in the cases of those fathers who, like the king of Mentón in *Zifar*, or Carmesina's father in *Tirant*, show inattentiveness or forbearance toward their daughters. These two scenarios, the coercive and the indulgent, both derive from the ascendancy of the ideology of female consent. Both would have represented a wish-fulfilment fantasy for women in the audience. The genre could thus be said to pander primarily to women, especially younger women, and secondarily to youthful males.

This indulgent regard for the rights of young women is a conspicuous common denominator of the four works studied here. For the heroes of these romances differ in many ways as much from one another as they do from the Cid of the *Poema*. Zifar is a family man who remains, in essence, faithful to his first wife despite a potentially bigamous second marriage. His son, Roboán, is a self-exiled prince who engages in knight-errantry. Betrothed to Princess Seringa, he never strays into covert sexuality. Tirant, a wandering knight who comes to the aid of a besieged empire, is secretly betrothed to Carmesina, but does not see their relationship sexually consummated until near the end of the story. Curial, banished through the displeasure of his mistress, likewise sees the realization of his desires only at the end of the tale, and after many vicissitudes. Only Amadís, of all these heroes, engages in a prolonged clandestine sexual relationship with his beloved.

What defines these romances as a group is, in large measure, their advocacy of the legal and social empowerment of women. This empowerment is dramatically endorsed as an ideal defended by the protagonists. The advancement of female prerogatives is represented in terms of a struggle between those who would perpetuate the subordination of women, and the knights who champion female liberation.

Because the chivalric romances foster permissiveness with regard to the sexuality and marital preferences of daughters, it is a serious misconception to view the Hispanic chivalric romance as a sexist or patriarchal genre. Ruth El Saffar speaks for all those who take this mistaken view when, dismissing chivalric romances as crudely supportive of machismo and male dominance, she compares Amadís and other chivalric heroes to Don Quijote, who experiences his lady as 'a distant image of beauty and refinement, so distinct from the familiar world of men as to be not only unattainable but scarcely human.' Categorizing the romance heroes, in effect, as quixotic in their infatuation, El Saffar argues, further, that the 'chivalric approach to the feminine is to put the woman out of sight and to engage in her name in a fascinating game of warfare with men'. What she calls the 'chivalric consciousness' is 'heavily overbalanced on the masculine side' (1984: 53).

Taking a somewhat similar approach to the Old French verse romances which exerted a significant influence on the Peninsular chivalric romances, Roberta L. Krueger rejects the notion, advanced by Gaston Paris and others, that courtly literature represented a 'Golden Age for women'. She allows that many works were dedicated to or inspired by women readers, and grants that a kind of 'female patronage or "matronage"' might well have presided over the composition and reception of medieval chivalric romances (2). However, she argues, courtly literature was written by clerics, and thus was not composed in the interest of women, but rather in furtherance of the 'values of male aristocratic culture'. The twelfth and thirteenth centuries to which she chiefly refers were thus a time when 'noblewomen's powers within feudal society and the family were in many respects declining'. Women's privileged status in romance was thus simultaneous with a '*displacement* from legal and social agency' (3; italics in original).

Krueger, like El Saffar, allows herself to be misled by the adventurous themes of the romances into disregarding the impact of consensual ideology on sexuality, gender roles, and social status. Fomented by the Church over several centuries, what we might call the consensual revolution prompted, from its inception, an empowerment of individual women within their family and clan. This would have been true in Spain, in France, and throughout Christendom. As already noted, this entitlement to matrimonial decision-making may well have been founded on the material and political interests of the Church, as Goody and others have suggested. Whatever the political implications of church policy in the area of marriage and family law, the Church's position on consent made it a powerful ally of young lovers everywhere. Young women would not have needed to focus on the political aspects of consent to perceive in it at least an extenuation of sexual misconduct, and at most, a defence of complete freedom in the selection of a mate.

Even if courtly literature, as Krueger supposes, were written exclusively by clerics — by no means a self-evident assumption — most such literary churchmen would have been excluded from the inner circles of patriarchal authority. The chiefs of aristocratic clans and of their vassal lineages, along with, perhaps, some eldest sons, would have constituted the membership of such a culture. Primogeniture and agnatic politics insured that younger sons probably formed the majority of the clergy; being unmarried, they did not qualify, by definition, for membership in this aristocratic power elite. At the same time, between those excluded from inheritance and the patriarchal elite that benefited from such exclusion, rivalrous estrangement was perhaps a more likely repercussion than solidary collaboration. Clerics were operatives of an institution whose system of family law was inimical to anything amounting to a coherent male aristocratic culture. When compelled to sustain their own families' lineal interests in cases of matrimonial dispute, clerics would have been subject to an inescapable conflict of interest. That this conflict might often have been settled by individual clergymen, for any number of reasons, in favour of family and clan, does not mean that the clergy as a whole acted as the dutiful agents of a monolithic 'male aristocratic culture'.

Assuming the existence of a solidary 'feudal society' acting in unitary resolve to propound and defend its interests, Krueger hypothesizes that the twelfth and thirteenth centuries reflect a general decline in noblewomen's 'legal and social agency'. At variance with this conjecture, the earlier French romances, of which those recounting the loves and adventures of Tristan and Lancelot are the most influential examples, represent an earlier phase in the ongoing consensual crisis, arising from the promulgation of the consensual model of marriage in ever broader sectors of society. Adultery could have been understood as a legitimate response to a repressive system that victimized women in the name of status, property, and family politics. An ideology of consent, furthermore, implies that where there is no consent, or where only nominal consent is achieved through familial coercion, there is no marriage. Where there is marriage in name only, there is no adultery. It is in light of this sort of casuistry that Christian audiences might have justified the actions of Arthur and Guinevere, of Tristan and Isolde.

The disparity between the social worlds of the *Poema de Mio Cid* and the chivalric romance, with regard to marital consent and vassalic solidarity, coincides with the contrast delineated by Denis de Rougemont between courtly chivalry and feudal law. The divergence of the two codes is highlighted, observes de Rougemont, by the conflicting characterization of informants. Feudalism held that a vassal was duty-bound to inform his lord of anything 'that might endanger the [lord's] rights or honor'. The vassal who refrained from so informing was a 'felon'. In conformity with the ethos of courtly love, the Tristan and Lancelot tales show denouncers of adultery — loyal and true vassals according to feudal morality — as the real felons (Rougemont 1983: 33).

Courtly love, according to a still prevalent theory, originated as a response to 'the brutal lawlessness of feudal manners'. Feudal barons employed marriage as a means of acquiring wealth and property. In response to this, courtly love envisioned a fealty, based on love alone, that transcended legal marriage. Courtly romances of the earlier period thus disparaged 'the social institution of marriage', while 'glorifying the virtue of men and women who love outside, and in despite of, marriage' (33–34).

The Cidian epic's viewpoint on informing barons is somewhat

similar to, but has an important difference from, the chivalric viewpoint on such treachery. The tale-bearers who seek the downfall of the Cid convey a simple calumny involving the Cid's betrayal of his lord. From the hints given in the story, we must assume that the Cid's detractors are liars. The rumour-mongers of the romances, by contrast, are telling the truth, in so far as they relate the mere facts of the hero's weaknesses. Fraudulent defamation, in other words, is the transgression of the Cid's *malos mestureros*, while malicious but factual gossip is the offence of their analogues in the romances. Zifar's detractors, for instance, disrupt the hero's relationship with his lord not on the grounds of any adulterous relationship with the lord's wife, nor on those of recreancy or malfeasance; rather, they persuade the monarch of the impropriety of Zifar's unfortunate tendency, the result of a curse on his line, to have his horses fall down dead at the end of every month. Roboán is nearly done in by malevolent courtiers who trick him into asking a forbidden question of his lord and host, the Emperor of Trigridia. Their envious counterparts in *Amadís* and *Curial* expose the love affair of the protagonist and his lady.

In real life, lovers might well have represented their amorous entanglement, to themselves as much as to others, as a marriage in the making. Matrimonial method, as enacted through clandestine marriage, exculpated carnal madness. Seemingly in accordance with such notions, the plots of the Tristan and Lancelot romances emphasize the injustice of the forced marriage, the predicament of the *mal mariée*. These earlier, adulterous romances, and the later, consensual ones such as the four discussed in the present study, could be said to represent distinct phases in the development of a genre defined by the consensual theme. Critchlow observes that the adventure romances reflect the ecclesiastical 'absorption' of the *sponsalia* — the central component of traditional, family-controlled marriage — into 'the sphere of the *matrimonium* formalities'. With the passage of time, and the increasing prestige and authority of the Church over all aspects of marriage, *sponsalia* and *matrimonium* were 'changed about in importance'. The *romans d'aventure* of the thirteenth and fourteenth centuries, he concludes, fall in 'the midpoint of this long transition' (1904–05: 499).

While the earlier texts justify apparent adultery in terms of a defective marriage contract, later romances rationalize amorous autonomy in terms of the prevention of nuptial duress. The earlier romances' essentially supportive depiction of adultery authorizes — or at least sympathizes with — female resistance to agnatic despotism. This implies a relative liberation compared to the epic's utter disregard for female consent in the making of marriage (as revealed in the *Poema de Mio Cid*'s handling of the hero's daughters, or in the *Chanson de Roland*'s perfunctory depiction of Aude, the hero's betrothed). The earlier French romances may be only midway between that epic world and the world of chivalric romance, which tells the tale of agnatic strategy circumvented or obstructed; they nonetheless represent a momentous break with clanic tradition, and an expansion, rather than a loss, of social and legal agency for women.

De Rougemont points out that a prevalent notion in earlier manifestations of courtly love was that of refraining from physical consummation as a sign of true amorous fealty. According to this notion, the 'claims of passion', such as those that play so potent a role in the Peninsular romances, were to be denied — the genuinely loyal lover would thus refrain from physical possession of his lady. Representative of this amorous paradox are those scenes in some versions of the Tristan romance in which the hero abstains from sexual intercourse with the beloved (1983: 35). One of the more controversial points of scholarship on medieval courtly love, the issue of whether courtly sexuality was meant to be understood as literal or figurative, cannot be resolved here. However, it is significant that a fourteenth-century Spanish version of the Tristan story frankly depicts the hero's rivalry with King Mark (before Tristan and Isolde fall victim to the love potion) over the attentions of a married noblewoman (Northup 1928: 98–99). A wounded Tristan, after defeating Mark in a duel, goes to meet the woman in her palace. There, we are told, 'fueronse echar'. The narrator then coyly addresses his readers: 'E luego si jugaron, non me lo demandedes'. Not waiting to be asked, the narrator informs us that Tristan had been a virgin before that night: 'Mas bien creo que fue vn tal juego que Tristan non lo auia jamas fecho, nin sabia que era'. We are left with little doubt as to the nature of their diversion: 'E ellos estodieron ally con grand alegria fasta la media noche' (99).

Toleration of adultery such as that depicted in the episode just cited might have marked an earlier phase of the consensual upheaval. Such expressions, however, could have continued to be popular, along with the newer, bolder expressions that involved outright consummation of physical passion, and a more tolerant view of matrimony. Juan García de Castrogeriz's mid-fourteenth-century reference to Tristan, Amadís, and Zifar as all the rage among youthful readers would indicate the ongoing and concurrent acceptance of these themes by audiences of the time (García de Castrogeriz 1947: III, 361).

We have seen that, in social history, hypergamic matches, expedited by accompanying dowry, typically required the out-marrying woman to renounce her patrimony. As Critchlow points out with regard to the *romans d'aventure*, the conflict arising from the woman's marrying out of her lineage, and thus out of the paternal domain, derives precisely from her empowerment before the law: 'to renounce [...] implies that a woman was possessed of the right of succession'. This right of succession, underlying a notion of women as potential vehicles of lineal identity, facilitates, as we have noted, such practices as the epiclerate. Paternal guardianship and a 'sister's right to succeed, equally with a brother, to her parent's estate' (Critchlow 1904–05: 500), both deriving from Roman law, were thus perceived to further agnatic interests. In practice, however, the increasing authority of the ideology of consent often set them at odds.

The struggle of women with their kinsmen was facilitated by what R. Howard Bloch terms 'the power of women to dispose'. Representing the increasing influence of ecclesiastical doctrine on social practice, at first along the Mediterranean littoral, then, gradually, in northern regions as well, this legal and social empowerment of women, especially with regard to inheritance and control of dowry, encroached on patriarchal and feudal control of property. Female dominion over family estates is attested by the recurrent appearance of matronymics, and by numerous documents showing transfers of property in women's names (Bloch 1991: 186–93).

Postulating a loss of female agency leads to misinterpretation of sexual and matrimonial themes expressed in the chivalric romances. Such an assumption dissociates kinship and marriage, as represented in this fictional literature, from the greater context of political and economic transformation. No character in these texts really has 'agency', in the sense of full legal and social empowerment. That is the whole point of the confrontation in these stories between fathers and daughters, between suitors and potential fathers-in-law, and between suitors and their beloveds. If fathers and other family interests in the romances were endowed with the agency imputed to them by Krueger, there would be no conflict, and thus no story. Nor can we assume that the concept of marital consent had only a theoretical impact on social practice. The frequency of clandestine marriage, one of the most vexatious issues in case law and in decretals, testifies to the repercussions, in social reality, of the ecclesiastical model of marriage (Brundage 1987: 189–90, 239–40, & 276–77).

Such real-world practices as primogeniture, *mayorazgo*, and the epiclerate were highly defensive strategies. The legalistic manifestation of a siege mentality on the part of the agnatic establishment, they bespeak weakness and vulnerability, rather than secure dominion. This defensiveness, of course, is precisely what might have instigated despotic treatment of women by their male kin. The social reality, then, was very possibly as oppressive, in many cases, as Krueger assumes. But we should not confuse that world with the world of a literature designed to provide escape from burdensome actuality. The romances show a world where women have leeway for outmanoeuvring their fathers — where fathers might even be brought to see reason.

While starting earlier in some regions than in others, the social trends alluded to in the present study became generalized throughout Western Europe. Certainly by the time of the composition of the earliest romance in our group (*Zifar*, early fourteenth century), the amorous dilemmas and familial dissensions they both provoked and reflected had become pervasive in European society. Readers of chivalric romances would have understood, therefore, that in the works of that genre the hero's lady embodied anything but El Saffar's 'distant image of beauty and refinement', or Krueger's female puppet of the clergy and aristocracy. She was all too human, a flesh-and-blood lover irresistible precisely because she was a familiar and attainable inhabitant of the knight's world. The lady in the chivalric universe is indeed frequently out of sight, and the hero does indeed fight in her name. However, the undoubted physical passivity and generally peripheral situation of women in the chivalric romances — in the sense of their non-participation in duels, jousts, or warfare — do not necessarily reflect an 'over-balancing on the masculine side'. In reality, this portrayal of woman as bystander endorses the notion of woman's power over man — a notion, again, that was promoted, rather than resisted, by the Church.

During the battle between Arcalaus's pagan coalition and Lisuarte's alliance, appreciative damsels marvel, like bullfight aficionados, at the exploits of Amadís: '¡Ea, caualleros, qu'él del yelmo blanco lo faze mejor!' (III, 728.890–91). As Amadís and his comrades prepare for the forthcoming war with Great Britain and the Roman allies of Lisuarte, the women in the hero's life — his beloved Oriana, his cousin Mabilia, Grasinda of Bohemia, queen Sardamira, and Briolanja — gather on Ínsula Firme, singing the hero's praises (IV, 1034–35.582–674). The same group of ladies and many other 'infantas y dueñas y donzellas' look on as avid spectators when the forces of Ínsula Firme set out to do battle (IV, 1080.128–33). Later, before the impending battle between Amadís and the giant Balán, we witness similar excitement among a larger, more variegated group of female onlookers. The parapets and windows of the fortress, we are told, are 'llenos de dueñas y donzellas' (IV, 1258.469–71).

Woman's physical passivity, as portrayed in the romances, might well have pandered to a prurient desire among the female audience to see men perform. In a culture obsessed by avoidance of the stigma of work, physical inactivity marks social superiority. It is the modern world, since the eighteenth century, that emphasizes enterprise and productivity — a 'work ethic' — as marks of status. The notion of a right to work, the liberty to choose a career, the freedom to compete — these would have been alien concepts to an audience in the medieval and early modern era. Career and work in such a context would have been the goals of artisans, lower-level clerics — in short, of the servile classes. Such aspirations are peculiar to the socially mobile workplace of later, intensively capitalized centuries. For women in the medieval audience, an empowering ambition and fantasy would have been to be the mistress of a large household, the princess of one's own domain, a presider over and evaluator of the labour of others. If women aspired, say, to be poets or artists, their aspiration would have taken the same form as the analogous objectives of their male counter-parts. They would have envisioned artistry not in terms of competitive struggle or of fastidious labour, but rather in those of leisured recreation, of status-enhancing performance unsullied by the contentious strife of the market-place.

Women in the romances are therefore happy to be spectators. Before the combat between Amadís and the grim Ardán Canileo, we read that

> toda la gente de la corte y de la villa estauan por ver la batalla en derredor del campo, y las dueñas y donzellas a las finiestras, y la fermosa Oriana y Mabilia a vna ventana de su cámara [...] (II, 531.848–53)

Based on the evidence of such scenes, we might be tempted to define chivalry, at least in these romances, as knightly deeds performed for the appreciation of women. The romances of chivalry understand society in terms of a symbiosis of the two sexes: men perform, women observe. From the viewpoint of the male, chivalry without the admiration of women is all in vain. Women, at the same time, are made complete by male performance on their behalf. This notion is expressed in Grasinda's reply to Amadís's declaration that, in defeating Salustanquidio and thus winning the crown of most beautiful for her, he has acquitted himself of the boon he had promised. She replies: 'no puedo yo hauer mayor descanso ni folgura en cosa que en ver vuestras grandes cauallerías' (III, 886.351–53).

The male need to impress and please women is exhibited even by Patín of Rome, the pompous suitor of Oriana. After his proposal of marriage, to which Lisuarte responds somewhat ambiguously, Patín sets forth 'por aquellas tierras a buscar los caualleros andantes para se con ellos combatir'. Assured of his betrothal to Oriana, complying with the dictates of chivalrous servility, he feels the compulsion to 'mostrar sus fuerças, creyendo ser con ello de aquella señora más amado [...]' (III, 790.599–605). The inexorable urge to impress the female is further seen in Amadís's attempt to reassure his squire and foster brother Gandalín, as the latter despairs of the hero's chances in the impending confrontation with the monster Endriago:

> Mi buen hermano, no tengas tan poca esperança en la misericordia

de Dios, ni en la vista de mi señora Oriana, que assí te desesperes;
que no solamente tengo delante mí la su sabrosa membrança, mas su
propia persona; y mis ojos la veen, y me está diziendo que la
defienda yo desta bestia mala. (III, 799.539–47)

The household envisioned by the knight is matrifocal. The
knight is errant, his beloved is stationary. Zifar and Tirant,
marrying into the families of royal heiresses, are literally uxorilocal, although the former, alone among the chivalric heroes
studied here, is not in love with the heiress he marries. However,
the kingdom that Zifar inherits through his spurious second union
is placed at the disposition of Grima, his real love. It is his
commitment to her and his family that determines his undertaking.
Even with apparent neolocality, the relationship and the residence
of the hero and his beloved are established on the woman's terms.
The knight describes an erratic orbit around the fixed star of the
heiress upon whom he depends. Roboán, Amadís, and Curial are
thus ostensibly neolocal in their pattern of residence, but for them,
strict amorous fidelity is the ethical equivalent of literal residence
in the female's domain.

Neolocal residence is a predictable literary fantasy in a society
where neither sex wants to be beholden to the other or to the
other's people. Men, especially, are beholden to women when the
most reliable means of practical social mobility for the ordinary
male — assuming minimal status credentials — is a good marriage.
Any sort of manual labour or mercantile activity caused the knight
to lose his status, not only in terms of loss of social standing but
also in terms of outright divestiture of chivalric title and privileges.

The neolocality of postmarital residence in *Amadís* and *Curial* is
in contrast to the Cid's territorial appropriation. He does establish a
new residence for himself and his family. But his is a well-earned
independence, as opposed to the fairy-tale acquisitions of Amadís
and Curial. The Cid, one could say, is a founder hero in more
senses than one, establishing as he does an independent community
that allows his followers to achieve social mobility and material
prosperity, while simultaneously establishing an influential and
prestigious lineage for his daughters and descendants.

In real-world family history it is often not the achieving climber
himself but his descendants who benefit, in terms of positive social
mobility. Property and power of themselves do not insure enhanced

status. 'The parvenu is never accepted by the privileged status groups', observes Max Weber, 'no matter how completely his style of life has been adjusted to theirs [... for] they will only accept his descendants who have been educated in the conventions of their status group and who have never besmirched its honor by their own economic labor' (Weber 1946b: 192).

The *Partidas*, expressing the mentality defined by Weber, denounce wealth gained through mercantile activity as a status disqualifier, declaring that 'non debe seer caballero home que por su persona andodiese faciendo mercadorias'. Wealth alone is inconsequential, in so far as enhancement of honour is considered, in that none may obtain 'honra de caballeria por precio de haber nin de otra cosa que diese por ella, que fuese como en manera de compra'. Knighthood, at the same time, is equated with lineage and nobility: 'Ca bien asi como el linage non se puede comprar, otrosi la honra que viene por nobleza non la puede la persona haber, si ella non fuere atal que la merezca por linage, ó por seso ó por bondat que haya en si' (XX.xxi.12).

Notions such as these shed light on woman's power to dispose. The power, in the case of the heiress, derived from her right to choose a consort. The power was not invariable or unconditional. It was a trump card only as useful to its possessor as her skill in deploying it. The game played between agnatic authority and female entitlement illuminates the concept of male dependency entertained by the romances. In historical reality, the suitor's chances are only as good as his sweetheart's tactical proficiency in dealing with her father and clan. The romances offer a utopic playground in which males escape dependency on the female, and in which daughters are absolved of the need for onerous subterfuge.

What could be called bondage of the male is seen even after the hero's reinstatement in the good graces of his beloved, after mis-understanding or temporary estrangement. Amadís, the most prominent example of this subservience, hangs on every word or look of Oriana. When, for example, she shows 'mal semblante' concerning some innocent remark he has made to Briolanja, he panics ('que della los ojos no partía'), feeling desperate regret at his having gallantly remarked to Briolanja that she herself should some day attempt the ordeal of the Arch of Faithful Lovers (II, 505.425–41). Later, Amadís, impatient for the arrival of Endriago, tells Gandalín that if he dies in the forthcoming encounter, the squire should convey to Oriana 'aquello que es suyo enteramente, que será mi coraçón [...] por no dar cuenta ante Dios de cómo lo ageno leuaua comigo' (III, 800.569–73). Bruneo de Bonamar speaks of his beloved Melicia, Amadís's sister, in similar terms: 'aquella que sin ella no pudiera yo sostener la vida' (III, 838.815–17).

In the *Poema de Mio Cid* it is the hero who sustains the female. Unlike the chivalric heroes, the epic Cid is not on the defensive. He performs not to impress his beloved, but to demonstrate to his family 'cómmo se gana el pan' (l. 1643). The contrast between the epic's sovereign breadwinner and the romances' reliant deliverer is brought out by a comparison of female spectators in the *Poema* and in the romances. The passage in which the Cid's wife and daughters watch him jousting and performing feats of horseman-ship from the ramparts of Valencia (*tirada* 86, ll. 1568–1609) seems at first to resemble scenes of female spectating in *Amadís* and the other chivalric texts. However, although he performs before his wife and daughters, the Cid has nothing to prove with regard to his manhood or suitability as a spouse. Jimena, moreover, has no power over him. It is he who sustains her, rather than the other way around. 'Sacada me avedes de muchas vergüenças malas', she lovingly acknowledges (1596). Her gratitude refers not to delivery from any specific emergency, as is so often the case with the romances' grateful females, but rather to the Cid's consummate ability to provide in all ways for all those dependent on him.

Of course, the chivalric heroes also rescue damsels from 'vergüenças malas'. But protecting and sustaining are two different ventures. The knight serves chiefly to safeguard women and other protected categories, such as widows and orphans. This chivalric hero's single-minded deliverer seems very specialized in compari-son to the Cid's eclectic provider. The fictional knight's hyper-specialization — reflected in the recurrence of such motifs as confrontations at crossroads, duels to the death, interventions on behalf of endangered damsels, challenges by bullies and upstarts, etc. — is yet another reflection of his real-world counterpart's essentially dependent character.

A present-day feminist reading might conclude that the romances' depiction of women as inactive spectators reflects the female loss of agency postulated by Krueger and others. The men in the romances are active, the women are passive. What could be more obvious? In reality, there is a subjugative dominance to this feminine onlooking. The tournament is the stylized simulacrum of the warfare that once had been the avenue of masculine autonomy and honourable social mobility. The romances' representations of chivalric combat are the textual correlative of such entertainments. For women in the chivalric romances, amorous devotion is not enough; the man must show not only fidelity but also unsurpassed martial prowess. The enchantment of the Ínsula Firme, we learn in *Amadís*, will last 'hasta tanto que vengan aquel y aquella que por su gran lealtad de sus amores, y gran bondad de armas del cauallero, en la fermosa cámara encantada entrarán, y ende fuelguen en vno' (II, 562.582–87). The romances polarize and reify sex roles. Manhood is founded on martial valour and unwavering fidelity, womanhood on exemplary beauty and attentive sedentarism.

Juan Manuel Cacho Blecua points out that *Amadís* seems to endorse that perspective on chivalry which is censured in Chrétien's *Erec et Enide*; namely, the knight's neglect of chivalric undertakings, in favour of a compliant service to the will of his lady (1979: 328). Armando Durán defines the contrast between Chrétien's *Erec* and his *Yvain* as an opposition between themes of the knight's disregard of chivalric duty through over-attentiveness to his beloved, and the knight's neglect of his love through obsession with chivalric obligations. In both cases, the knight puts himself to a test that will permit the sensible mediation of the two extremes (1973: 80–81).

There is, however, an important distinction to be made between the Spanish romance's depiction of the amorous knight's conflict of obligations, and the analogous dilemma in Chrétien's works. The predicament does not arise, for Amadís, until the very end of his tale, after he and Oriana are married. In Chrétien's *Erec*, most of the story, by contrast, is devoted to the quandary that confronts a married couple. Erec's story, unlike Amadís's, begins with his marriage. As Cacho Blecua observes, for Amadís, marriage 'supondrá un cambio de vida para el heroe' (1979: 328n1).

In the Spanish chivalric romances, we find little hint of Chrétien's compromise between chivalric commitment and amorous devotion. Except for the special case of Zifar, the wandering of the knights in these works is conditioned, one way or another, by the protagonists' response to the women in their lives. When the chivalric romance depicts women as spectators, they have something of the power of Roman matrons beholding a gladiatorial spectacle; this power within the narrative corresponds to an analogous power enjoyed by propertied women in the audiences of the genre. In neither context — the ancient Roman, the medieval chivalric — do sedentary female spectators lose agency due to non-participation in the combat observed.

The important differences between the two historical examples of combat before spectators bring out certain aspects of the medieval context. Fighters in the ancient Roman arena performed for a diverse demography of spectators in state-sponsored mass entertainments, while medieval tournaments were more limited in their audience, more modest in the dimensions and complexity of the spectacle offered. The combatants of ancient Rome fought for survival, the medieval knights, for status.

Sportive chivalry, in addition to its function as an enhancement of the male's standing among fellow competitors, was erotic display contrived to entertain and beguile the female. In a social setting in which conventional labour of any kind tarnishes or obliterates reputation, and in which, consequently, heiress-hunting is the only viable avenue of improving one's lot, any enhancement of reputation augmented the knight's chances of attracting the favourable attention of the maximum number of desirable females in a given audience. Excellence in the tournament can be presumed to be erotically appealing to at least a sizeable minority of females attending the spectacle. At the same time, the representation of female enthusiasm for such spectacles was very possibly a futile projection of the desperate male vanity of impecunious knights.

The female's staying in one place while the knight ranges far and wide is the narrative correlative of the relationship of knights to women in social history. Chivalric spectacle, whether as actual tournament or as its idealized military equivalent in literature, functioned as advertising for the marriage market, in both the historical and the fictional dimensions. By virtue of his exhibition of skill before an audience of female connoisseurs of chivalry, the knight's performance in the tournament assured his potential, as a lover or suitor, to a broad spectrum of eligible observers. The competitor publicized his efficacy and his virtuosity, hoping thereby to increase his chances for the best possible match. Again, even if the attraction is physical, female approval, decoding as consent, vindicates eventual amorous dalliance as a marriage in the making. One can detect a situation that is the opposite of the modern world's amorous cliché, whereby men obtain sexual favours by feigning interest in marriage. In the medieval context, men projected erotic appeal in order to secure an advantageous marriage.

There are two fantasies expressed: one, the female, imagines males in servitude to the judgment of women. The social reality, as we have seen, was that males tended to bide their time in finding a mate, and that women were often made to settle for both hypogamous marriage and a dowried exclusion from the patrimony. Nor were all men dependent on women for social advancement or acquisition of property. Some must have remained unmarried; some must have had marriages arranged for them by their own families. To imagine all men — especially all desirable and glamorous men — as beholden to discerning, exacting females is to appeal to female fantasies of the ideal match.

The other fantasy, male, was that women would be, first of all, impressed enough by martial prowess — the most that the average knight had in his favour — to consider the performing male as a suitable lover and husband. Although some women must have been unimpressed by mere success at tournaments, must often have been even repulsed by the excessive violence and posturing of chivalry's day-to-day business, many women must have been eroticized by the spectacle of the tourney, while some men did indeed realize the fantasy of landing an heiress by means of performance at tournaments.

Only a minority of men, presumably, were good at jousting or warfare, or even allowed to participate in such activities. However, even when men were not warriors or jousters, they could respond to a chivalric literature that glamorized courage, martial aptitude, forthrightness, integrity, and manly good looks. These virile attributes were appealing features of chivalric characters because such traits permitted — as do their analogues in such modern escapist genres as the thriller, the martial arts adventure, the space opera — the clear affirmation of the hero's superiority. Distinguishing winners from losers, such manly qualities are unmistakable criteria of merit. They offer, in tantalizing contrast to the drab inequity of real life, the illusion of a winnable game governed by intelligible rules.

The chivalric romance thus panders to boys who dream of winning the love of beautiful, socially superior girls through heroic deeds, and to girls who dream of being fair damsels rescued by handsome, audacious, athletic males. Genuine knightly prowess and superlative female beauty would have been rare in real life; this rarity was beside the point. The occasional chivalric success story, and the presence of appreciative females in the audiences of tournaments, while not improving the chances of individual male participants in the marital lottery, did constitute an example to be envied and emulated. Women were the jackpot, men the gamblers. By definition, gamblers outnumber jackpots. For the vast majority of contestants, then, the game must have seemed rigged in favour of the house. However, since the whole point of jackpots is their rarity, and since this scarcity does not prevent hordes of suckers from overrunning casinos or buying lottery tickets, we may assume there must have been many eager players in the matrimonial sweepstakes.

Although the romances show a society where men implicitly compete for women, real-world society was probably somewhat different, with many men abstaining from or postponing participation in the matrimonial competition. Authors thus appealed to female audiences by this depiction of men ever on the defensive. Because the male characters have something to prove, and the female characters are generally infallible judges of male excellence, the genre's readership must therefore have included a sizeable percentage of women. At the same time, the allure of these tales of knights-errant and their attainment of fame and fortune is that the adventures and vicissitudes of heroes and heroines provide a narrative analogue of the hopes and aspirations of readers seeking to become spouses, householders, and parents. The Spanish chivalric romances endorse notions of consent and hypogamy not through simple imitation of French models, in the form of the many similar romances catalogued by Critchlow and others. We must assume that the authors of the original French romances were prompted by the same motives as those who translated so many

French texts into Peninsular languages. These motives included an expectation of comprehension and of receptivity to these themes on the part of their audiences.

According to Leach's general model of traditional marriage, and Duby's specifically medieval paradigm, fathers control daughters for the good of the lineage. What do fathers do that mimics their children's passion? What corresponds to clandestine marriage as a stratagem that furthers parental gamesmanship? Fathers coerce, while daughters connive. The couple invokes consent; fathers of brides invoke honour. The constant surveillance of parents who themselves performed in their youth before a faultfinding community, and continue to feel its continual surveillance; the ever-present hazard of observant tale-bearers, personified by the slanderous courtiers that beset the hero and his beloved at every turn — all these elements conduce to a compunctious regard for public opinion whose sanctions and incentives we categorize as elements of shame culture. The ideology of consent makes for a circumvention of the whole system of behavioural constraints prescribed by shame. Consent underwrites egocentrism: the marriage made by the couple is for them, and not for their families or even their offspring. In my introduction I pointed out the paradox arising from a mentality of shame. A clue to the authorial intentions of chivalric romances may be discerned in Caro Baroja's observation that the cohesion of the lineage deteriorates precisely because of contradictions arising when clanic segments contend for honour and property (1966: 89 & 92–93). A society governed by shame, argues Caro Baroja, promotes among its members 'a fierce individualism' that tends to erode the lineage system from within.

The Church's policy on consent, along with its array of statutes concerning such related matters as cousin marriage, abetted the fierce individualism inherent in traditional societies. The core ideology of consent implicitly nurtured a live-for-the-moment disregard for the political and economic realities in which kinship had to be managed. Not that all youth succumbed, but that the possibility of personal happiness unfettered by social reality hung always before the young people of the time, a fruit forbidden by kin-ordered tradition, but tantalizingly approved by churchly doctrine. This was the social and legal environment that nurtured the chivalric romances of the later Middle Ages and the early modern era.

We close our discussion by recognizing that our findings support a none too controversial judgement as to the contrast between the epic and the chivalric romances. The former genre, sympathetic to the patriarch, is masculine in its outlook, while the latter, supportive of women's issues, presents a somewhat feminized perspective. Perhaps slightly more controversial is the assertion that the detectable feminization of the chivalric romances somewhat diminishes the apparent contrast between these works and the sentimental romances. The chivalric hero's dependency on the female would undoubtedly have annoyed many men of the day. There would thus have been little to choose, for the traditional male concerned with maintaining sex roles, between the sentimental and chivalric variations of a single womanized genre unfit for manly consumption. While the real-world dependency of ambitious males on women's power to dispose was mitigated by numerous behavioural and political factors, that power to dispose is exaggerated in the chivalric romances. It is exaggerated in order to please an audience in which women predominated morally if not numerically.

Abbreviations

AA	*American Anthropologist*
AE	*American Ethnographer*
AHAM	*Anales de Historia Antigua y Medieval*
AHDE	*Anuario de Historia del Derecho Español*
AnnRevS	*Annual Review of Sociology*
ARA	*Annual Review of Anthropology*
ASAM	Association of Social Anthropologists, Monographs
ASR	*American Sociological Review*
BAE	Biblioteca de Autores Españoles
BHS	*Bulletin of Hispanic Studies*
C	*La Corónica*
CA	*Current Anthropology*
CCa	Clásicos Castalia
CCE	Colección de Crónicas Españolas
CFMA	Classiques Français du Moyen Âge
CHE	*Cuadernos de Historia de España*
CSIC	Consejo Superior de Investigaciones Científicas

CSSA	Cambridge Studies in Social Anthropology
CSSH	*Comparative Studies in Society and History*
Eth	*Ethnology*
His	*Hispania* (Madrid)
HR	*Hispanic Review*
HSMS	Hispanic Seminary of Medieval Studies
IESS	*International Encyclopedia of the Social Sciences*
JFH	*Journal of Family History*
JIES	*Journal of Indo-European Studies*
LH	Letras Hispánicas
MH	*Medievalia et Humanistica*
N	*Neophilologus*
NCSRLL	North Carolina Studies in Romance Languages and Literatures
NRFH	*Nueva Revista de Filología Hispánica*
P&P	*Past & Present*
PL	Patrologiae Cursus Completus: Series Latina, ed. J.-P. Migne (Paris: Migne & Garnier)
PMLA	*Publications of the Modern Language Association of America*
PUF	Presses Universitaires de France
R	*Romania*
REH	*Revista de Estudios Hispánicos* (USA)
RenQ	*Renaissance Quarterly*
RH	*Revue Hispanique*
RLC	*Revue de Littérature Comparée*

RPh	*Romance Philology*
SJA	*Southwestern Journal of Anthropology*
UP	University Press

Bibliography

ABERLE, David F., 1961. 'Navaho', in Schneider & Gough 1961: 96–201.

ALESANDRO, John A., 1971. *Gratian's Notion of Marital Consummation* (Rome: Officium Libri Catholici).

ALFONSO EL SABIO, 1861. Real Academia de la Historia, *Siete Partidas del rey don Alfonso el Sabio*, 5 vols (Paris: Librería de Rosa y Bouret). Repr. of 1807 ed. in 3 vols (Madrid: Imprenta Real).

ALVAR, Carlos, 1991. 'Mujeres y hadas en la literatura medieval', in Lacarra 1991: 21–33.

ARCHIBALD, Elizabeth, 1991. *Apollonius of Tyre: Medieval and Renaissance Themes and Variations: Including the Text of the 'Historia Apollonii regis Tyri' with an English Translation* (Cambridge: D. S. Brewer).

ASENJO GONZÁLEZ, María, 1984. 'Las mujeres en el medio urbano a fines de la Edad Media: el caso de Segovia', in Segura Graiño 1984: 109–24.

AVALLE-ARCE, Juan Bautista, 1952. 'El arco de los leales amadores en el *Amadís*', *NRFH*, 6: 149–56.

——, 1982. 'El nacimiento de Amadís', in *Essays on Narrative Fiction in the Iberian Peninsula in Honour of Frank Pierce*, ed. R. B. Tate (London: Dolphin), pp. 15–25.

——, 1985. '*Tirant lo Blanc, Amadís de Gaula* y la caballeresca medieval', in *Studies in Honor of Sumner M. Greenfield*, ed. Harold L. Boudreau & Luis T. González del Valle (Lincoln, NE: Society of Spanish & Spanish-American Studies), pp. 17–31.

262

——, 1990. *'Amadís de Gaula': el primitivo y el de Montalvo* (México: Fondo de Cultura Económica).

AYLWARD, Edward T., 1985. *Martorell's 'Tirant lo Blanch': A Program for Military and Social Reform in Fifteenth-Century Christendom*, NCSRLL, 225 (Chapel Hill: Dept of Romance Languages, Univ. of North Carolina).

BACHOFEN, Johann Jakob, 1948. *Das Mutterrecht*, ed. Karl Meuli et al., 2 vols (Basel: Beno Schwabe).

BAKHTIN, M. M., 1981. *The Dialogic Imagination: Four Essays*, tr. Michael Holquist (Austin: University of Texas Press).

BARBERO, Abilio, & Marcelo VIGIL, 1974. *Sobre los orígenes sociales de la reconquista* (Barcelona: Ariel).

BARBERO, Alessandro, 1984. 'Lignaggio, famiglia ed entourage signorile nel *Cantar de Mio Cid*', *Annali della Scuola Normale Superiore di Pisa: Classe di Lettere e Filosofia*, 14.1: 45–117.

BARLAU, Stephen B., 1976. 'Germanic Kinship', *JIES*, 4: 97–129.

BARTH, Fredrik, 1973. 'Descent and Marriage Reconsidered', in Goody 1973b: 3–19.

BARTLETT, Robert, & Angus MACKAY, ed., 1989. *Medieval Frontier Societies* (Oxford: Clarendon Press).

BASEHART, Harry W., 1961. 'Ashanti', in Schneider & Gough 1961: 270–97.

BEEKES, Robert S. P., 1976. 'Uncle and Nephew', *JIES*, 4: 43–63.

BELL, Claire H., 1922. *Sister's Son in the Medieval Epic*, Univ. of California Publications in Modern Philology, 10 (Berkeley: University of California Press).

BELMARTINO, Susana M., 1968. 'Estructura de la familia y "edades sociales" en la aristocracia de León y Castilla según las fuentes literarias e historiográficas (siglos X–XIII)', *CHE*, 47–48: 256–328.

BELTRÁN, Rafael, 1991. 'Relaciones de complicidad ante el juego amoroso: *Amadís*, *Tirant*, y *La Celestina*', in Lacarra 1991: 103–26.

BENDIX, Reinhard, 1970. 'Tradition and Modernity Reconsidered', in *Essays in Comparative Social Stratification*, ed. Leonard Plotnicov & Arthur Tuden (Pittsburgh: University of Pittsburgh Press), pp. 273–336.

——, & Seymour M. LIPSET, ed., 1966. *Class, Status, and Power*, 2nd ed. (New York: Free Press).

BENSON, Larry D., 1984. 'Courtly Love and Chivalry in the Later Middle Ages', in *Fifteenth-Century Studies: Recent Essays*, ed. Robert F. Yeager (Hamden, CT: Archon), pp. 237–57.

BLACKSTONE, William, 1979. *Commentaries*, 4 vols (Chicago: University of Chicago Press). First publ. 1765–69.

BLOCH, Marc, 1961. *Feudal Society*, tr. L. A. Manyon, 2 vols (Chicago: University of Chicago Press).

BLOCH, Maurice, 1973. 'The Long Term and the Short Term: The Economic and Political Significance of the Morality of Kinship', in Goody 1973b: 75–87.

BLOCH, R. Howard, 1977. *Medieval French Literature and Law* (Berkeley: University of California Press).

——, 1983. *Etymologies and Genealogies: A Literary Anthropology of the French Middle Ages* (Chicago: University of Chicago Press).

——, 1991. *Medieval Misogyny and the Invention of Western Romantic Love* (Chicago: University of Chicago Press).

BOHANNAN, Paul, ed., 1967. *Law and Warfare: Studies in the Anthropology of Conflict* (Austin: University of Texas Press).

——, & John MIDDLETON, ed., 1968a. *Kinship and Social Organization* (Garden City, NY: The Natural History Press).

——, & ——, ed., 1968b. *Marriage, Family and Residence* (Garden City, NY: Natural History Press).

BOHIGAS BALAGUER, Pedro, 1949. 'Orígenes de los libros de caballerías', in *Historia general de las literaturas hispánicas*, ed. Guillermo Díaz-Plaja, I (Barcelona: Editorial Barna), pp. 521–41.

BONILLA Y SAN MARTÍN, Adolfo, ed., 1912. *Libro del esforçado cauallero don Tristán de Leonís y de sus grandes fechos en armas (Valladolid, 1501)*, Sociedad de Bibliófilos Madrileños, 6 (Madrid: SBM).

BOSSEN, Laurel, 1988. 'Toward a Theory of Marriage: The Economic Anthropology of Marriage Transactions', *Eth*, 27: 127–144.

BOURDIEU, Pierre, 1977. *Outline of a Theory of Practice*, tr. Richard Nice, CSSA, 16 (Cambridge: Cambridge UP).

——, 1984. *Distinction: A Social Critique of the Judgement of Taste*, tr. Richard Nice (Cambridge, MA: Harvard UP).

BREMMER, Jan, 1976. 'Avunculate and Fosterage', *JIES*, 4: 65–75.

BROOKE, Christopher N. L., 1989. *The Medieval Idea of Marriage* (Oxford: Oxford UP).

BROOKS, Peter, 1984. *Reading for the Plot* (New York: Random House).

BRUNDAGE, James A., 1987. *Law, Sex and Christian Society in Medieval Europe* (Chicago: University of Chicago Press).

BULLOUGH, D. A., 1969. 'Early Medieval Social Groupings: The Terminology of Kinship', *P&P*, 45: 3–18.

BUMKE, Joachim, 1982. *The Concept of Knighthood in the Middle Ages*, tr. W. T. H. Jackson & Erika Jackson (New York: AMS Press).

BURTON, Richard, tr., 1886. 'The King Who Lost Kingdom and Wife', in *Supplemental Nights to the Book of the Thousand Nights*, 6 vols (London: The Burton Club), I, pp. 319–31.

CACHO BLECUA, Juan Manuel, 1979. *Amadís: heroismo mítico cortesano* (Madrid: Cupsa).

——, 1986. 'El entrelazamiento en el *Amadís* y en las *Sergas de Esplandián*', in *Studia in honorem prof. M. de Riquer*, I (Barcelona: Quaderns Crema), pp. 235–71.

——, ed., 1987–88. Garci Rodríguez de Montalvo, *Amadís de Gaula*, LH, 255–56 (Madrid: Cátedra).

——, 1991. 'La iniciación caballeresca del *Amadís*', in Lacarra 1991: 59–79.

——, 1996. 'Los problemas del *Zifar*', in Rico & Ramos 1996: 57–94.

CARDONA DE GIBERT, Ángeles, & Joaquín RAFEL FONTANALS, ed., 1969. *Amadís de Gaula* (Barcelona: Bruguera).

CARLÉ, María del Carmen, 1961. 'Infanzones e hidalgos', *CHE*, 33–34: 56–100.

——, 1981. 'Caminos del ascenso en la Castilla bajo-medieval', *CHE*, 65–66: 207–76.

CARO BAROJA, Julio, 1966. 'Honour and Shame: A Historical Account of Several Conflicts', tr. R. Johnson, in *Honour and Shame: The Values of Mediterranean Society*, ed. John Peristiany (Chicago: University of Chicago Press), pp. 81–137.

——, 1969. *Ensayo sobre la literatura de cordel* (Madrid: Editorial Revista de Occidente).

——, 1986. *Realidad y fantasía en el mundo criminal*, Biblioteca de Dialectología y Tradiciones Populares, 19 (Madrid: CSIC).

CARRIAZO, Juan de Mata, ed., 1940. *Hechos del condestable don Miguel Lucas de Iranzo*, CCE, 3 (Madrid: Espasa-Calpe).

CASEY, James, 1989. *The History of the Family* (Oxford: Basil Blackwell).

CERVANTES, Miguel de, 1968. *Don Quijote de la Mancha*, ed. Martín de Riquer (Barcelona: Editorial Juventud).

CHRÉTIEN DE TROYES, 1968. *Erec et Enide*, ed. Mario Roques, CFMA, 80 (Paris: Champion).

——, 1973–75. *Le Conte du graal (Perceval)*, ed. Félix Lecoy, CFMA, 100 & 103 (Paris: Champion).

——, 1982. *Cligés*, ed. Alexandre Micha, CFMA, 84 (Paris: Champion).

CINTRA, Geraldo Ulhoa, ed., 1946. *Crónica de Palmeirim de Inglaterra*, 3 vols (São Paulo: Anchieta).

COOPER, Louis, ed., 1979. *Gran conquista de Ultramar*, 4 vols (Bogotá: Instituto Caro y Cuervo).

COROMINAS, Joan, & José A. PASCUAL, 1980–91. *Diccionario crítico etimológico castellano e hispánico*, 6 vols (Madrid: Gredos).

COROMINES, Joan, Joseph GULSOY, & Max CAHNER, 1980–91. *Diccionari etimològic i complementari de la llengua catalana*, 9 vols (Barcelona: Curial Edicions Catalanes & la Caixa).

CRITCHLOW, F. L., 1904–05. 'On the Forms of Betrothals and Wedding Ceremonies in the Old French *Romans d'aventure*', *Modern Philology*, 2: 497–537.

DEYERMOND, Alan, 1971. *A Literary History of Spain: The Middle Ages* (London: Ernest Benn; New York: Barnes & Noble).

——, 1981. 'The Interaction of Courtly and Popular Elements in Medieval Spanish Literature', in *Court and Poet: Selected Proceedings of the Third Congress of the International Courtly Literature Society, Liverpool, 1980*, ed. Glyn S. Burgess et al. (Liverpool: Francis Cairns), pp. 21–42.

——, 1984. 'Divisiones socio-económicas, nexos sexuales: la sociedad de *Celestina*', *Celestinesca*, 8.2: 3–10.

——, 1988. 'La sexualidad en la épica medieval española', *NRFH*, 36: 767–86.

——, 1989. 'Emoción y ética en el *Libro de Apolonio*', *Vox Romanica*, 48: 153–64.

DILLARD, Heath, 1984. *Daughters of the Reconquest* (Cambridge: Cambridge UP).

DONAHUE, Charles, 1983. 'The Canon Law in the Formation of Marriage and Social Practice in the Later Middle Ages', *JFH*, 8: 144–58.

DOUGLASS, William A., 1988. 'Iberian Family History', *JFH*, 13: 1–12

DOYLE, Thomas P., 1985. Introd. and commentary to Title VII, 'Marriage', cc. 1055–1165, in *The Canon Law: A Text and Commentary*, ed. James A. Coriden, Thomas J. Green, & Donald E. Heintschal (New York: Paulist Press), pp. 737–833.

DUBY, Georges, 1973a. 'Dans la France du Nord-Ouest au XIIe siècle: les "Jeunes" dans la société aristocratique', in his *Hommes et structures du Moyen Âge* (Paris: Mouton), pp. 213–25.

——, 1973b. 'Les origines de la chevalerie', ibid., pp. 325–41.

——, 1973c. 'Stuctures de parenté et noblesse dans la France du Nord aux XIe et XIIe siècles', ibid., pp. 267–85.

——, 1976a. 'La diffusion du titre chevalresque sur le versant méditerranéen de la Chrétienté latine', in *La Noblesse au Moyen Âge: xie–xve siècles: essais à la mémoire de Robert Boutruche*, ed. Philippe Contamine (Paris: PUF), pp. 39–70.

——, 1976b. 'Lineage, Nobility, and Chivalry in the Region of Mâcon during the Twelfth Century', in *Family and Society: Selections from the 'Annales'*, ed. Robert Forster & Orest Ranum (Baltimore: Johns Hopkins Press), pp. 16–40.

——, 1977a. 'Le mariage dans la société du haut Moyen Âge', in *Il matrimonio nella società altomedievale: Settimane di Studio del Centro Italiano di Studi sull' Alto Medioevo* (Spoleto: Sede del Centro), II, pp. 15–39.

——, 1977b. 'Présentation de l'enquête sur famille et sexualité au Moyen Âge', in *Famille et parenté dans l'occident médiéval*, ed. Duby & Jacques Le Goff (Rome: École Française de Rome), pp. 3–11.

——, 1978. *Medieval Marriage: Two Models from 12th-Century France*, tr. Elborg Forster (Baltimore: Johns Hopkins UP).

——, 1980. *The Three Orders*, tr. Arthur Goldhammer (Chicago: University of Chicago Press).

——, 1983. *The Knight, the Lady and the Priest*, tr. Barbara Bray (New York: Pantheon Books).

DUMONT, Louis, 1980. *Homo Hierarchicus: The Caste System and its Implications*, tr. Mark Sainsbury, Louis Dumont, & Basia Gulati (Chicago: University of Chicago Press).

DURÁN, Armando, 1973. *Estructura y técnicas de la novela sentimental y caballeresca* (Madrid: Gredos).

EGGAN, Fred, 1968. 'Kinship: Introduction', *IESS*, 8: 390–401.

ELLIOTT, J. H., 1963. *Imperial Spain 1469–1716* (London: Edward Arnold).

EISENBERG, Daniel, 1982. 'Who Read the Romances of Chivalry?', in his *Romances of Chivalry in the Spanish Golden Age* (Newark, DE: Juan de la Cuesta), pp. 89–117. First publ. *Kentucky Romance Quarterly*, 20 (1973): 209–33.

EL SAFFAR, Ruth S., 1984. *Beyond Fiction: The Recovery of the Feminine in the Novels of Cervantes* (Berkeley: University of California Press).

EMBER, Melvin, & Carol R. EMBER, 1971. 'The Conditions Favoring Matrilocal vs. Patrilocal Residence', *AA*, 73: 571–94.

ENTWISTLE, William J., 1949–50. '*Tirant lo Blanch* and the Social Order of the End of the Fifteenth Century', *Estudis Romànics*, 2: 149–64.

ESMEIN, Adhémar, 1968. *Le Mariage en droit canonique*, 2 vols (New York: Burt Franklin). First publ. Paris, 1891.

Estudio 1976. *Estudio sociológico de la familia española* (Madrid: Confederación Española de Cajas de Ahorros).

EVANS, Dafydd, 1981. 'Wishfulfilment: The Social Function and Classification of Old French Romances', in *Court and Poet: Selected Proceedings of the Third Congress of the International Courtly Literature Society, Liverpool, 1980*, ed. Glyn S. Burgess et al. (Liverpool: Francis Cairns), pp. 129–34.

FARNSWORTH, William O., 1913. *Uncle and Nephew in the Old French Chansons de Geste* (New York: Columbia UP).

FATHAUER, George H., 1961. 'Trobriand', in Schneider & Gough 1961: 234–69.

FLANAGAN, James G., 1989. 'Hierarchy in Simple Egalitarian Societies', *ARA*, 18: 245–66.

FLETCHER, Richard, 1990. *The Quest for El Cid* (New York: Knopf).

FOGELQUIST, James Donald, 1982. *El 'Amadís' y el género de la historia fingida* (Madrid: José Porrúa Turanzas).

FORDE, Daryll, 1968. 'Double Descent Among the Yakö', in Bohannan & Middleton 1968a: 179–91. First publ. as chaps 3 & 4 of his *Yakö Studies* (London: Oxford UP, 1964).

FORTES, Meyer, 1969. *Kinship and the Social Order: The Legacy of Lewis Henry Morgan* (Chicago: Aldine).

——, & E. E. EVANS-PRITCHARD, 1940. Introduction to *African Political Systems*, ed. Fortes & Evans-Pritchard (London: Oxford UP), pp. 1–9.

FOULCHÉ-DELBOSC, Raymond, 1906. 'La plus ancienne mention d'Amadís', *RH*, 15: 806.

FOX, Robin, 1967. *Kinship and Marriage: An Anthropological Perspective* (Harmondsworth: Penguin Books).

FRANCESCHETTI, A., 1982. 'Tra letteratura e realtà: la presa di Constantinopoli e la tradizione narrativa della letteratura cavalleresca', in *Il Rinascimento: aspetti e problemi attuali*, ed. Vittore Branca, Claudio Griggio, et al. (Firenze: Olschki), pp. 403–18.

FRAPPIER, Jean, 1959. 'The Vulgate Cycle', in Loomis 1959: 295–318.

FREEMAN, John Derek, 1968. 'On the Concept of the Kindred', in Bohannan & Middleton 1968a: 255–72.

——, 1973. 'Kinship, Attachment Behavior and the Primary Bond', in Goody 1973b: 109–19.

FRIEDL, Ernestine, 1963. 'Some Aspects of Dowry and Inheritance in Boetia', in Pitt-Rivers 1963: 113–35.

FRIEDRICH, Paul, 1966. 'Proto-Indo-European Kinship', *Eth*, 5: 1–36.

FUMAROLI, Marc, 1985. 'Jacques Amyot and the Clerical Polemic Against the Chivalric Novel', *RenQ*, 38: 22–40.

GAGARIN, Michael, 1986. *Early Greek Law* (Berkeley: University of California Press).

GARCIA, Michel, 1983. *Obra y personalidad del canciller Ayala* (Madrid: Alhambra).

GARCÍA DE CASTROJERIZ, Juan, 1947. *Glosa castellana al 'Regimiento de príncipes' de Egidio Romano*, ed. Juan Beneyto Pérez, 3 vols (Madrid: Instituto de Estudios Políticos).

GARCÍA DE CORTÁZAR, José Ángel, 1976. *La época medieval*, 3rd ed., Historia de España Alfaguara, 2 (Madrid: Ediciones Alfaguara).

GARCÍA DE ENTERRÍA, María Cruz, 1985–86. 'Libros de caballerías y romancero', *Journal of Hispanic Philology*, 10: 103–15.

GARCÍA DE VALDEAVELLANO, Luis, 1963. 'Las instituciones feudales en España', in Ganshof 1963: 229–300.

GAYANGOS, Pascual de, ed., 1857. *Las sergas del muy esforzado caballero Esplandián*, in *Libros de caballerías*, BAE, 40 (Madrid: Rivadeneyra), pp. 403–561.

GEROULD, Gordon Hall, 1904. 'Forerunners, Congeners, and Derivatives of the Eustace Legend', *PMLA*, 19: 335–448.

GIBERT SÁNCHEZ, Rafael, 1947. 'El consentimiento familiar en el matrimonio según el derecho medieval español', *AHDE*, 18: 706–61.

GIDDENS, Anthony, 1982. 'Class Structuration and Class Consciousness', in *Classes, Power, and Conflict*, ed. Giddens & David Held (Berkeley: University of California Press), pp. 157–74.

——, 1986. *The Nation-State and Violence* (Berkeley: University of California Press).

GIRARD, René, 1965. *Deceit, Desire, and the Novel*, tr. Yvonne Freccero (Baltimore: Johns Hopkins UP).

GLICK, Thomas F., 1979. *Islamic and Christian Spain in the Early Middle Ages* (Princeton: Princeton UP).

GOLDHAMER, Herbert, 1968. 'Social Mobility', *IESS*, 14: 429–38.

GONZÁLEZ, Cristina, 1984. *'El Cavallero Zifar' y el reino lejano* (Madrid: Gredos).

GOODY, Jack, 1961. 'The Classification of Double Descent Systems', *CA*, 2: 3–12.

——, 1968. 'Descent Groups', *IESS*, 8: 401–08.

——, 1969. 'The Mother's Brother and the Sister's Son in West Africa', in his *Comparative Studies in Kinship* (London: Routledge & Kegan Paul), pp. 39–90.

——, 1970. 'Marriage Prestations, Inheritance, and Descent in Pre-Industrial Societies', *Journal of Comparative Family Studies*, 1: 37–54.

——, 1973a. 'Bridewealth and Dowry in Africa and Eurasia', in Goody & Stanley J. Tambiah, *Bridewealth and Dowry*,

270

Cambridge Papers in Social Anthropology, 7 (Cambridge: UP), pp. 1–58.

——, ed., 1973b. *The Character of Kinship* (Cambridge: Cambridge UP).

——, 1973c. 'Strategies of Heirship', *CSSH*, 15: 3–20.

——, 1976. *Production and Reproduction: A Comparative Study of the Domestic Domain*, CSSA, 17 (Cambridge: Cambridge UP).

——, 1983. *The Development of the Family and Marriage in Europe* (Cambridge: Cambridge UP).

——, Joan THIRSK, & E. P. THOMPSON, ed., 1976. *Family and Inheritance: Rural Society in Western Europe, 1200–1800* (Cambridge: Cambridge UP).

GOUGH, Kathleen, 1961a. 'Nayar: Central Kerala', in Schneider & Gough 1961: 298–384.

——, 1961b. 'Nayar: North Kerala', ibid: 385–414.

——, 1961c. 'Mappilla: North Kerala', ibid.: 415–42.

——, 1961d. 'Descent-Group Variation Among Settled Cultivators', ibid.: 457–521.

——, 1961e. 'Variation in Residence', ibid.: 545–76.

——, 1961f. 'Variation in Interpersonal Kinship Relationships', ibid.: 577–613.

GRATIAN, 1891. *Decretum Magistri Gratiani*, PL, 187.

GREGORY IX, 1959. *Decretales Gregorii IX*, 2nd ed., in *Decretalium Collectiones*, ed. A. Richter & A. Friedberg, Corpus Iuris Canonicis, 2 (Leipzig: Tauchnitz). First publ. 1881.

GUGLIELMI, Nilda, 1963–64. 'Cambio y movilidad social en el *Cantar de mio Cid*', *AHAM*, 12: 43–65.

GUICHARD, Pierre, 1977. *Structures sociales 'orientales' et 'occidentales' dans l'Espagne musulmane*, Civilisations et Sociétés, 60 (Paris: Mouton).

HAJNAL, John, 1965. 'European Marriage Patterns in Perspective', in *Population in History: Essays in Historical Demography*, ed. David V. Glass & D. E. C. Eversley (London: Edward Arnold), pp. 101–43.

HALLETT, Judith, 1984. *Fathers and Daughters in Roman Society: Women and the Élite Family* (Princeton: Princeton UP).

HANNING, Robert W., 1972. 'The Social Significance of Twelfth-Century Chivalric Romance', *MH*, ns, 3: 3–29.

——, 1977. *The Individual in Twelfth-Century Romance* (New Haven: Yale UP).

——, 1981. 'The Audience as Co-Creator of the First Chivalric Romances', *Yearbook of English Studies*, 11: 1–28.

HARNEY, Michael, 1982–83. 'The Geography of the *Libro del Caballero Zifar*', *C*, 11: 208–19.

——, 1983. 'The Literary Geography of the *Libro del Cauallero Zifar*', doctoral thesis (University of California, Berkeley). *Dissertation Abstracts International*, 45A (1984–85): 841.

——, 1987. 'Class Conflict and Primitive Rebellion in the *Poema de Mio Cid*', *Olifant*, 12: 171–219.

——, 1987–88. 'More on the Geography of the *Libro del Caballero Zifar*', *C*, 16: 76–85.

——, 1989. 'Estates Theory and Status Anxiety in the *Libro de los estados* and Other Medieval Spanish Texts', *REH*, 23: 1–29.

——, 1989–90. 'The *Libro del Caballero Zifar*: Recent Editions and a Recent Monograph', *RPh*, 43: 569–601.

——, 1990. 'The *Libro del Caballero Zifar* as a "Refraction" of the Life of St. Eustace', in *Saints and their Authors: Studies in Medieval Hispanic Hagiography in Honor of John K. Walsh*, ed. Jane E. Connolly, Alan Deyermond, & Brian Dutton (Madison: HSMS), pp. 71–82.

——, 1992. 'Movilidad social, bandolerismo y la emergencia del estado en el *Poema de Mio Cid*', in *Mythopoesis: literatura, totalidad, ideología*, ed. Joan Ramon Resina (Barcelona: Anthropos), pp. 65–101.

——, 1993a. *Kinship and Polity in the 'Poema de Mio Cid'*, Purdue Studies in Romance Literatures, 2 (West Lafayette: Purdue UP).

——, 1993b. 'Mythogenesis of the Modern Super Hero', in *Modern Myths*, ed. David G. Bevan (Amsterdam: Rodopi), pp. 189–210.

——, 1994. 'Economy and Utopia in Medieval Hispanic Chivalric Romance', *HR*, 62: 381–403.

——, 1995. 'Siege Warfare in Medieval Hispanic Epic and Romance', in *The Medieval City under Siege*, ed. Ivy Corfis & Michael Wolfe (Woodbridge: Boydell Press), pp. 177–90.

HARREL, Steven, & Sara A. DICKEY, 1985. 'Dowry Systems in Complex Societies', *Eth*, 24: 105–20.

HARRISON, A. R. W., 1968. *The Law of Athens*, I: *The Family and Property* (Oxford: Clarendon Press).

HART, Thomas R., 1993. 'Tirant lo Blanc: Between Romance and Epic', in *Letters and Society in Fifteenth-Century Spain: Studies Presented to P. E. Russell on his Eightieth Birthday*, ed. Alan Deyermond & Jeremy Lawrance (Llangrannog: Dolphin), pp. 59–68.

HATCH, Elvin, 1989. 'Theories of Social Honor', *AA*, 91: 341–53.

HEERS, Jacques, 1977. *Family Clans in the Middle Ages*, tr. Barry Herbert (Amsterdam: North-Holland Publishing).

HERLIHY, David, 1983. 'The Making of the Medieval Family: Symmetry, Structure and Sentiment', *JFH*, 8: 116–30.

——, 1985. *Medieval Households* (Cambridge, MA: Harvard UP).

——, & Christiane KLAPISCH-ZUBER, 1985. *Tuscans and their Families: A Study of the Florentine Catasto of 1427* (New Haven: Yale UP).

HOMER, 1967. *The Odyssey of Homer*, tr. Richmond Lattimore (New York: Harper & Row).

HUGH OF ST VICTOR, 1880. *De sacramentis christianae fidei*, in PL, 176, cols 174–618.

HUGHES, Diane Owen, 1978. 'From Bridewealth to Dowry in Mediterranean Europe', *JFH*, 3: 262–96.

INFANTES, Victor, 1991. 'La narración caballeresca breve', in Lacarra 1991: 165–81.

ISIDORE OF SEVILLE, 1911. *Etymologarium sive originum*, ed. W. M. Lindsay, 2 vols (Oxford: Clarendon Press).

JORDAN, Leo, 1908. 'Die Eustachiuslegende, Chistians Wilhelms-leben, Boeve de Hanstone, und ihre orientalische Verwandten', *Archiv für das Studium der Neueren Sprachen und Literaturen*, 121: 341–67.

JOYCE, George Hayward, 1948. *Christian Marriage: A Historical and Doctrinal Survey* (London: Sheed & Ward).

JUAN MANUEL, 1974. *Libro de los estados*, ed. R. B. Tate & I. R. Macpherson (Oxford: Clarendon Press).

——, 1982. *Libro del cauallero et del escudero*, in Juan Manuel, *Obras completas*, ed. José Manuel Blecua (Madrid: Gredos), I, pp. 39–116.

——. 1985. *El conde Lucanor*, ed. José Manuel Blecua, CCa, 9, 4th imor. (Madrid: Castalia).

KEEN, Maurice, 1984. *Chivalry* (New Haven: Yale UP).

KERTZER, David I., 1984. 'Anthropology and Family History', *JFH*, 9: 201–16.

——, 1991. 'Household History and Sociological Theory', *AnnRevS*, 17: 155–79.

——, & Caroline BRETTELL, 1987. 'Advances in Italian and Iberian Family History', *JFH*, 12: 87–120.

——, & Jennie KEITH, ed., 1984. *Age and Anthropological Theory* (Ithaca: Cornell UP).

KORTEKAAS, G. A. A., ed., 1984. *Historia Apollonii Regis Tyri* (Groningen: Bouma's Boekhuis).

KRUEGER, Roberta L., 1993. *Women Readers and the Ideology of Gender in Old French Verse Romance* (Cambridge: Cambridge UP).

LACARRA, María Eugenia, ed., 1991. *Evolución narrativa e ideológica de la literatura caballeresca: Seminario sobre literatura caballeresca, Vitoria, 1988* (Bilbao: Universidad del País Vasco).

LASLETT, Peter, & Richard WALL, ed., 1972. *Household and Family in Past Time* (Cambridge: Cambridge UP).

LAUMANN, Edward O., Paul M. SIEGEL, & Robert W. HODGE, ed., 1970. *The Logic of Social Hierarchies* (Chicago: Markham Publishing Company).

LAWRANCE, Jeremy, 1985. 'The Spread of Lay Literacy in Late Mediaeval Castile', *BHS*, 62: 79–94.

LEACH, Edmund, 1961. *Rethinking Anthropology* (London: Athlone Press).

——, 1965. *Political Systems of Highland Burma* (Boston: Beacon Press). First publ. 1954.

——, 1973. 'Complementary Filiation and Bilateral Kinship', in Goody 1973: 53–58.

LÉVI-STRAUSS, Claude, 1963. 'Structural Analysis in Linguistics and Anthropology', in his *Structural Anthropology*, tr. Claire Jacobson & Brooke Grundfest Schoeff (New York: Basic Books), pp. 31–54.

——, 1969. *The Elementary Structures of Kinship*, revd ed., tr. James Harle Bell & John Richard von Sturmer, ed. Rodney Needham (Boston: Beacon Press).

LEVY, Harry L., 1963. 'Inheritance and Dowry in Classical Athens', in Pitt-Rivers 1963: 137–43.

LEYSER, Karl, 1968. 'The German Aristocracy from the Ninth to the Early Twelfth Century: A Historical and Cultural Sketch', *P&P*, 41: 25–53.

——, 1970. 'Maternal Kin in Early Medieval Germany: A Reply', *P&P*, 49: 126–134.

LIDA DE MALKIEL, María Rosa, 1952–53. 'El desenlace del *Amadís* primitivo', *RPh*, 6: 283–89.

——, 1959. 'Arthurian Literature in Spain and Portugal', in Loomis 1959: 406–18.

LISÓN TOLOSANA, Carmelo, 1966. *Belmonte de los Caballeros: A Sociological Study of a Spanish Town* (Oxford: Clarendon Press).

LOOMIS, Roger Sherman, ed., 1959. *Arthurian Literature in the Middle Ages: A Collaborative History* (Oxford: Clarendon Press).

LOWIE, Robert H., 1949. Review of Bachofen 1948, *AA*, 51: 628–29.

LUCÍA MEGÍAS, José Manuel, 1996. 'Los testimonios del *Zifar*', in Rico & Ramos 1996: 97–136.

MACKAY, Angus, 1976. 'The Ballad and the Frontier in Late Mediaeval Spain', *BHS*, 53: 15–33.

——, 1977. *Spain in the Middle Ages: From Frontier to Empire* (London: Macmillan).

——, 1986. 'The Lesser Nobility in the Kingdom of Castile', in *Gentry and Lesser Nobility in Late Medieval Europe*, ed. Michael Jones (Gloucester: Alan Sutton; New York: St Martin's Press), pp. 159–75.

MCNERNEY, Kathleen, 1984. 'Elements of Courtly Romance in *Tirant lo Blanc*', in Mermier 1984: 151–60.

MARAVALL, José Antonio, 1978. 'Interés personal por la casa propia en el Renacimiento', *RLC*, 53: 255–66.

MARRIOT, McKim, & Ronald B. INDEN, 1974. 'Caste Systems', *Encyclopedia Britannica*, 15th ed., III, pp. 982–91.

MARTÍNEZ MARCOS, Esteban, 1966. *Las causas matrimoniales en las 'Partidas' de Alfonso el Sabio* (Salamanca: CSIC).

MAUSS, Marcel, 1967. *The Gift* (New York: W. W. Norton).

MAYER, Adrian C., 1966. 'The Significance of Quasi-Groups in the Study of Complex Societies', in *The Social Anthropology of Complex Societies*, ed. Michael Banton, ASAM, 4 (London: Tavistock Press), pp. 97–122.

MEINHARD, H. H., 1975. 'The Patrilineal Principle in Early Teutonic Kinship', in *Studies in Social Anthropology: Essays in Memory of E. E. Evans-Pritchard by his Former Oxford Colleagues*, ed. J. H. M. Beattie & R. G. Lienhardt (Oxford: Clarendon Press), pp. 1–29.

MENÉNDEZ PIDAL, Ramón, ed. 1955. *Primera crónica general de España que mandó componer Alfonso el Sabio y se continuaba bajo Sancho IV en 1289*, 2nd ed., 2 vols (Madrid: Seminario Menéndez Pidal & Gredos).

——, 1956. *La España del Cid*, 5th ed., 2 vols (Madrid: Espasa-Calpe).

MERÊA, Manuel Paulo, 1952a. 'O dote nos documentos dos seculos XI–XII', in his *Estudos de direito hispânico medieval* (Coimbra: Universidade), I, pp. 59–150.

——, 1952b. 'Sobre a palavra "arras"', ibid.: 32–57.

MEYER, Paul, ed., 1891–1901. *Histoire de Guillaume le Maréchal*, 3 vols (Paris: Société de l'Histoire de France).

MICHAEL, Ian, ed., 1978. *Poema de mio Cid*, CCa, 75, 2nd ed. (Madrid: Castalia).

——, 1989. '"From Her Shall Read the Perfect Ways of Honour": Isabel of Castile and Chivalric Romance', in *The Age of the Catholic Monarchs, 1474–1516: Literary Studies in Memory of Keith Whinnom*, ed. Alan Deyermond & Ian Macpherson (Liverpool: Liverpool UP), pp. 103–12.

MIQUEL I PLANAS, R., ed., 1932. *Curial e Güelfa* (Barcelona: Biblioteca Catalana).

MITRE FERNÁNDEZ, Emilio, 1979. *La España medieval: sociedades, estados, culturas*, Ciclos y Temas de la Historia de España, Colección Fundamentos, 63 (Madrid: Ediciones Istmo).

MOLL, Francesc de Borja, 1982. *Els llinatges catalans*, 2nd ed., Els Treballs i els Dies, 23 (Mallorca: Editorial Moll).

MOLLER, Herbert, 1958–59. 'The Social Causation of the Courtly Love Complex', *CSSH*, 1: 137–63.

MONEDERI, Carmen, ed., 1987. *Libro de Apolonio*, CCa, 156 (Madrid: Castalia).

276

MORGAN, Lewis Henry, 1871. *Systems of Consanguinity and Affinity of the Human Family* (Washington, DC: Smithsonian Institution).

MOXÓ (Y ORTIZ DE VILLAJOS), Salvador de, 1969. 'De la nobleza vieja a la nobleza nueva: la transformación nobiliaria castellana en la Baja Edad Media', *Cuadernos de Historia*, 3: 1–210.

——, 1970. 'La nobleza castellano-leonesa en la Edad Media', *His*, 30: 5–68.

——, 1970–71. 'La nobleza castellana en el siglo XIV', *Anuario de Estudios Medievales*, 7: 493–511.

——, 1975. 'La promoción política y social de los "letrados" en la corte de Alfonso XI', *His*, 35: 5–29.

MURDOCK, George Peter, 1968. 'Cognatic Forms of Organization', in Bohannan & Middleton 1968a: 235–53.

MURRAY, Alexander, 1983. *Germanic Kinship Structure* (Toronto: Pontifical Institute of Mediaeval Studies).

NADER, Helen, 1979. *The Mendoza Family in the Spanish Renaissance 1350 to 1550* (New Brunswick: Rutgers UP).

NALLE, Sara T., 1989. 'Literacy and Culture in Early Modern Castile', *P&P*, 126: 65–95.

NEEDHAM, Rodney, ed., 1971. *Rethinking Kinship and Marrriage*, ASAM, 11 (London: Tavistock Press).

NERLICH, Michael, 1987. *The Ideology of Adventure*, tr. Ruth Crowley, Theory and History of Literature, 42–43 (Minneapolis: University of Minnesota Press).

NORTHUP, George Tyler, ed., 1928. *El cuento de Tristán de Leonís, Edited from the Unique Manuscript Vatican 6428* (Chicago: University of Chicago Press).

ORCASTEGUI GROS, Carmen, 1984. 'Ordenanzas municipales y reglamentación local en la Edad Media sobre la mujer aragonesa en sus relaciones sociales y económicas', in Segura Graiño 1984: 13–18.

PARSONS, Talcott, 1966. *Societies* (Englewood Cliffs, NJ: Prentice-Hall).

PERISTIANY, J. G., ed., 1966a. *Honour and Shame: The Values of Mediterranean Society* (Chicago: University of Chicago Press).

——, 1966b. 'Introduction', in Peristiany 1966a: 9–18.

PERRY, Ben Edwin, 1967. *The Ancient Romances: A Literary-Historical Account of their Origins*, Sather Classical Lectures, 37 (Berkeley: University of California Press).

PESCADOR, Carmela, 1961–64. 'La caballería popular en León y Castilla', *CHE*, 33–34 (1961): 101–238; 35–36 (1962): 156–201; 37–38 (1963): 88–198; 39–40 (1964): 169–260.

PETER LOMBARD, 1981. *Sententiae in iv libris distinctae*, 2 vols (Roma: Grottaferrata).

PHILLPOTTS, Bertha Surtees, 1913. *Kindred and Clan in the Middle Ages and After* (Cambridge: UP).

PIERS, Gerhart, & Milton B. SINGER, 1971. *Shame and Guilt* (New York: Norton).

PITT-RIVERS, Julian, ed., 1963. *Mediterranean Countrymen: Essays in the Social Anthropology of the Mediterranean* (The Hague: Mouton).

——, 1966. 'Honour and Social Status', in Peristiany 1966a: 21–77.

——, 1968. 'Pseudo-Kinship', *IESS*, 8: 408–13.

——, 1971. *The People of the Sierra*, 2nd ed. (Chicago: University of Chicago Press).

——, 1973. 'The Kith and the Kin', in Goody 1973b: 89–105.

PLACE, Edwin B., ed., 1959–69. *Amadís de Gaula*, 4 vols (Madrid: CSIC).

POSPISIL, Leopold, 1974. *The Anthropology of Law: A Comparative Theory* (New Haven: Human Relations Area Files Press). First publ. New York: Harper & Row, 1971.

POWERS, James F., 1988. *A Society Organized for War: The Iberian Municipal Militias in the Central Middle Ages* (Berkeley: University of California Press).

PRAT, Joan, Ubaldo MARTÍNEZ, et al., ed. 1991. *Antropología de los pueblos de España* (Madrid: Taurus Universitaria).

QUINTANILLA RASO, María Concepción, 1982. 'Estructuras sociales y familiares y papel político de la nobleza cordobesa (siglos XIV y XV)', in *Estudios en memoria del profesor D. Salvador de Moxó*, ed. Miguel Angel Ladero Quesada, I, En la España Medieval, 4 (Madrid: Universidad Complutense), pp. 331–52.

RADCLIFFE-BROWN, A. R., 1965. 'On Joking Relationships', in his *Structure and Function in Primitive Society* (New York: Free Press), pp. 90–104. First publ. 1952.

RAHEJA, Gloria Goodwin, 1988. *The Poison in the Gift* (Chicago: University of Chicago Press).

RAMOS, Rafael, 1996. 'Invitación a la lectura del *Libro del caballero Zifar*', in Rico & Ramos 1996: 15–54.

RENOIR, Alain, 1986. 'Oral-Formulaic Rhetoric and the Interpretation of Literary Texts', in *Oral Tradition in Literature: Interpretation in Context*, ed. John Miles Foley (Columbia: University of Missouri Press), pp. 103–35.

REUTER, Timothy, ed., 1978. *The Medieval Nobility* (Amsterdam: North-Holland Publishing).

RHEUBOTTOM, David B., 1988. '"Sisters First": Betrothal Order and Age at Marriage in Fifteenth-Century Ragusa', *JFH*, 13: 359–76.

RICO, Francisco, & Rafael RAMOS, ed., 1996. *'Libro del caballero Zifar': códice de París: estudios* (Barcelona: M. Moleiro).

RÍOS Y RÍOS, Ángel de los, 1979. *Ensayo histórico etimológico filológico sobre los apellidos castellanos*, Biblioteca de Filología Hispánica, Onomástica y Toponimia, 3 (Barcelona: El Albir).

RIQUER, Martí de, 1964. *Història de la literatura catalana*, I–III (Barcelona: Ariel).

——, ed., 1969. Joanot Martorell & Martí Joan de Galba, *Tirant lo blanc* (Barcelona: Seix Barral).

——, 1973. 'Cervantes y la caballeresca', in *Suma cervantina*, ed. J. B. Avalle-Arce & E. C. Riley, Colección Támesis, A14 (London: Tamesis), pp. 272–87.

——, 1987. *Estudios sobre el 'Amadís de Gaula'*, Biblioteca General, 3 (Barcelona: Sirmio).

——, 1992. *'Tirant lo blanch', novela de historia y de ficción* (Barcelona: Sirmio).

RIVERA GARRETAS, Milagros, 1984. 'Normativa y litigios en torno a la dote durante la época de Jaime II', in Segura Graíño 1984: 19–25.

ROUGEMONT, Denis de, 1983. *Love in the Western World*, revd ed., tr. Montgomery Belgion (Princeton: Princeton UP).

RUBIN, Zick, 1970. 'Do American Women Marry Up?', in Laumann, Siegel, & Hodge 1970: 633–43.

RUIZ DE CONDE, Justina, 1948. *El amor y el matrimonio secreto en los libros de caballerías* (Madrid: Aguilar).

SAHLINS, Marshall D., 1965. 'On the Ideology and Composition of Descent Groups', *Man*, 65: 104–07.

——, 1966. 'The Segmentary Lineage: An Organization of Predatory Expansion', in Bendix & Lipset 1966: 89–119.

SAN PEDRO, Diego de, 1985. *Obras completas*, II: *Cárcel de Amor*, ed. Keith Whinnom, CCa, 39, 3rd ed. (Madrid: Castalia).

SÁNCHEZ ALBORNOZ, Claudio, 1956. *España: un enigma histórico*, 2 vols (Buenos Aires: Sudamericana).

SCHAPS, David M., 1979. *Economic Rights of Women in Ancient Greece* (Edinburgh: Edinburgh UP).

SCHEFFLER, Harold W., 1966. 'Ancestor Worship in Anthropology: Observations on Descent and Descent Groups', *CA*, 7: 540–98.

——, 1970. '*The Elementary Structures of Kinship*, by Claude Lévi-Strauss: A Review Article', *AA*, 72: 251–68.

——, 1974. 'Kinship, Descent, and Alliance', in *Handbook of Social and Cultural Anthropology*, ed. J. J. Honigmann (New York: Rand McNally), pp. 747–93.

SCHLEGEL, Alice, & Rohn ELOUL, 1988. 'Marriage Transactions: Labor, Property, Status', *AA*, 90: 291–309.

SCHMID, Karl, 1978. 'The Structure of the Nobility in the Earlier Middle Ages', in Reuter 1978: 37–59.

SCHNEIDER, David M., 1961a. 'Introduction', in Schneider & Gough 1961: 1–29.

——, 1961b. 'Truk', ibid.: 202–33.

——, & E. Kathleen GOUGH, ed., 1961. *Matrilineal Kinship* (Berkeley: University of California Press).

SCHUSKY, Ernest L., 1972. *Manual for Kinship Analysis*, 2nd ed. (New York: Holt, Rinehart & Winston).

SEALEY, Raphael, 1990. *Women and Law in Classical Greece* (Berkeley: University of California Press).

SEGURA GRAIÑO, Cristina, ed., 1984. *Las mujeres en las ciudades medievales: Actas de las III Jornadas de Investigación Interdisciplinaria* (Madrid: Seminario de Estudios de la Mujer, Universidad Autónoma).

SIEBER, Harry, 1985. 'The Romance of Chivalry in Spain, from Rodríguez de Montalvo to Cervantes', in *Romance: Generic Transformation from Chrétien de Troyes to Cervantes*, ed. Kevin Brownlee & Marina Scordilis Brownlee (Hanover: UP of New England), pp. 203–19.

SMITH, Charles Edward, 1940. *Papal Enforcement of Some Medieval Marriage Laws* (Baton Rouge: Louisiana State UP).

SMITH, Raymond T., 1973. 'The Matrifocal Family', in Goody 1973b: 121–44.

——, 1984. 'Anthropology and the Concept of Social Class', *ARA*, 13: 467–94.

——, 1988. *Kinship and Class in the West Indies*, CSSA, 65 (Cambridge: Cambridge UP).

SOLIDAY, Gerald L., Tamara K. HAREVEN, et al., ed., 1980. *History of the Family and Kinship: A Select International Bibliography* (Millwood, NY: Kraus International).

SOUTHALL, Aidan, 1968. 'Stateless Society', *IESS*, 15: 157–68.

SPACCARELLI, Thomas D., 1987. 'The Symbolic Substructure of the *Noble cuento del enperador Carlos Maynes*', *Hispania* (USA), 30: 1–19.

SPINELLI, Emily, 1983–84. 'Chivalry and Its Terminology in the Spanish Sentimental Romance', *C*, 12: 241–53.

STANESCO, Michel, & Michel ZINK, 1992. *Histoire européenne du roman médiéval: esquisse et perspectives* (Paris: PUF).

STEVENS, John, 1973. *Medieval Romance: Themes and Approaches* (London: Hutchinson).

STEWARD, Julian H., 1955. *Theory of Culture Change* (Urbana: University of Illinois Press).

STIMMING, Albert, ed., 1911–20. *Der festländische 'Beuve de Hantone'*, Gesellschaft für Romanische Literatur, 25, 30, 34, & 42 (Dresden: Gesellschaft für Romanische Literatur).

STOCK, Brian, 1983. *The Implications of Literacy: Written Languages and Models of Interpretation in the Eleventh and Twelfth Centuries* (Princeton: Princeton UP).

STRAYER, Joseph P., 1970. *On the Medieval Origins of the Modern State* (Princeton: Princeton UP).

Studia philologica 1960–63. *Studia philologica: homenaje ofrecido a Dámaso Alonso por sus amigos y discípulos con ocasión de su 60o aniversario*, 3 vols (Madrid: Gredos).

SUÁREZ FERNÁNDEZ, Luis, 1972. 'The Kingdom of Castile in the Fifteenth Century', in *Spain in the Fifteenth Century*, ed. Roger Highfield, tr. Frances M. López-Morillas (London: Macmillan), pp. 80–113.

TAMBIAH, Stanley J., 1973. 'Dowry and Bridewealth, and the Property Rights of Women in Southeast Asia', in Jack Goody & Tambiah, *Bridewealth and Dowry*, Cambridge Papers in Social Anthropology, 7 (Cambridge: Cambridge UP), pp. 59–169.

TERRY, Emmanuel, 1972. *Marxism and 'Primitive Societies'*, tr. Mary Klopper (New York: New Left Review Press).

THOMAS, Henry, 1920. *Spanish and Portuguese Romances of Chivalry* (Cambridge: Cambridge UP).

THOMPSON, I. A. A., 1985. 'Neo-Noble Nobility: Concepts of *hidalguía* in Early Modern Castile', *European Historical Quarterly*, 15: 379–406.

THOMPSON, Stith, 1955–58. *Motif-Index of Folk Literature: A Classification of Narrative Elements in Folktales, Ballads, Myths, Fables, Mediaeval Romances, Exempla, Fabliaux, Jest-Books, and Local Legends*, 2nd ed., 6 vols (Bloomington: Indiana UP; Copenhagen: Rosenkilde & Bagger).

TIEMANN, Hermann, ed., 1977. *Der Roman von der Königin Sibille* (Hamburg: Ernst Hauswedell).

TRAUTMANN, Thomas R., 1987. *Lewis Henry Morgan and the Invention of Kinship* (Berkeley: University of California Press).

TUMIN, Melvin, 1966. 'Some Principles of Stratification: A Critical Analysis', in Bendix & Lipset 1966: 53–58. First publ. *ASR*, 18 (1953): 387–93.

TURNBULL, Colin, 1972. *The Mountain People* (New York: Simon & Schuster).

VAN BEYSTERVELDT, Antony, 1981. 'El amor caballeresco del *Amadís* y del *Tirante*', *HR*, 49: 407–25.

——, 1982. *Amadís-Esplandián-Calisto: historia de un linaje adulterado* (Madrid: José Porrúa Turanzas).

VERKAUTEREN, Fernand, 1978. 'A Kindred in Northern France in the Eleventh and Twelfth Centuries', in Reuter 1978: 87–101.

VICENS VIVES, Jaime, 1969. *An Economic History of Spain*, 3rd ed., tr. Frances M. López-Morillas (Princeton: Princeton UP).

VINAVER, Eugène, 1971. *The Rise of Romance* (Oxford: Clarendon Press).

WAGNER, Charles Phillip, 1903. 'The Sources of the *Libro del caballero Çifar*', *RH*, 10: 5–103.

——, ed., 1929. *El libro del cauallero Zifar (El libro del cauallero de Dios)*, University of Michigan Publications: Language and Literature, 5 (Ann Arbor: University of Michigan).

WALKER, Roger M., 1974. *Tradition and Technique in 'El libro del cavallero Zifar'*, Colección Támesis, A36 (London: Tamesis).

WEBER, Wax, 1946a. 'Structures of Power', in *From Max Weber: Essays in Sociology*, tr. & ed. H. H. Gerth & C. Wright Mills (New York: Oxford UP), pp. 159–60.

——, 1946b. 'Class, Status, Party', ibid.: 180–95.

——, 1946c. 'Bureaucracy', ibid.: 196–244.

——, 1968. 'The Nature of Charismatic Authority and its Routinization', in *On Charisma and Institution Building*, ed. Schmuel Eisenstadt (Chicago: University of Chicago Press), pp. 48–65.

WEIGAND, Rudolf, 1981. 'Liebe und Ehe bei den Dekretisten des 12. Jahrhunderts', in *Love and Marriage in the Twelfth Century*, ed. Willy Van Hoecke & Andries Welkenhuysen, Mediaevalia Lovaniensia, 1.8 (Leuven: Leuven UP), pp. 41–58.

WERNER, Karl Ferdinand, 1977. 'Liens de parenté et noms de personne', in *Famille et parenté dans l'occident médiéval*, ed. Georges Duby & Jacques Le Goff (Rome: École Française de Rome), pp. 25–34.

WHINNOM, Keith, 1980. 'The Problem of the "Best-Seller" in Spanish Golden Age Literature', *BHS*, 67: 189–98.

WHITEHEAD, F., ed., 1970. *La Chanson de Roland* (Oxford: Basil Blackwell).

WILLIAMSON, Edwin, 1984. *The Half-Way House of Fiction: 'Don Quijote' and the Arthurian Romance* (Oxford: Clarendon Press).

——, 1991. 'Cervantes y Chrétien de Troyes: la destrucción creadora de la narrativa caballeresca', in Lacarra 1991: 145–63.

WINCH, Robert F., 1968. 'Marriage: Family Formation', *IESS*, 10: 1–8.

Index